The London Dream

Migration and the Mythology of the City

The London Dream

Migration and the Mythology of the City

Chris McMillan

Winchester, UK
Washington, USA

JOHN HUNT PUBLISHING

First published by Zero Books, 2020
Zero Books is an imprint of John Hunt Publishing Ltd., No. 3 East St., Alresford,
Hampshire SO24 9EE, UK
office@jhpbooks.com
www.johnhuntpublishing.com
www.zero-books.net

For distributor details and how to order please visit the 'Ordering' section on our website.

ISBN: 978 1 78904 420 1
978 1 78904 421 8 (ebook)
Library of Congress Control Number: 2019945266

A CIP catalogue record for this book is available from the British Library.

Design: Stuart Davies

UK: Printed and bound by CPI Group (UK) Ltd, Croydon, CR0 4YY
US: Printed and bound by Thomson-Shore, 7300 West Joy Road, Dexter, MI 48130

We operate a distinctive and ethical publishing philosophy in
all areas of our business, from our global network of authors to
production and worldwide distribution.

Contents

to Hudson and Huxley.

this book was written while your wonderful mother was
growing you.
It was edited while I was trying to get you to sleep, so
apologies to the reader.

Acknowledgements

This book was carried by the same illusions that propel the London dream: I loved the idea of writing it, despite all rationality, and its primary site of production was coffee shops across the city. Furthermore, like the London dream, my ambitions relied on the labour of others.

Writing a book, it is said, is the process of transforming a bundle of books into one. That has been the case here. As the reader will see, I have been heavily reliant on Jerry White's extensive histories of London, as well as Peter Ackroyd's biography of the city. Lindsey German and John Rees' *A People's History of London* was also invaluable and comes highly recommended. I have also borrowed the wisdom and research of numerous others.

It goes without saying that I am deeply indebted to those who gave up their time to tell their story of London, to answer difficult questions, and to endure my company. I can only hope that I have captured your dreams faithfully.

I am also thankful to Zero Books for taking a chance on the project and to my copy editor, John Romans, for his thoughtful edits and comments.

To Richard Boardman, Andy Lewin and Martyn Winslade, thank you for your early thoughts on the project and your continued contribution to discussions about capitalism, social justice and cricket. That you are wrong about most things does not lessen the quality of your friendship.

I am also deeply grateful to my family, who have provided me with the love and support that enables everything I do. Now that I am on the other side of the equation, I love and appreciate you more every day. The greatest downside of my London dream is not the commute or the dodgy contracts, but being away from you. A special thanks goes to my mother, Sue McMillan, who painstakingly and effectively proofread the text.

Thanks also to my employer, Arcadia University in London, not only for allowing me to look forward to coming to work but also in providing funding to support the process. My colleagues have been a continuous source of support, solidarity, gossip and goodwill.

The reader will also see that there are regular references to my students at both Arcadia University and New York University in London, whose enthusiasm for London is a constant source of joy. It also allows me to see the city through new eyes every semester.

And, most importantly, my heart goes to my wife and my twins, Hudson and Huxley.

Boys, as I write this in June 2019, you are blissfully sleeping beside me and I can't imagine being happier. I eagerly await the adventures that lie ahead of us, even if tonight that means changing your stinky nappies.

Victoria, you are my penguin. Your support throughout this process has meant more than you can imagine. I love you.

You and our HuHu grubs are my dream come to life.

Previous Title

Žižek and Communist Strategy (Edinburgh University Press, 2012) Paperback ISBN: 978-0748682331

Preface

This project began as a rather bleak critique of working conditions in London. I sought to argue that the logic of capitalism and of London's economy had not much changed since the inequities and indignities of Victorian London. My first few interviews pursued confirmation of this argument. I kept pressing for stories of woe and they were forthcoming. And yet, there was always a tension, a hesitancy in our discussions. Sure, those that sat across from me were disgruntled with London life but their lack of gruntlement was not the narrative my Londoners wanted to convey.

Of course, London life was hard for them at times. It still is and we spent time swapping horror stories. But they wanted, almost needed, to tell me that they love it here. In spite of it all, they love London. These loyal and lingering Londoners were telling me that they are on the way up. They were telling me of their hopes and dreams. They were telling me, however humbly, that they were on the cusp of something better. Often they were; many of the characters encountered in this book have moved on to better things in London.

The persistence of hope where there might otherwise be despair tells us much about the human condition and the power of the stories we tell ourselves about our current discontent. This is the hope that if we can just overcome this obstacle or fulfil that desire, then life would suddenly be better. You might be making endless flat whites at an East End café now but maybe one of those coffees will lead to a contact that will lead to a flat white economy job. Sure, your rent takes up half your pay but it will all be worth it when you get a *proper* job.

London, and capitalism, runs on this paradoxical partnership of hope and desire, despair and discontent. The couplet of capital and city has long driven people to London for all the city has to

1

offer; civility, consumption, cool and the prospect of prosperity. Or just the safety of community. This is the London dream, one at once invigorating, invasive and exploitative.

Section 1

The Place to Be

The London Dream

'Tired of London, tired of life' has become a cliché suitable only for the most hackneyed travel blog. Possibly one about things to do in Hackney.

That it has become so clichéd reveals an enduring mythology of London.

The commodification of Samuel Johnson's original (reported) utterance was not predestined to be the title of a myriad of books, blogs and brochures; the workhouse was as much a feature of Georgian London as Johnson's intellectual glamour.

Dr Johnson, who should be better remembered as a literary titan and the creator of the preeminent dictionary of his time, is recorded to have said something like it to his friend, and future biographer, James Boswell. Boswell included it on page 286 of his *The Life of Samuel Johnson* as part of a story about his time with Johnson in Ashbourne, a market town outside of Derby, in 1777. Boswell reports that on the morning of Saturday 20 September he and Johnson had a 'serious conversation' about the latter's growing sense of 'melancholy and madness'. Boswell appears to have had no sympathy for his friend's concerns.

He was pleased, however, to have 'entered seriously upon a question of much importance to me, which Johnson was pleased to consider with friendly attention'[1]. Then based in Scotland, Boswell wrote that he spoke to Johnson of a concern that '…if I were to reside in London, the exquisite zest with which I relished it in occasional visits might go off, and I might grow tired of it'[2].

Johnson had little time for such folly, responding:

Why, Sir, you find no man, at all intellectual, who is willing to leave London. No, Sir, when a man is tired of London, he is tired of life; for there is in London all that life can afford[3].

5

This idea of London, one of everlasting possibility, has launched millions of migrant journeys and kept Londoners in place when they are tired of life itself and the grime and misery the city offers. It is the sense that if one is to 'make it', they can make it in London. That no matter how hard life is in London, there is always the sense that, with a little fortune, it could get better.

It is the London dream.

It exists in the sentiments of British journalist Tony Parsons, who ended his 2016 *GQ* polemic *London is the Greatest City in the World* with:

> *Everything they say about London is true. To live here you must take on all comers. What they once sang about New York is actually truer of London today - if you can make it here then you can make it anywhere. But scatter my ashes on Hampstead Heath. Let my dust blow across those green fields forever, may it be carried by the wind from the bathing ponds to Kenwood House to Parliament Hill. It will take everything you have, this city, this capital of the world, this centre of the universe, but London will be worth it.*
>
> *Love it or leave it*[4].

Such dreams are not limited to Johnson's 'at all intellectual' man or Parsons's privileged Hampstead mornings. The London dream may be stronger among those recent arrivals wearily pouring Parsons's espresso and making his suits. We see it in Sam Selvon's description of Galahad's reaction to Piccadilly Circus in his 1956 novel *The Lonely Londoners*:

> *Always, from the first time he went there to see Eros and the lights, that circus have a magnet for him, that circus represent life, that circus is the beginning and the ending of the world. Every time he go there, he have the same feeling like when he see it the first night, drink coca-cola, any time is guinness time, bovril and the fireworks, a million flashing lights, gay laughter, the wide doors of theatres, the*

huge posters, everready batteries, rich people going into tall hotels,
people going to the theatre, people sitting and standing and walking
and talking and laughing and buses and cars and Galahad Esquire, in
all this, standing there in the big city, in London.
Oh Lord[5].

The London dream is a myth, but not in the sense that it is a mere illusion. It is one of those stories that humanity uses to make sense of the social world; a story we tell ourselves about ourselves. Whether it is true does not depend on its relationship to an objective reality but whether it resonates with those who tell it.

We would not get far telling the Doncaster dream, but the American dream and the idea of a 'shining light on the hill' is a story that has gripped migrants and the migrated for centuries. Likewise, the London dream has stoked imaginations since the Romans arrived almost two thousand years ago. It has brought migrants from across the Isles, the continent, the Commonwealth and the world[6]. Or just students returning from their adolescent adventures at northern universities.

This London dream is why students flock to the capital after graduation in search of excitement and opportunity. It is why recent arrivals endure the most precarious of lives and refugees flow back into London, despite being officially 'dispersed' around the country by the UK government[7].

It is also why Londoners are able to enjoy a cornucopia of consumption and employers are able to push the boundaries of pay rates and working conditions.

This story is the story of the London dream.

Living the Dream

I have lived the London dream.

Like many Londoners before me, I migrated in search of hope and economic opportunity and inadvertently found myself on

7

the margins of employment and in the midst of my national diaspora.

London provided me with a second chance at youth. It has (eventually) offered meaningful and well-paid employment, a base to travel and a community of friends who have become like family. I love the sense of being at the centre of the world. For me, London is the place to be.

But it has not always been like this for me. It is not like this for a good proportion of Londoners.

Unable to pay our rent and without secure employment prospects in our native New Zealand, my wife and I sold our possessions and bought a one-way ticket to London, secure in our belief that everything would be better once we arrived in the big city. We will not be the last to rest our fate on such naivety.

Having quickly discovered that we could not afford our own place – although the Foxtons agents who eagerly drove us around the city in their Minis were keen to persuade us otherwise – we moved into a converted Victorian mansion with 11 others. It would be difficult to find a more apt metaphor for life in London. Migrants from Portugal, Ireland, Australia and New Zealand shared the same space in occasional harmony and an efficiency that only came from getting out of each other's way. Small communities formed, the house turned over at a remarkable rate and we came together as one only when disrupted by an unnecessarily outspoken alarm. Friendships were forged, enemies were made and despair and triumphs were shared in equal measure. Everyone left as soon as their contract allowed. Some moved on to brighter things. Others went back to their city of origin with stories to tell of London's brutality.

Work life wasn't much easier. Agency contracts were the norm, either as a first step into a desired industry or as a way of surviving. My wife kept us afloat through these contracts. A recent teaching graduate, she would wake at 5:30am, call a collection of the education recruitment companies she had registered with and wait for a call back by 6:30am. By 6:45am, hopefully, she would be using a Transport for London (TfL) map to work out how to get to a new part of London to try to control a class and maintain her sanity – and our London foothold – for another day.

Four days of work meant that we could pay our rent, 5 days allowed for leisure spending (who saves in London?) and 3 days meant a week of worry. Some of the most difficult moments of our life were waiting for the phone to ring in the unusually hot summer mornings of June 2010.

Such precariousness pushes you into doing things you don't want to do. I signed up to be a film extra, but was reluctant to pay the £10 registration fee. I walked from Shepherd's Bush to Bloomsbury for £5 to participate in psychological research. Inspired by my new stream of revenue, I registered to participate in medical research; £3000 to test a new flu medication and all I had to do was not move for a week. It wouldn't necessitate much of a change in lifestyle. My family strongly disagreed and a deposit from New Zealand, both resented and gratefully received, arrived in my bank account. Few migrants receive such a privilege.

Work was required, however. My PhD fell off my CV and long forgotten student retail work took its place. I found myself answering an ad for a hospitality recruitment firm and invested in the commute across London for an interview and a mass training day. Having shown myself to be a warm body with a National Insurance number, I entered into the world of zero-hours contracts. Anachronistically, we received a letter in the mail with an offer of work for a coming event. We had a day to phone and confirm our availability and there was no guarantee that the work would still be on offer.

Many of the gigs were horse racing events that required a train into London's commuter belt. Absorbing a £15 return ticket was not worth the 4 hours of minimum wage work. An England vs. Pakistan cricket test match in South London was much more appealing for a life-long fan of the game. Yet, while I knew the rhythms of cricket, my years of retail work had not prepared me for the misery of precarious employment in London.

Upon arriving at the event space, we were harried into a holding room where we were forced to give up our phones and wallets before trading our clothes for a standard issue uniform - black trousers, white shirt – and a brown bag for lunch.

During our four 10-hour shifts, paid at not a penny above the minimum wage, we were prevented from leaving the premises. Anyone who rejected these conditions would not be employed for the day, nor would they likely be invited back. Our crew was at once motley and overqualified. Among us were students, partially employed creatives (most with post-graduate qualifications) and hospitality workers looking for a way to find extra shifts. We were grateful for the work.

Weeks later, with relief and resentment in equal measure, I took on a temporary contract at Waterstone's, joining the ranks of recent graduates and bookstore lifers earning less than London's living wage. A mass of unanswered job applications gave way to an unsuccessful job interview at Brunel University's Learning Support department, which became successful when an employee moved on months later. It might have been part-time, and temporary, but it was a foothold and meaningful work with wonderful people. This led to offers of sociology teaching on hourly contracts that were as exploitative as any role. Vitally though, it provided the experience for me to apply for other teaching work. Seven years after arriving in London I secured full-time, permanent employment in my field.

London now provides me with an opportunity to travel, to have our own place, to meet friends for dinner and to do new and interesting things when the opportunity presents itself. It has become the first home for our twins. Our lives are still lived month to month, but such security is a privilege in London.

Hard work and resilience were required. Work was harder and required far more resilience when it was precarious. Few migrants can fall back on their educational qualifications, the privileges of Whiteness and middle-class mores. Not everyone is able to have the option of begging their families for rent if the need ever arises.

Moreover, as much as I try to mitigate against it, I benefit from the kind of exploitation and vulnerability I once experienced when I consume. I benefit from low wages when I nip into a supermarket or go to the cinema. As much as I avoid Uber, I benefit from its excessive presence when I take any other taxi service home after a night out. I am guilty of taking into account cheap delivery prices on my take out, which no doubt attributes to the criminal compensation given to my delivery driver. Sure, I might kick my guilt down the road by giving a tip, but what good is that against the interests of businesses big and small and a city of consumers searching for the best price in order to survive?

For many of the Londoners who service these forms of consumption in London, life is a matter of toil and mental degradation, held together by necessity and hope. The consumption of cosmopolitan culture and commodification cool is matched by the production of misery. This is no aberration waiting to be overcome by further development of the city. It is the very dynamic that propels London's economy. Karl Marx knew it both intimately and intellectually.

Marx(ism) in London

In his painfully and painstakingly constructed *Das Kapital*, Marx argued that the

Accumulation of wealth at one pole is, therefore, at the same time accumulation of misery, agony of toil, slavery, ignorance, brutality, mental degradation, at the opposite pole[8].

Living and writing in Victorian-era London, this was not an

unreasonable assertion for him to make. One of many European radicals fleeing the continent – in a letter to his daughters in June 1871, Marx wrote that our 'cousins from the country' were 'thronging [London's] streets. You recognize them at once by their bewildered air'[9] – he sought refuge in London in 1849 after the defeat of the German revolution, remaining there until his death in Hampstead in 1883.

Although Marx spent much of his time surrounded by the spoils of Empire in the Reading Room of the British Museum, his life in London was defined by the kind of precarity experienced by many Victorian families. He was not exaggerating when he wrote to his follower Joseph Weydemeyer in 1851 to complain of the 'wretched circumstances in which we are vegetating here'[10]; from 1850 to 1855 Marx and his wife Jenny lost three children to poverty-related conditions[11].

The Marxes were not alone in their misery. Captivated by a now all-encompassing capitalism, nineteenth-century London was creating a new form of human existence, one with great accumulations of wealth and of misery. As English journalist and playwright Blanchard Jerrold was to inscribe in his *London, a Pilgrimage*, 'The aged, the orphan, the halt, the blind, of London would fill an ordinary city'[12].

For Marx, it was the desperation of those who filled the capital city and the city of capital who were the key to its expansion; the misery of many is the key to the accumulation of some. Marx's identification of urban inequality was hardly new. Plato had remarked in *The Republic* that, 'Any city, however small, is in fact divided into two, one the city of the poor, the other of the rich'[13]. For Marx, though, widespread destitution was not a natural part of the human condition. Nor was it an aberration to be overcome with further development. Instead, Marx's foundational claim was that inequality was part of the grammar of capitalism.

The London Dream does not dispute this claim. We might, however, expand Marx's key thesis. It is not only the accumulation of wealth that is dependent upon the exploitation of the most vulnerable, especially in the twenty-first century. The consumption of a civilised, 'cool' and cosmopolitan London is also predicated upon the misery of those who work to reproduce this cool economy.

This was applicable in *Londinium*, with its glistering forum and thriving slave market. It could be seen in the lit streets of Georgian London which opened up the night and only made the presence of workhouses even darker. It was in existence in the simultaneous splendour and squalor of Victorian London. It drives the sense of cool that compels young people to migrate to London and entrenches the precarious lives of the new working classes who service this economy.

The jarring juxtaposition of excitement and exploitation is dependent upon the grip of the London dream. Those buying into the mythology of the city as a place of opportunity, prosperity and excitement continue to flow into London, in turn perpetuating the narrative of London as the place to be. In doing so, they provide as steady a stock of potential workers to London as any agricultural clearances, supplying what Marx called a 'mass of human material' vulnerable to exploitation in the creative sector as much as the service sector.

These Londoners, both the fresh and the faithful, serve to increase the vulnerability of an already precarious workforce through the knowledge, shared by employer and employee alike, that there is always a ready and willing supply of replacement workers available. Just as every toiling docker could see the desperation of those wanting to take on their miserable work, every Uber driver knows that someone else is logged in and available to fill the rides they turn down. Likewise, every newly arrived theatre graduate serves as a potential replacement for those on the margins of creative London. This is London's new reserve army of labour. Not the strictly unemployed but the underemployed and overqualified, working while waiting for more exciting and more profitable ways to be exploited.

And still, they come: London's population is growing at a rate of 100,000 per year, despite the ruthless turnover of young people. They come in search of the seemingly inextinguishable London dream.

In a city of entrenched poverty, businesses feed off the propagation of this fantasy. But hope is not merely an illusion fostered into mere dupes. Workers need it too. They need hope in the face of adversity and of cool rationality.

The only thing worse than being exploited in London is not being exploited. And not being in London.

Looking Ahead

The struggle between the hope of the London dream and the exploitation it fuels is the focus of *The London Dream*. Through encounters with people[14] and places in London, I tell the story of a city in which excitement and opportunity, exploitation and degradation, are inextricably linked. There are no public figures here, no big names, just Londoners living lives at once unique and clichéd.

Moreover, *The London Dream* does not pretend to represent all of London, although it does evoke a mythology that is distinctly London. There are no property developers or construction workers here, nor civil servants, scientists and nurses. These stories are certainly important, particularly those from below, and they have been done well elsewhere. I particularly recommend *Looking to London* by Cynthia Cockburn[15] and *This is London* by Ben Judah[16]. Our focus, however, is on the mythology of London and its part in the reproduction of a civilised, cosmopolitan, cool city beholden to consumer capitalism.

The story begins by exploring how London began as the place to be for Huguenots and hipsters alike. We then move to London's transformation into a post-industrial powerhouse. Here London's twenty-first century economy is animated by a sense of subversive cool that attracts creative and service workers alike. Often it attracts the creative classes who become service workers.

This is the second part of the story of twenty-first century London; that of a reserve army of aspiring creative workers toiling in the service classes. In turn, this creates greater competition for service roles that results in precarious conditions and the brutality and degradation of the gig economy.

And yet, not only do they continue to come to London, but those who are here are ready to battle for their hopes and for the prospects of their fellow Londoners.

The London Dream is about the accumulation of wealth and the toil of those workers, visible and invisible. It is about the exploitation of the poor and the exclusion of the most vulnerable. It is about the consumption of cool and the misery it produces. It is about an oceanic urban expanse seemingly capable of absorbing all newcomers and of a rising tide that drowns those not in the same boat. It is about the hopes and struggles of those seeking a better life and employers who benefit from these dreams.

Chapter 1

Beyond British Dreams

Theresa May's attempt to cast off her 'Maybot' image after her disastrous 2017 election campaign did not go as well as she might have hoped, although it went as well as most people expected.

In her post-election speech at the Conservative Party Conference, the then UK Prime Minister tried to turn apology into aspirational hyperbole by earnestly explaining that she had joined the Conservative Party because:

> ...it had at its heart a simple promise that spoke to me, my values and my aspirations: that each new generation in our country should be able to build a better future. That each generation should live the British Dream.
> And that dream is what I believe in.

The response was wonderfully British: ruthlessly dry mockery. On Twitter, the perfect medium for such mirth, responses to the question of 'What on earth is the British dream?' ranged from 'a pot full of teabags' and 'a Wetherspoons on every corner' to the delightfully grim 'Isn't the British dream the one where we turn up naked and unprepared for an important exam? Or Brexit, as it's otherwise known[17].'

More sedately, although without any more sympathy, in *The Guardian*, Nesrine Malik argued that, 'even among all the new puffed-up nativism of Brexit, the phrase still jars. It's just so embarrassing. So try-hard. So un-British both in overstatement and mawkishness. Its forced grandiosity reveals its threadbare shabbiness[18].' Even the Maybot must have felt the burn.

It did not help that May's speech was interrupted by her constant cough, letters from the backdrop of 'A Country that

Works for Everyone' falling off and a prankster delivering a P45 end of employment form. The language may have been distinctly American but this was a very British farce.

Beyond its appalling presentation and grating rhetoric, the critical reception May's speech received brought the lack of an aspirational British story to the surface[19]. At best, we might think of a British social contract; pay your taxes, keep your head down and the government will look after you when necessary. The absence of an aspirational narrative is not just the absence of rags to riches tales – the British like their rags and riches kept quite separate, thank you very much – but the absence of a hopeful migrant story[20].

Indeed, the popularity of relocation TV shows like *A House in the Sun* and *Wanted Down Under* shows that perhaps a stronger example of the British migrant dream has been the desire to leave the country and recreate a fantasy of a Britain left behind. Where Brits once took long voyages to the colonies, they now hop on budget airlines heading for the sunshine of Southern Europe and construct communities seemingly based around warm ales, marmite and the shared pain of sunburn.

London, that City of Nations, has a different story, one more New York than York. The city has always had a symbiotic relationship with migrants. Unable to organically replenish its stocks of willing and able working bodies, London is hungry for migrants to feed its economy[21]. Equally, since the Romans bridged the Thames some 2,000 year ago, there has been no shortage of migrants eager to be thrown into the capital in search of the London dream.

Réfugié Dreams

London was able to be settled by the invading Romans because they were initially tolerated by local tribes while those in the West, Wales and the North were openly hostile[22]. This was the first step in the formation of a city of migrants. The Romans brought with them soldiers and administrators, slaves and merchants. In turn, they attracted migrants from across the Isles[23].

London's population might have ebbed more than it flowed during the tumultuously desolate years after the fall of *Londinium* in the fifth century, but migrants continued to drift sporadically into the city so that in the thirteenth century London was described as 'over-flowing with Italians, Spanish, Provencals and Poitevins'[24].

The most anxious Brexiter might have the same observation about East London today, although the Poitevins have been replaced by hipsters and Bangladeshis. For most Londoners, however, this hyper-diversity of humans thrown together into trying arrangements of their own choosing is not discombobulating, chaotic as it might be. It is simply the whirlpool of London life. It is instructive that while England voted 52 per cent to 48 per cent to leave the EU, in London 60 per cent voted to remain. In the London Borough of Tower Hamlets, two-thirds opted to remain[25].

Sitting on the site of a Roman burial ground just outside the North-Eastern boundary of the City of London, Tower Hamlets is a smorgasbord of cultures that has played host to the dreams of migrants throughout London's history. In the Ward of Spitalfields and Banglatown, only 27 per cent of residents claimed White British ethnicity in the 2011 census, compared to 81 per cent in England. Given the Ward's name, it should not be a surprise that Bangladeshis are currently the predominant ethnic group[26].

For over 300 years, Spitalfields has been a sanctuary for the poor and the persecuted, or just those looking to forge a different life. In the 1970s it was Bangladeshis. In the early years of the twenty-first century, it was hipsters escaping perceptions of cultural normativity by forming communities of shared values. For much of Spitalfields' history, though, the area has played host to waves of Europe's unwanted.

These newcomers were at once resented, admired, emulated and absorbed. They took on the jobs unwanted by 'native' Londoners and were blamed for their willingness to be exploited in order to survive[27]. Their customs were strange and perceived to be incompatible with those of their new community. It soon became difficult to conceive of London without them. Who can imagine a London without curry houses or Irish bars, Uber drivers and ambitious baristas?

It was the French Huguenots who fled into Spitalfields that have had the longest lasting legacy, even if no geographically defined Huguenot communities exist in London anymore. Between 40,000 and 50,000 Huguenots poured into protestant England between 1677 and 1710 after their already precarious existence was made impossible by King Louis XIV's revocation of the Edict of Nantes in 1685, which had allowed them to worship in specific places. The Huguenots had been offered sanctuary by Charles II, suspicious as he was of the French and eager for the skills and wealth these migrants would bring[28]. A total of 25,000 came into a city rebuilding in brick after the Great Fire of 1666, some to Soho and most to Spitalfields[29].

They came to Spitalfields because the seeds of a silk industry were growing there – many of the Huguenots had been involved in elements of the silk industry in their former lives – and because they were able to operate outside of the Guild system that protected trades within the city walls. Mainly they also came to Spitalfields because others had come before them. It is out of such historical accidents that the patchwork of London has been sewn.

The Huguenots have often been positioned as ideal immigrants; grateful to their host and quick to assimilate. Their initiation was not quite so rosy though. The first wave clung to their language and religion, as those communities fleeing areas in which they had specifically come under threat are want to do.

Not everyone was ready for these new influences. Like today's

Brexiting stiff-upper-lip football fan abusing an over-dramatic foreign striker, these cultural differences challenged 'those who equated a tide of luxurious effeminacy with a corrupting foreign influence'[30]. There were anti-French riots in 1675, 1681 and 1683, and an MP described the Huguenots as a 'plague of Frogs'[31].

Huguenot customs might have been ridiculed but they were also adopted, adding a welcome layer of cultural vibrancy. Well educated and highly skilled, the Huguenots transformed Spitalfields from the economic and physical margins of London to the thriving, if chaotic, hub of the silk industry. In the great London tradition, the Huguenots' economic success was not so much in raw production. Instead, they supplemented the products of the empire (much of the silk sewn in Spitalfields came from the East Indies[32]) with creative flair and technical skill. Or, in the language of today's East London techno-capitalists, the Huguenots disrupted these traditional industries.

It was not just their silk that was popular with London's increasingly refined consumers. A rising service economy of hairdressers, interior designers, dentists and tailors developed[33], adding a degree of cosmopolitanism that continues to propel ideas of London. With time these cultural differences became just another weave in the cultural tapestry of London. The Huguenots dispersed into the suburbs as they became more prosperous like so many migrant communities that would follow. They left behind a garment industry that continues today in Spitalfields, if with a distinctly vintage-hipster edge. There also remain physical hints of their existence. From Fournier Street to Fleur de Lis Street, their Huguenot names and houses – distinguished by large attic windows to maximise light for weavers – define the streets of Spitalfields. So too remain Huguenot names such as 'Farage', despite many of them being Anglicised over time.

These houses would not be the Huguenots' most lasting legacy. That lies with the introduction of the word *refugee* into the English language. Refugee originates in the French réfugié, meaning those 'gone in search of refuge'[34]. More specifically, réfugié referred to the plight of the Huguenots. Their spirit has been inhabited by a wave of post-Cold War asylum seekers and refugees who make their way to London, so powerfully captured in Cynthia Cockburn's *Looking to London*[35].

While most asylum seekers arrive in London, they are deliberately dispersed around the country; government support is conditional upon these most vulnerable of migrants moving outside of London. Yet, while the government claims that 92 per cent of asylum seekers are outside of London[36], as soon as that support expires or they can escape the authorities, most make their way back to London to join their national diasporas and to have a better chance of finding work[37]. This is the power of the London dream.

While today these most vulnerable of Londoners would not be able to afford to live in Spitalfields, the next generation of exiles to follow the Huguenots, European Jews, made their way there specifically because of its cheapness. They were not so well received.

Jews had been encouraged into London by William the Conqueror in 1066 and played an important role in the establishment of banking in the City[38]. The twelfth and thirteenth centuries, however, saw increasingly violent prejudice against the Jewish population, marked by a number of pogroms and finally the expulsion of 16,000 Jews in 1290[39].

A Jewish community had re-established itself in London after Oliver Cromwell had allowed them to worship openly in 1656, although strong prejudice was still in existence. The community consolidated during the eighteenth century but Jewish London was established in earnest when the city absorbed many of the two million Jews who fled widespread economic hardship and persecution in Eastern Europe between 1881 and 1914[40]. Most sought the American dream, often arriving in London and moving onto Liverpool to sail across the Atlantic[41]. Nonetheless, a sizeable proportion remained and by 1901 there were 140,000 Jews in the city, 95 per cent of them around Wentworth Street in the Spitalfields area[42].

These new Londoners improvised a living on the streets and in markets, with many finding themselves in the garment work established by their Spitalfields predecessors. This trade continued to be carried out in workshops attached to homes, although these Huguenot homes were now densely sub-divided. The wretched poor working in the garment industry in the developing world would easily recognise the 'sweating' conditions that they were forced to endure.

London's Jews also had to endure continued discrimination. As is the way, their customs were found to be strange and they were accused of refusing to integrate, a cruel demand of a people fleeing persecution for maintaining their way of life. Protests, especially in the East End, were widespread. The 1905 Aliens Act, which brought into British law the first meaningful immigration controls, was a response to an ominous protest by the fascist British Brothers' League calling for Britain to stop acting as 'the dumping ground for the scum of Europe'[43].

With time, though, the Jews became wealthier and more accepted, particularly after World War II. Those who had not left for the suburbs already were bombed out by the Luftwaffe[44]. It was this bombing that would bring the next generation of London dreamers from across the Commonwealth.

The Mother City

Luftwaffe bombs created a new mythology of London – the Blitz Spirit – that would be reproduced through terroristic attacks, tube strikes and flurries of snow. Nonetheless, in the 1950s the London dream was fading fast for its traditional constituents. London needed to be rebuilt, revigorated and reimagined. A different source of bodies, and hopes, was required. Britain turned to the fast-dissolving empire and changed the cultural shape of the city forever. Although long flush with migrants from across the British Isles, and sporadic waves from the continent, in 1951, 95 per cent of Londoners were British born. Those remaining foreigners were perceived to be 'white'[45].

The 1948 British Nationality Act changed everything. The status of 'citizen of the United Kingdom and Colonies' was created, allowing free movement from the 'Commonwealth of Nations', first from the Caribbean and then from the Indian Subcontinent. This new legal status entrenched the rights of Commonwealth citizens to move to the UK, which some 500,000 non-white migrants did between 1948 and 1962. Three-quarters settled in London[46].

A new London, and a new Britain, was born. The city was transformed from the 'alloy of the people of Britain' to an alloy of the world in a couple of generations[47]. In 40 years the number of foreign-born Londoners had risen from 5 per cent to 20 per cent in 1991[48]. In 2017 it was over a third, with two-thirds of all children born in the capital having at least one foreign-born parent[49].

Like the Huguenots and migrant communities to follow, Caribbean migrants had added to the cultural vibrancy of the city which, in turn, encouraged others to move to London and find their place. They were followed by Indian migrants who would congregate in Southall from the 1950s and the Bangladeshi migrants who continued the legacy of the Huguenots and the Jews by settling around Spitalfields, especially in Brick Lane.

For Jerry White, this migration 'changed the face of the Londoner more significantly than any event since the Norman conquest'[50]. Where pre-war London could only truly be considered cosmopolitan in Soho and in the East End, migrant communities were forming and mixing across the capital. Far from watching Britain 'heaping up its own funeral pyre' as Enoch Powell infamously postulated in his 1968 *Rivers of Blood* speech[51], London's post-war migrants constructed the contemporary, cool capital.

The hopes of those who had grown up believing themselves to be British subjects and imagining London as 'the centre of the world they learned about in school'[52] were clear from the moment the 500 Caribbean passengers of the *Empire Windrush* disembarked at the Tilbury Docks. BBC cameras stopped to capture Calypso King Aldwyn Roberts', better known as Lord Kitchener, impromptu performance of the openings stanzas of 'London is the Place for Me'. He sang:

London Is The Place For Me
London this lovely city
You can go to France or America, India, Asia or Australia
But you must come back to London City

Well, believe me, I am speaking broad-mindedly
I am glad to know my mother country
I've been to travelling to countries years ago
But this the place I wanted to know
London That's The Place For Me

What better example could there be of the London dream? Across London new migrants sang their version of this song. They also experienced the tension between their image of the Mother Country and the Western world and their experience of cramped living conditions, menial jobs and everyday discrimination. Many, especially those from South Asia, had come from more privileged backgrounds (and were thus able to pay for their journey) and found the experience particularly galling[53].

The Poles and Lithuanians who surged into London on budget airlines and at coach stations when British borders opened to the Eastern regions of the EU in 2004, would no doubt sympathise. These EU-born workers, willed and willing to be exploited in the big city, not only hold 600,000 jobs in London but act as a ready reserve of labourers willing to paint houses and clean cars. The presence of their countrymen on cardboard boxes around central London is a continual reminder of their vulnerability.

Their vulnerability gives material form to both dimensions of the dark side of the London dream. On one hand, the city and its businesses are built upon the exploitation of those preferring to toil in London rather than their home towns, whether near or far. On the other, many Londoners blame their misery on the arrival of those chasing their own dreams. It is this blame that haunted the Huguenots and the Jews, the West Indians and the Bangladeshis. It is a fear that drove the festering spectre of the National Front in the 1970s.

Anxiety about the presence of alien cultures, from their customs to the paradoxical resentment of migrants simultaneously taking 'our' jobs and taking advantage of 'our' welfare state, was a core current of Brexit. Thankfully much of this Brexiting bigotry lies beyond the geographical and cultural margins of the city. Nonetheless, we must tackle it directly before proceeding.

Chapter 2

Competing Dreams

When the American author Jack London intrepidly entered the slums of the East End in 1902 he did so 'with an attitude of mind which I may best liken to that of the explorer'[54]. Disguised as a down on his luck American sailor, he found 'The streets were filled with a new and different race of people, short of stature, and of wretched or beer-sodden appearance[55].'

London chronicled his experiences in *People of the Abyss*, writing that he halted his wandering around Mile End when he came across a group of 'workmen of the better class' heatedly arguing. The topic of conversation was quickly evident, as he recalls:

'But 'ow about this 'ere cheap immigration?' one of them demanded. 'The Jews of Whitechapel, say, a-cutting our throats right along?'
'You can't blame them,' was the answer. 'They're just like us, and they've got to live. Don't blame the man who offers to work cheaper than you and gets your job.'
'But 'ow about the wife an' kiddies?' his interlocutor demanded. 'There you are,' came the answer. 'How about the wife and kiddies of the man who works cheaper than you and gets your job? Eh? How about his wife and kiddies? He's more interested in them than in yours, and he can't see them starve. So he cuts the price of labour and out you go. But you mustn't blame him, poor devil. He can't help it. Wages always come down when two men are after the same job. That's the fault of competition, not of the man who cuts the price.'[56]

Over a century later, this debate continues on the Eastern fringes of London, although they are so Eastern that they are more Essex than London. And the Jews of Whitechapel are now the Muslims.

Or the Poles. Or the Romanians. Or just 'Them'.

It is always them.

This is the playing field of the new politics of the West: who should be blamed for life getting harder for working people in advanced capitalist societies? Who should be blamed for real wages falling over the past decade[57] when it appears that the wealthiest are only getting wealthier[58]? Why are we receiving warnings of a return to *Victorian* levels of inequality[59]? This is a battle of narratives, a political battle to explain discontent.

The basic question is the same as that overheard in Mile End: Are migrants unjustly adding to the numbers competing for jobs and resources for which locals should be prioritised? Or are workers all in the same boat, all just trying to make a living and being eagerly exploited by employers? In this case, the fault lies with those who benefit from the competition, not those who compete.

At the moment, outside of London and the global cities of the world, one side is clearly winning. 'They' are at fault.

Greg knows which side of the debate he is on and he is keen to tell me.

I'm Heartbroken for London

Grey-bearded and compact, Greg has the kind of countenance to which you immediately warm. But he has not warmed to the new London. Born in post-war Notting Hill, Greg is 'heartbroken about London'. Sipping a Guinness in a draughty pub that will soon be overtaken by the creative types that now occupy his part of North London, he is determined to tell me why.

Because the Londoners have gone. People like me. You know? In less than a generation, so 20 years, or 25 years. Just gone. I miss them

The London he claims to miss is Cockney London. *Real*, 'indigenous' London. The Cockney reputation for London-ness was established during the great Victorian migration. At this time, Jerry White asserts, migration to the city – particularly of unmarried young women – meant that by the mid-nineteenth century, having two London-born grandparents would have been 'inherently improbable'[60].

And yet, although Victorian newcomers tended to settle on the greener edges of London, often in close proximity to the railway station they arrived from[61], an increasingly compacted section of the East End held Londoners of a longer lineage. This was especially true of Bethnal Green, where the 1851 census showed that 82 per cent of residents were London born, compared to 62 per cent in the city as a whole[62].

For an indigenous community, though, their roots were rather recent. This most London of districts was simply a more entrenched migrant community; Bethnal Green was originally an overspill of the eighteenth-century Huguenot silk weaving community, eventually developing what we have come to know as a Cockney dialect[63]. It does not take long to become a Londoner.

But Greg has a frozen view of what a Londoner is and I'm not sure that I meet his criteria. He mourns the loss of the Cockney accent, the rhyming slang where he could turn to a stranger and start up a conversation in the same vernacular. He insists that we have 'lost our London accent now' and he is nonplussed by the new 'Jamaican type of accent' (Multicultural London English or 'Jafaican') now favoured by London's working classes.

In his grand time before the fall, before the migrants arrived and our resources ran dry:

It was a Londoners' city. And I'm talking about, you know, working-class, middle-class Londoners.

But not anymore. Londoners, he claims, 'got to feel isolated in their areas, because they weren't surrounded by Londoners anymore'. This, to his mind, is criminal.

If they had been heritage buildings, or something like that, people would have been protected on heritage.

Greg pauses while he stares into his Guinness and repeats his mantra with the melancholic earnestness of the aged:

Absolutely heartbroken

It is no wonder that Greg's love of London has cooled, although perhaps not for the reasons he believes. Expelled from school, Greg worked his way up through an electrical apprenticeship. This was back when there was 'so much opportunity for non-academic kids', before the demise of apparent working-class London and the working-class Londoners Greg holds so dear.

He attributes some of this change to Margaret Thatcher, who turned London away from manufacturing and into a service economy. He was a socialist then, he 'hated racial hatred' and 'one of the happiest days of [his] life was when Tony Blair's Labour Party got into government'.

Life was good, then.

It took a turn for the worst with the banking crisis. Made redundant from his facilities management job, he headed overseas to 'ride out the recession', eventually teaching English in South-East Asia. Then he got sick, a stomach ulcer that put him in hospital for weeks. The bills almost bankrupted him and he returned to London. Despite his years away, London had not yet recovered from the recession and jobs were hard to come by. Greg was unemployed, again. He was also denied benefits because he had been out of the UK for too long and was now deemed to be a foreign national.

Despite having, 'paid in all my life', he found the Job Centre absolutely unwilling to help him. In a painful irony for Greg, he thought himself to be 'the only English person' in this place, being denied benefits because of his newfound non-nationality while 'people who were new arrivals to Britain, who haven't paid into the system, were entitled to all the benefit that came with it'.

Work was hard to come by and the Job Centre was a brutal experience. They tried to force him to do unpaid work. They tried to force him to be a cleaner but he couldn't do it; the stigma was too much. Short-term contracts in the recruitment industry were found to be equally demeaning, and unsuccessful. Other applications went unanswered.

Soon enough Greg became part of London's 'Hidden Homeless' population; those not on the streets but without formal housing, existing through the charity of friends and family. The *London Assembly* estimates that there are 12,500 Londoners in this situation on any given night[64].

But charity can only last so long. He was out of options and into the cold.

After almost half a century in the workforce, Greg found himself desperate and one of 8,000 Londoners braving the streets[65]. Now in his mid-fifties, he was surviving in libraries and on public transport during the day. At night he was dodging addicts and having to stay awake at night to keep himself warm and safe. This wouldn't have happened in the London he loved, one of community, working-class solidarity and migrants who knew their place.

His local council refused to provide housing assistance but he found salvation in shelters. They offered compassion not found in the newly austerity-orientated administrative apparatus, providing food, community and a kind word. Food banks would later supply much needed sustenance. If Greg had experienced the worst of London – a banking crisis and recession, austerity and a hostile application of immigration policy – he was also experiencing the remnants of the best.

Greg is in a better place now, helped into a job that allows him to express his charisma and share some of his experiences. His bitterness remains.

We can see good reason for his heartbreak. There is no denying that Greg's life has taken a turn for the worse, mostly for reasons outside of his control. But the reader can interpret a number of causes for Greg's bitterness and the trauma caused by the disruption in his firmly embedded sense of place. We might identify Thatcher's battle against manufacturing and, along with Tony Blair, support for bankers and neo-liberal economics. We could blame the austerity policies of the 2010 Conservative-Liberal Democrat coalition, policies which have led to a 44 per cent funding cut for London boroughs from 2010-2015[66]. We might blame an economic system that allowed the banking industry to continue to thrive while workers like Greg were out in the cold.

For Greg, the answer is clear. The problem is migration and living in London has been 'like an invasion or losing a war'. Greg is not the first Londoner to hold these opinions. Despite the city long being considered an 'aggregate of various nations, distinguished from each other by their respective customs, manners, and interests'[67], there is a long history of tension between newcomers and those more established in London.

The complaints follow a familiar pattern.

'Their customs are strange.'

'They refuse to adapt to our way of life.'

'They stick to themselves.'

'They are taking our jobs.'

When the first wave of Jewish migrants took on the money lending Christians were forbidden to do, for example, they were attacked and eventually violently expelled from the city[68]. A similar suspicion was cast over Italian merchants in the sixteenth century[69]. Huguenots provoked alarm by their numbers and their unfamiliar language. They were also accused of taking up 'the fairest houses, in the city, divid[ing] and fit[ting] them for serval uses [and] tak[ing] into them several lodgers and dwellers'[70].

Such fears continue today, although they are generally dismissed as hopelessly anachronistic. This is seen in the reaction to the BBC documentary *The Last Whites of the East End*, which led viewers like Nicci Kay to ask 'Why are we forced to pay for racist views to get aired on TV?'[71] Set in the London Borough of Newham, once a Cockney stronghold but now the area with the lowest White British population in the UK[72], the documentary explored the attitudes of residents who felt threatened and are engaging in 'white flight' further East into Essex. Here one resident, secretary of the East Ham Working Men's Club Peter Bell, expressed similar concerns to the accusations against the Huguenots in the early eighteenth century, stating:

> I mean no disrespect to the Muslim community, but I don't think they want to be part of the traditions here. I hear words like multiculturalism and community and I think it's nonsense. We are in an area that has massive unemployment and that is about to become overcrowded and you feel ostracised.

The reference to overcrowding and unemployment is instructive. It highlights one of the paradoxes of attacks on impoverished migrants; they are stereotyped as being both lazy and living off hand-outs, and taking 'our' jobs at the same time[73].

The *Express* tabloid, for example, made a typically alarmist claim that:

> European nationals are more likely to claim tax credits and child benefits than British born people, whilst still accessing public services like the NHS. They are also contributing less in tax than working Britons because they are working for lower pay, undercutting wages in a number of sectors from building to

manufacturing.[74]

The *Express,* with front page headlines such as 'Migrants Rob Young Britons of Jobs' and 'Migrants Pay Just £100 to Invade Britain' embodies the enduring logic of populist politics. In response to discontent, an enemy – 'them' – is positioned as the cause. In these narratives, eliminating the enemy would eliminate discontent. We do not have to turn to Nazi Germany and 'the Jewish Question' to see this logic in action. Donald Trump's positioning of Muslims, Mexicans, Crooked Hillary and the Liberal Elite was the basis of his 2016 election to the US Presidency[75]. Afterwards, Fake News, MS-13 and the FBI have played this role.

The Brexit referendum ran according to a similar logic of 'us' against the EU and the fear of foreigners, particularly those of colour. These sentiments certainly still exist in London, though they are not as prominent a feature of politics in the capital as elsewhere. Greg is right, his London is gone. As linguist Susan Fox found, Cockney accents are more likely to be found in areas like Basildon in the East End[76]. Perhaps those who are most heartbroken no longer live in London.

Perhaps the dislocation of Greg's sense of place is just what happens if you live in London for long enough: the city leaves you behind if you do not change with it. Life in the capital is far too transient to cling to the monolithic identities. In a city whose popular de facto slogan is #Londonisopen, those who Greg does not consider to be Londoners would not recognise his views as those of a true Londoner.

Why is London Open?

Violence and discrimination against newcomers has always been a part of London life. It is unfair to paint London as some sort of cosmopolitan utopia. Many migrants, especially those of colour, continue to experience sustained discrimination. It is challenging to be a migrant when the Conservative government is actively creating a 'hostile environment'[77]. In such a fluid city it is easy to forget that this is the capital of the United Kingdom and remaining in the country in the long term requires forms, tests and considerable sums of money. And the infinite patience required to negotiate the surely deliberately unresponsive immigration system.

But London continues to be a place where 'they open the door'. Becoming a Londoner can be a matter of months, rather than years and there are certainly no forms to fill in. For every Notting Hill riot, there is a Notting Hill Carnival. For every anti-migrant protest, there is a Battle of Cable Street or 'Refugees Welcome Here' rally.

When the Conservative Party Mayoral candidate Zac Goldsmith's 2016 campaign ran a fear campaign that played on anti-Muslim prejudices, claiming that his opponent had 'repeatedly legitimised those with extremist views'[78], he woefully underestimated Londoners. Just 6 weeks before the Brexit vote, Sadiq Khan, the son-of-a-bus-driver Labour Party candidate, won by 57 per cent of the vote to become the first Muslim Mayor of London. His Pakistani migrant parents would have been proud (as he kept telling us).

Few groups ever stay a 'them' for long in London. In the face of violence and exclusion, most migrant communities have slowly slid into the London waters. They have adapted to customs, they have traded with others and they have spread into the suburbs, becoming just another tile in the mosaic of the city[79]. Culturally life is difficult, particularly for the first wave and first generation of migrants. But they adapt to the city and the city adapts to them, embracing a vibrancy absent outside of this global city. Perhaps the reason it does, however, is that employers need their work ethic and their wallets.

It is here that we see another layer to the #LondonisOpen mantra. On the campaign website created in response to the EU referendum, Mayor Sadiq Khan writes of Londoners:

We don't simply tolerate each other's differences, we celebrate them. Many people from all over the globe live and work here, contributing to every aspect of life in our city. We now need to make sure that people across London, and the globe, hear that #LondonIsOpen. I urge everyone to get involved with this simple but powerful campaign to send a positive message to the world[80].

Wonderfully inspirational. It is not just diversity that is being celebrated, however. While the Mayor wants to 'reassure the more than one million foreign nationals who live in London that they will always be welcome, and that any form of discrimination will not be tolerated', he also wants to show the world that:

London remains entrepreneurial, international and full of creativity and possibility...London is the best city in the world. We're entrepreneurial, international and outward looking

London is certainly open, but it is open to businesses and bodies willing to work above anything else. Indeed, contra to the tabloid headlines, a report from PWC showed that London's 1.8 migrant workers have a significantly positive influence on London's economy, generating £83 billion in economic value each year[81]. It is no wonder that London's employers are so keen for London to stay open to migrants.

These migrants, whether from Peterborough or Poland, are the fulcrum of London's new economy; a high-tech and creative economy that is reliant not only on the arrival of talented newcomers but those for whom servicing this economy is better than what they have left behind, no matter the conditions they endure in their new home.

There is nothing new about London's employers embracing newcomers willing to be exploited. It was the very basis for

London's nineteenth-century metamorphosis into the world's greatest metropolis.

Chapter 3

The Dreams of Capital

In his monumental *The Condition of the Working Class in England*, Marx's great collaborator Fredrich Engels writes of mid-nineteenth-century London with some awe:

> *A town, such as London, where a man may wander for hours together without reaching the beginning of the end, without meeting the slightest hint which could lead to the inference that there is open country within reach, is a strange thing. This colossal centralisation, this heaping together of two and a half millions of human beings at one point, has multiplied the power of this two and a half millions a hundredfold; has raised London to the commercial capital of the world, created the giant docks and assembled the thousand vessels that continually cover the Thames. I know nothing more imposing than the view which the Thames offers during the ascent from the sea to London Bridge. The masses of buildings, the wharves on both sides, especially from Woolwich upwards, the countless ships along both shores, crowding ever closer and closer together, until, at last, only a narrow passage remains in the middle of the river, a passage through which hundreds of steamers shoot by one another; all this is so vast, so impressive, that a man cannot collect himself, but is lost in the marvel of England's greatness before he sets foot upon English soil*[82]

Engels was not wrong about the stupendous scale of the monstrosity that was Victorian London. In an ungodly experiment on the human condition, nineteenth-century Londoners were thrust into close proximity on an unprecedented scale, propelling an incomprehensible diversity of ways of life and ways of surviving.

Nor was Engels alone. For the first intrepid chroniclers of early-modern London, there was always something unfathomable about what Henry Mayhew called the 'Bricken Wilderness' of the metropolis[83].

London was expanding rapidly and exhibiting the fineries of industrialisation while attempting to control the chaos of its own creation. The city also had a sophomoric relationship to darkness and disorder. Today's digital technologies mean that no corner of the city goes unmapped and no pop-up goes unreviewed. In an environment in which one was as likely to stumble on an elegant estate as a rotting rookery, the streets harboured a sense of mystery that was at once exciting and foreboding. The unmapped was not just unknown, it was dangerous and laden with immorality.

This fear of the unknown was rampant in the bewildered descriptions of a rapidly expanding London. In particular, references to Africa – the frontier of empire – to darkness, and to untamed humanity were common[84]. Commenting on the irregularity of London's design in his 1751 pamphlet *An Enquiry into the Causes of the Late Increase of Robbers*, the English novelist Henry Fielding claimed that if the city had been:

…intended for the very purpose of concealment, [it] could not have been better contrived. Upon such a view the whole appears as a vast wood or forest in which the thief may harbour with as great security as wild beasts do in the deserts of Arabia and Africa[85].

Moreover, William Booth, the founder of the Salvation Army, directly compared the 'submerged tenth' of London's population with 'darkest Africa', arguing

As there is a darkest Africa, is there not also a darkest England…May we not find a parallel at our own doors, and discover within a stone's throw of our cathedrals and palaces similar horrors to those which

[Henry] Stanley has found existing in the Great Equatorial forest?[86]

London was a city of light and of dreams. The darkness of the squalor concealed within it loomed large. As much as the Victorians tried to keep this residuum of the city in place, it could not be contained and by the mid-nineteenth century evidence was discharging out onto its streets. At the end of the century, these unwashed masses were protesting on these pavements.

'The paradox here', Peter Ackroyd argues, 'is that the imperial city, the city which maintained and financed a world empire, contained within its heart a population more brutish and filthy than any of the races it believed itself destined to conquer[87]'.

Perhaps there is no paradox. Wealth and poverty, squalor and splendour have always been part of London's mix. These contradictions were driven onto the streets of Victorian London, becoming inescapably visible for the first time.

The Inescapable Poor

It was not just the scale and density of London's streets that was bewildering for the Victorians; it was the sheer concentration of the misery that was seeping to the surface and lying on these streets. London has always harboured the outcasts of the world, those with no place in the social fabric and those existing in a state of abject poverty. What was new to the Victorian world was the density of this suffering and its jarring proximity to wealth. Moreover, as London's economy boomed, the presence of the poor did not dissipate with the rising tide. When the economy crashed in the 1840s and in the 1870s, this jetsam of the city were inescapable.

For London's poor, life was short, precarious and improvised. In his *Life and Labour of the London Poor*, Mayhew had estimated in 1865 that there were 30,000 making a living on the streets and that 3 days' rain could bring them to the brink of starvation[88]. Conditions were such that many boys in the East End were found to be unfit to fight in the Boer War at the conclusion of the nineteenth century, creating considerable public consternation and triggering health reforms[89].

The abject misery of London's lost children and its paupers was immortalised by the literature of Charles Dickens. In his *Oliver Twist*, Dickens described Oliver's first impressions of London:

> *A dirtier or more wretched place he had never seen. The street was very narrow and muddy, and the air was impregnated with filthy odours. There were a good many small shops; but the only stock in trade appeared to be heaps of children, who, even at that time of night, were crawling in and out at the doors, or screaming from inside. The sole places that seemed to prosper amid the general blight of the place, were the public-houses; and in them, the lowest orders of Irish were wrangling with might and main[90].*

Life expectancy for a boy born in London in the 1850s was 35. It was lower still in the slums, where children sharing a bed with their parents were regularly recorded to have been suffocated[91]. Putting children to work was a necessity for many families and a boon for those who employed their little hands. Even more troublesome was the presence of thousands of orphaned children on the streets. Often existing in improvised colonies, they would become part of those scrambling an improvised living on the streets. If they made it that far.

They were selling wares in markets. They were begging on the streets and sleeping on benches. These were the wasted lives of Victorian London. Lives lived in filth and surviving on scraps. Often they were lives where the only means of subsidence was in banishing the waste products of the wealthy, searching the pavement for scraps and taking away night soil.

This refuse of humanity was inescapable. Handling the waste products rendered by civilised consumption is a very London problem. Roman London, with its desire to create a civilised society, had complex methods and regulations to contend with the excesses of urban life. Even as civilised life in London became problematic during the middle-ages, waste was confined to designated grounds. In the thirteenth century, for example, regulations are said to have required that 'no one shall place dun or other filth in the streets or lanes, but cause the same to be taken by the rakes to the places ordained'[92]. This legacy can still be seen in the existence of street names such as 'Pudding Lane', even if the names Shiteburn Ave and Pissing Alley have been consigned to history[93].

The growing consumption of the Victorian middle classes, however, meant that their waste products could no longer be contained. The increases in the scale of the economy caused smog that was often so thick that residents would get lost within metres of their homes[94]. Infectious diseases, caused both by a lack of hygienic waste disposal and because many Londoners were forced to source their water from the euphemistically 'Brownish' Thames, haunted those Londoners without a private supply of water. Moreover, while these diseases were concentrated in the poorest areas of the capital, they were spread by the poor[95]. Along with the 'Great Stink' in the summer of 1858, which led to Joseph Bazalgette's revolutionary sewers that continue to run under contemporary London, the spread of disease and the resulting fear ensured that Londoners were in the filth together.

Just as London struggled to contain its waste matter, its poor could not be confined to the designated darkness. London's slums and rookeries, its streets and workhouses may have felt like another country to those who explored them, but they were also starting to encroach on territories unused to the unwashed. Not only were there areas in which the 'well-to-do' and those experiencing 'chronic want' closed in on the powerful Cities of London and of Westminster[96] but the very existence of the poorest was becoming increasingly evident as this residuum flowed onto the streets and into the senses.

The all-to-common association between these forms of residuum was evoked by Jack London, who wrote with some bewilderment of the 'Carter and Carpenter' he spent time with on his exploration, noticing that they walked with their eyes on the pavement. He was startled to find out why:

> From the slimy, spittle-drenched, sidewalk, they were picking up bits of orange peel, apple skin, and grape stems, and, they were eating them. The pits of greengage plums they cracked between their teeth for the kernels inside. They picked up stray bits of bread the size of peas, apple cores so black and dirty one would not take them to be apple cores, and these things these two men took into their mouths, and chewed them, and swallowed them; and this, between six and seven o'clock in the evening of August 20, year of our Lord 1902, in the heart of the greatest, wealthiest, and most powerful empire the world has ever seen[97].

Thus, as much as the city concealed the darkness within it, the flow of newcomers and the need to leave the slums to find substance meant that the poorest Londoners were increasingly visible. Outside of the enclaves of the wealthy, the poor could always be felt, even if they existed in the shadows. They represented, as Ackroyd observes, 'almost a city within a city, and such a large aggregate of human misery could not be ignored'[98]. The darkest of African had come to the streets of London.

And still, they came like never before. That the appeal of London was stronger than ever, despite the readily apparent suffering, speaks of the compelling grip of the London dream and its instantiation in the Victorian imagination. Aware of the risk of ending up on the streets, workers were flowing into the city for the chance to be exploited in a workplace.

In 1801, there were one million Londoners[99]. By 1861 another two million squeezed into an area barely beyond today's Zone

2, making London the most populous city in the world. Notably, at least 38 per cent of Londoners were new to the city[100]. While its sides bulged with newly minted suburbs facilitated by an expanding railway network, its streets filled with paupers and its air thickened with smog. But neither the discontent nor the desolation of the poorest Londoners stopped others from joining their ranks; London's population grew from 2.6 million in 1851 to 6.5 million in 1901[101].

It was upon these Londoners that the city depended and it was vital that they did not become conscious of their universal class status, or take inspiration from their revolting continental comrades.

As Jerry White writes[102], what to do about the poor, the diseases they spread, the crimes they committed and the political instability they provided were the most pressing questions of the 1830s. A civilising mission was required, one of distinctly imperial virtues.

Civilising Savages

At the start of Queen Victoria's reign, there was no widespread sympathy for the poor, at least not from those with the power to do something about it. The labouring classes certainly had no political power of their own. There was no Labour Party or World Bank. There was not even a Bono to 'Make Poverty History' or to create an anti-poverty campaign led by wealthy celebrities without a hint of self-awareness.

Instead, the moral failing was attributed to the poor. They were idle. They were irresponsible. They were just plain immoral. Who could defend a street urchin who could not even bother to wash their clothes or to develop a basic knowledge of the classics? No one can be helped who does not want to be helped. Perhaps their suffering was just the natural order of things, like the divine right of kings or a wet English Summer.

This strange sense of morality was the basis for the 1834 Poor

Law Amendment Act. After the previous iteration was widely resented because it was seen to be redistributing taxes to the idle and encouraging them to have children, the updated laws ruled that the poor had to enter a workhouse in order to receive any relief. A minimum of clothing and food were provided in exchange for hard, and generally pointless, labour. The idleness of the poor, it was supposed, could be cured by making the support system worse than the suffering it was theoretically relieving.

This is the logic of the workhouse that Dickens ascribes with adroit irony in *Oliver Twist* to the 'very sage, deep, philosophical men' running a Ward workhouse, who '...established the rule, that all poor people should have the alternative (for they would compel nobody, not they) of being starved by a gradual process in the house, or by a quick one out of it'[103].

These workhouses were dreaded and seen as a last resort, just as the authorities had wanted. Lines were long; Jack London recorded the despair and desperation of lines outside 'the Spike':

First of all, I must beg forgiveness of my body for the vileness through which I have dragged it, and forgiveness of my stomach for the vileness which I have thrust into it. I have been to the spike, and slept in the spike, and eaten in the spike; also, I have run away from the spike.

After my two unsuccessful attempts to penetrate the Whitechapel casual ward, I started early, and joined the desolate line before three o'clock in the afternoon. They did not 'let in' till six, but at that early hour I was number twenty, while the news had gone forth that only twenty-two were to be admitted. By four o'clock there were thirty-four in line, the last ten hanging on in the slender hope of getting in by some kind of a miracle. Many more came, looked at the line, and went away, wise to the bitter fact that the spike would be 'full up.'[104]

This was certainly an effective way of distancing oneself from the misery of those with whom you shared a city. Conservative politicians around the world continue to deploy it. Iain Duncan Smith, for example, the former leader of the UK Conservative Party and founder of the cruelly named Centre for Social Justice, responded to spiralling poverty in the UK in his role as Work and Pensions Secretary by claiming, 'Getting a family into work, supporting strong relationships, getting parents off drugs and out of debt — all this can do more for a child's well-being than any amount of money in out-of-work benefits'[105]. How wonderfully Victorian of him.

But this confinement of the poor could not and would not hold. Researchers and reformers like Booth and Mayhew were painstakingly mapping and classifying poverty. This very Victorian method of social control, while completed with no little condescension, bewilderment and pity, brought the suffering of Londoners into the public sphere. Similarly, the compelling virtue of Dickens' work in particular evoked poverty in a different light and the first shoots of a social conscience appeared as the century developed[106].

In 1848, soon to be Prime Minster Lord Palmerton proclaimed:

Our duty, our vocation is not to enslave, but to set free; and I may say without any vainglorious boast, or without great offence to anyone, that we stand at the head of moral, social and political civilisation. Our task is to lead the way and direct the march of other nations.

The first solutions to the 'threat' of the poor were to bring them into the realm of the state, harshly prosecuting crimes against property and instituting public health improvements, if slum clearances could be included in that category.

London's poor had some other answers. At the beginning of the nineteenth century, there was already a long history of radical politics in London[107]. Although London's diverse economy restricted the kind of tight class consciousness that emerges when a single industry dominates a place, radical political petitions, pamphlets, newspapers and rallies were commonplace. At a time when the vote was restricted to property owning men and corruption was endemic, much of this political energy was focused on political reform rather than economic revolution[108].

This energy coalesced in the Chartist movement, whose People's Charter produced six demands for political reform. Most prominently, they called for the vote for every man aged 21 or over. The relative comforts of London meant that the Chartist movement was initially stronger in the North. By mid-century, however, with London's economy weakening and misery stockpiling during the 'hungry 40s', Chartism had built a popular following[109].

The Chartist movement was given further impetus by the 1848 European revolutions. While the Chartist's demands were more modest than those of the Springtime of the Peoples, they presented a sharp message to Britain's elite. Crown and capital alike needed a way to quell the anger of those with no public voice and receiving no apparent benefit from the expansion of industrial capitalism.

Their strategy was two-part. The Chartists, forced into a potential insurrectionary confrontation with the state, were defeated[110]. This political defeat was only ever going to be temporary, however. Crushing of rebellion does not crush the spirit that drives it. Another solution was required to quell the peoples' anger.

If the state has a way to deal with worrisome political desires, capitalism has another. Workers and non-workers, Londoners and potential Londoners had to be made to feel like they were part of a great leap forward. Some of this was achieved through real and imagined material advancement. The rest was conjured through the dark magic of capitalism; an embodied, if unconscious, buy-into a narrative of progress and the London dream.

This is not to say that the working classes were not restless. Their struggles, along with the intersecting women's movement, were continuous. Rebellion continued to be ruthlessly crushed and the organisation of an atomised, exhausted and not-always-employed working class proved difficult. But control of violence was not the only reason that Chartists' demonstrations went no further. The other reason relied on a shift in consciousness and the mobilisation of the London dream.

Exhibiting the Dream

One of the primary drivers of this shift was the Great Exhibition or, to give it its full name, The Great Exhibition of the Works of Industry of All Nations. Opening on May Day in 1851 in the temporary 'Crystal Palace' installed in Hyde Park, the Great Exhibition was the first international display of manufacturing and design. Or, as Karl Marx is reported to have said, an 'emblem of the capitalist fetishism of commodities'[111].

The Exhibition encompassed 100,000 exhibits by 15,000 contributors, including a hydraulic press, adding machines and the world's first voting machine. 'Retiring Rooms', built by George Jennings, the inventor of the first public flush toilets, were also present. These were the wonders of capitalism and, naturally, Britain occupied half of the floor space[112]. Also featured was a printing press turning out 5,000 copies an hour of the *Illustrated London News*, which of course gave the Exhibition celebratory reviews, describing it as turning 'the capital of a great nation, [into] the metropolis of the world'.

This celebration of industrial capitalism was a tremendous triumph, attracting six million visitors, a remarkable third of the country[113]. Visitors marvelled at the scale and the grandiose novelty of the exhibits. The author Charlotte Bronte, for example, wrote in wonderous terms to her father about her second visit to the Exhibition:

> We remained in it about 3 hours, and I must say I was more struck
> with it on this occasion than at my first visit. It is a wonderful
> place – vast, strange, new and impossible to describe. Its grandeur
> does not consist in one thing, but in the unique assemblage of all
> things. Whatever human industry has created you find there. It
> seems as if only magic could have gathered this mass of wealth from
> all the ends of the earth – as if none but supernatural hands could
> have arranged it this, with such a blaze and contrast of colours and
> marvellous power of effect. The multitude filling the great aisles
> seems ruled and subdued by some invisible influence. Amongst the
> thirty thousand souls that peopled it the day I was there not one
> loud noise was to be heard, not one irregular movement seen; the
> living tide rolls on quietly, with a deep hum like the sea heard from
> the distance[114].

Given the state of unrest among the working classes, there
were initial fears that London's poor would not take well to
the Exhibition. A total of 10,000 troops were moved into the
London area, the Metropolitan Police force was strengthened
and a Working Classes Central Committee was formed out of
prominent (but not strictly working-class) Londoners[115]. Instead,
the event attracted those at both ends of the manufacturing
process, with the working classes (if not those eking out an
existence of the streets) coming in huge numbers on 'Schilling
Day'. For those whose experience of industry was dirty and
thankless, the machinery on display suggested a brighter future.

The Exhibition installed London at the heart of the global
imagination and introduced provincial Britons to the possibility
of the city. Visitors were enabled by the emergence of a national
railway system with London as its hub, with stations opening
at Euston (1837), King's Cross (1852), Paddington (1854) and
Waterloo (1848). These railways created ready access to the

city for goods and for people so that in 1850 *The Times* claimed 'Thirty years ago not one countryman in one hundred had seen the metropolis. There is now scarcely one in the same number who has not spent the day there[116].'

These visitors returned home either determined to join the whirlpool of the capital or with tales to inspire others. Perhaps they never came back at all. As White notes, 'moving to London was one of the great social facts in the life of the nation'[117]. New aspirants were arriving from all over the country, averaging 30,000-50,000 per year during the Victorian era[118].

As towns across the country were developing connections with London, so was London growing in the collective consciousness of Britain and of the world. Outsiders were able to read letters from those they knew in London, or perhaps catch up on stories during visits. Most influentially, perhaps, they were able to engage with a glamorised version of London produced in literature. Here the likes of Pierce Egan's immensely popular *Life in London* told stories of adventure and opportunity[119].

So developed a 'London Season' from the beginning of May to the end of July, a season now observed by today's global elite and still featuring many of the anchor events of the original season: Ascot, Wimbledon, Henley and the Chelsea Flower Show. In the nineteenth century, this season 'brought thousands of bourgeois and upper-middle-class families' who found 'attendance in the London for the season indispensable'[120]. They came for the parties and the fashion, visiting Regency-era shopping arcades and new-fangled department stores like Harrods (1853).

They also came because it was the thing to do and London was the place where everything that could be done was done. A place where the civilisations of the world met and a city that provided an opportunity to escape the misery of elsewhere. One that, in English barrister, politician and writer Robert Plumer Ward's words, offered the 'contagion of numbers, the sense of something going'.[121] A place to live out London dreams.

These fabled dreams of a city of splendour and opportunity installed London as *the* global city, a modern Babylon that '... seemed to contain within itself all previous civilisations'[122]. It is the apparent presence of these civilisations that continues to pull migrants and tourists alike.

It is this Victorian dream that continues to animate contemporary London, which tells a story of itself as the centre of the universe, a modern metropolis where 'you really can live in London for years and years and still find something new each day'[123]. As of 2018, London's population has never been higher and the city has never been richer, with economic output double the rest of the UK[124] and an economy comfortably bigger than that of the Netherlands[125].

London may no longer be the undisputed 'Greatest City in the World', as Victorians claimed it to be. And yet, even as they cram into tube carriages on their morning commute, their minds absorbed in technology that allows them to escape the misery of intense proximity to others, most Londoners would grudgingly acknowledge that there is no place they would rather be. Even when they are daydreaming about being anywhere else.

This aspirational suffering is as much part of London's story as the accumulation of wealth and the consumption of culture. Just as the Victorians, Tony Parsons claimed that:

...if you are going to live in London, then you have to take on the world. You have to compete - and it doesn't matter if you are a self-made millionaire or a van driver. The long-term Londoners who work hard are now contending with newcomers who work seven days a week. Londoners who fly first class are suddenly vying - for houses, for school places, for restaurant tables - with people who fly in private planes. In this new London, there is always someone richer than you, there is always someone who is prepared to work harder than you do, there is always someone who wants it much more than you do[126].

This is the stuff of the London dream, an aspirational narrative that has long drawn migrants to the city and allowed Londoners to justify their suffering. It is the idea that things can always get better. That the city will provide opportunities unavailable elsewhere. That the misery of some of its inhabitants is only an aberration.

The city is hungry for this new blood, for new bodies and new dreamers. It should not be surprising that the grip of London's mythology is strongest with the youngest among us, even if it moves more destitute bodies to the city.

Chapter Four

The Three Rebirths of Modern London

Victorian London did not end with Queen Victoria's death, it just took on an Edwardian label and launched into the twentieth century without breaking stride, excusing a few Royal hiccups. By 1939 London's population had reached 8.6 million, a peak that would not again be reached until 2015. London did better than the rest of the country during the depression and migrants flooded in so much that, in Jerry White's words, '…between the wars the age-old lure of London as a city where the streets were paved with gold was burnished more brightly than for generations before'[127].

As with Britain itself, the Second World War changed everything. Within a decade not only would an emboldened America take its place as the global superpower with imperial ambitions, but many of Britain's most notable colonies would achieve independence. As America's 'greatest generation' was forging ahead, the British were still operating ration books.

For much of the latter half of the twentieth century, it looked like the capital would go the same way as its country.

While World War I had centralised London's power, its sequel had the opposite effect. A third of the floor space in the city was destroyed and from 1939-1945 businesses moved out of London at a rate unseen since the Great Fire. The destruction and post-war zoning regulations significantly restricted industry in the East End. In any instance, firms had learnt to exist outside of London and continued to move away during the 1950s.

The 1951 Festival of Britain provided a welcome fillip, with eight million visiting the South Bank exhibition. It was not to have the lasting influence of the Great Exhibition. Instead, the Festival acted as a farewell party to the empire rather than the welcome launch of a century earlier.

If London had been at the forefront of industrial capitalism, it was now experiencing some of the worst of the 'urban crisis'. During the 1970s and 1980s deindustrialisation led to unemployment, dislocated communities and crime. The industrial jobs that had kept London's working classes in humble conditions were drifting away: 80 per cent of manufacturing jobs in London were lost between 1966 and 1996[128].

Overall, London lost 30 per cent of all jobs from 1962 to 1994[129]. Crime rose by 46 per cent from 1981 to 1991[130]. Despite the glamour of the Swinging Sixties in the West of the city and the intrigue of new migrant communities, London's shine was fading. It could no longer claim to be the centre of the world. London's population dropped remarkably, falling to 6.6 million in 1981 as city dwellers escaped to distant suburbs and the garden towns planned to move the focus of the UK's economy away from London.

But this would not be the end of the London dream. It just needed new believers.

As we have seen, they first came from around the Commonwealth, introducing widespread ethnic diversity in London for the first time. These migrants not only helped to rebuild the city, they also reinvigorated its mythology. By embracing London as the place to be, they transported this narrative to an ever-wider range of potential Londoners. Moreover, the newness of these Caribbean migrants also engendered a sense of cosmopolitan cool that, along with the presence of 'Americans in the flesh', recreational drug use and the teenage musical revolution, dragged London's nightlife back from the brink of the blitz[131]. It was this sense of cool and possibility that was at the centre of London's next rebirth in the 1960s.

Swinging into Life

It is not hard to be enthralled by Piri Halasz's reading of 1960s

London. Writing in *Time* magazine, her article *You Can Walk Across It On the Grass* enshrined the phrase 'Swinging City' in the global imagination. Halasz breathlessly claimed that 'every decade has had its city'. Paris owned the 1920s. Berlin had its time in the 1930s before handing off to New York and then Rome. The 1960s were London's time in the global spotlight.

The story of London as the place to be was being revived as the city took its first steps into a post-industrial world. This revival was a counter-cultural revolt against a disciplinary society and its fading empire. Where older Britons were depressed by lingering rationing and the Suez crisis of 1956, London's youths simply felt repressed by the self-sacrificing dullness of the Blitz Spirit. Teenage gangs, the faux-Edwardian Teddy Boys, hit the streets and race riots sparked[132]. Out of this tension emerged the Mods and a 'cult of smartness and cool sophistication'[133] that spread across the world. There was something in the air and it was no longer just industrial smog.

Describing London in a series of scenes, Halasz exuberantly explored 'a once sedate world of faded splendour, everything new, uninhabited and kinky is blooming at the top of London life'. This city was the place to go and the place to be, one where:

Ancient elegance and new opulence are all tangled up in a dazzling blur of op and pop. The city is alive with birds and beatles, buzzing with minicars and tellystars, pulsing with half a dozen separate veins of excitement. The guards now change at Buckingham Palace to a Lennon and McCartney tune, and Prince Charles is firmly in the longhair set...faded splendor, everything new, uninhibited and kinky is blooming at the top of London

Halasz mapped their scene through the West End, from Soho to Mayfair and Chelsea. Only remnants remain. King's Road is now far too posh to be fashionable. Carnaby Street is a commodified memorial to its time. While Soho still sells its liberating culture, rental prices tell a different story. In the 1960s, though, it was the epicentre of London's symbolic, if not economic, revival.

Halasz quotes the iconic gallery owner Robert Fraser, otherwise known as 'Groovy Bob', who told her that 'everybody wants to be there. There's no place else. Paris is calcified. There's an indefinable thing about London that makes people want to go there.' He was not alone. Reflecting on his time in London in the 1960s, actor Michael Caine recalled in his documentary *My Generation* '[London] is where everyone who wanted to be somebody wanted to be. You might be out of work. You might be broke. But it was cheap and you lived within two miles of Buckingham Palace'[134]. Newcomers living that close to the Palace today are in one of two categories: homeless or the global elite.

It was the arrival, or at least the prominence, of people like Caine that led Halasz to announce the rise of what the celebrity urbanist Richard Florida would later call the 'creative class'[135], a 'new and surprising leadership community; economists, professors, actors, photographers, singers, admen, TV executives and writers – a swinging meritocracy' replacing the 'old Tory-Liberal Establishment'. Caine echoed this sentiment, remembering that:

For the first time in British history, the young working class, people like me, stood up for ourselves and said, 'We are here, this is our society and we are not going away.'[136]

It is no coincidence that the Swinging City arose at a time in which Britain was liberalising laws around gender and sexuality. The availability of The Pill was a revolution for women, even if the objectification of 'birds' was part of the fabric of the 1960s. But the cultural and legal spirit of the times did not swing everywhere. While this revolution occurred in London, other parts of the country experienced a much more conservative reaction. This only made London, and the London dream, more compelling; in the face of post-war conformity, London was the place to be yourself.

Here Halasz claimed that:

For all its virtues, which are many, and its faults, which are considerable, London has a large measure of that special quality that was once the hallmark of great cities: civility in the broadest sense. It takes away less of a person's individuality than most big cities, and gives the individual and his rights more tolerance than any.

This sense of individuality, this sense that you have the power to be yourself or to reinvent yourself, is why the London dream is so appealing to so many migrants. This power comes in many forms. The first post-war migrants had come because they were free to chase work unavailable at home, and perhaps to see if the capital of the mother country lived up to their expectations. The next generation of migrants were young people seeking their chance at freedom, even if it only meant moving from the East to the West of the city.

The 1960s were not to last, as tends to happen. The decades that followed were some of the most worrisome and quarrelsome in the history of modern London. But something was building out of the husks of the once great city and the recession of the early 1990s. This was not a revival of industry or of empire, although the financial industry and migrants from the empire certainly played their part. Instead, it was inspired by the spirit of the 1960s. This time the vibe, and the economy within which it was intertwined, was here to stay. More importantly, it was spreading out of the West End and into places like New Cross and Hackney, led by young people fleeing the safe lives their parents had established in the suburbs. There is coincidence that they came when London's economy seemed to be at its lowest ebb, with unemployment at 11.6 per cent in 1991.

Reborn, Again

It was another American magazine that thrust London back into the international imagination. With their splash cover, *Newsweek* announced that 'London Rules!' Mirroring the enthusiasm of Haslaz's *Time* feature 30 years earlier, *Newsweek's* spread exclaimed that 'Hot fashion, a pulsating club scene and lots of new money have made this the coolest city on the planet[137].' *Vanity Fair* was to go further a year later in annoucing that 'London Swings! Again!'[138] London in the 1990s was certainly catching America's attention, something director Richard Curtis exploited with his London-based films *Four Weddings and a Funeral* (1994) and *Notting Hill* (1999), both of which would feature American actors in key roles.

These magazines were right to celebrate London. The city was being revived from within. A wave of artist expression forged in the late 1980s by the likes of Damien Hirst spread across the city, only to be co-opted by the Blair government. Riffing on the eighteenth-century imperial song Rule, Britannia! the term Cool Britannia came into vogue. Such a pun was apt; the iconic 1966 *Time* article cited the loss of empire as vital to the emergence of cool, rather hastily claiming that 'Britain has lost an empire and lightened a pound. In the process, it has also recovered a lightness of heart lost during the weighty centuries of world leadership.'

If those remaking London in the Swinging Sixties were throwing off the weight of the empire, by the 1990s the empire felt like a distant relic to London's youth. Strangely, it was, as the *Newsweek* authors Stryker McGuire and Michael Elliott were to assert, in 'the least British place of all' that this patriotic cultural renaissance would emerge.

They may not have been as openly patriotic, but the explosion of the loosely grouped Young British Artists (YBAs), with their philosophy of 'conquer by shock', was equally influential in the rise of a Cool Britannia. While they may have been labelled *British* artists, London became their scene. Some, like Hirst[139], came out of Goldsmiths via Leeds and others, like Tracey Emin, from the Royal College of Art in Kensington via Margate. Emin moved into East London in the early 1980s, which she described as a 'giant bombsite' [140]. Despite that, Emin recalled, she has always 'felt at ease'. It is a common refrain; artists and the artistically inspired found a home and a community in London that they did not even know existed. London provided them with possibilities unthinkable at home and they helped to create a city where the unthinkable could be profitably exhibited.

The YBAs exhibited and occupied once thriving and now abandoned factories and warehouses in the East of the city, particularly in Hoxton, Shoreditch and the Docklands. It was the use of these industrial spaces that inspired the later conversion of Bankside Station into the Tate Modern, which would itself go on to exhibit the works of the YBAs and celebrate them through the revived Turner Prize.

The music industry was similarly London-centric. As White suggests:

Even those not bred in London had to come there to record; and usually, for sensible business reasons of accessibility to studios and session musicians, agents and tour promoters, photographers and journalists, ended up living there, if only for a time[141]

London produced 20 per cent of hitmakers between 1950 and 2017, although only 7 per cent were born in the city[142]. Many of the Brit-pop bands of the early 1990s came out of London universities. Blur was formed at Goldsmiths. The members of Suede meet at University College London. Describing their eponymous debut album, bassist Mat Osman, himself a graduate of the London School of Economics, recalled that:

London was a touchstone for everyone in the band, so the album became about us being placed in this city of sex, drugs and poverty after living in these suburban satellite towns. London is full of a certain kind of arts professional—people in bands whose parents bought them guitars when they were 12 and went to state school.[143]

London's fashion industry, represented by rising icons like Alexander McQueen and Stella McCartney, also boomed. Again. Recreational drugs, as they had in the 1960s, were commonplace and 'cocaine fell on London like snow'[144]. An underground rave scene developed in warehouses and parking lots as industrial spaces were organically repurposed by those enjoying chemically enhanced lives.

If you were young, cool and creative, or just looking to make a quid, London was the place to be. *Time's* claim that 'No other city offers a wider variety of ways in which to pass the time, and Londoners pursue their pleasures as relentlessly as people anywhere in the world'[145] had never been truer than in the late 1990s. This time it was here to stay.

By 1991, the city's population had fallen to 6.4 million. After decreasing by 4 per cent in the previous decade, it would rise by 13 per cent during the 1990s, reaching 8.2 million in 2001. Reversing a decades-long trend, most of this growth came in Inner London. Alan Ehrenhalt called this the Great Inversion[146], where the youth sought out the innermost part of global cities across the world. In London, young people flowed into the city in numbers not seen since Edward was on the throne. Where their grandparents had fled to the suburbs and their parents to the commuter belt or New Towns, their offspring caused the inner city to grow by almost a quarter during the 1990s[147].

New infrastructure emerged, most notably the London Eye and the Millennium Bridge. London had a centralised government again. Thatcher and the 18 years of Tory rule were over as New Labour won the 1997 election in a landslide. It is hard to conceive of now, but Prime Minister Tony Blair was popular. Welcome at entertainment awards. Cool, almost.

This was a new, Cool, Britannia, and London was at the centre of it all. Again.

It is not all plain sailing. London frees and alienates in equal measure, sometimes on the same tube ride. For many, the hurly-burly of metropolitan life is the appeal; to come to the big city and see if you can make it. The cost and pace of living were all part of the fantasy of London life, just as hangovers, noodle dinners and empty pubs are part of chasing your big break.

So, they come. They come to make it big, whatever it takes. For Carley, Patrick and the rest of *Torture and the Desert Spiders*, New Cross is the place where they can start to make it happen.

Youthful Crossroads

When Halasz praised the pleasures of a 'Swinging City' where 'ancient elegance and new opulence are all tangled up in a dazzling blur of op and pop' [148], the scenes she described for *Time Magazine* were far from New Cross. The post-war vibe of this South-Eastern corner of London did not fit with her exalting imagination of a city 'seized by change, liberated by affluence, graced by daffodils and anemones'.

Little has changed. It is grey, not green, that dominates the grim (or is that gritty?) New Cross high street. Kebab shops and sporadic graffiti, untroubled by artistic aspiration, liberate the streets from any hints of affluence. This is not a spot that can be seen in the opening credits of Hollywood romantic comedies set in London. Newly discovered princesses go to Kensington. They certainly do not cross the river.

But today New Cross is at the vanguard of the changing fabric of the capital. It was central in the rise of Brit Pop in the 1990s, with soon to be iconic bands like Blur, Oasis and Radiohead playing at the re-established *Venue* bar. Then came so-called New Wave and the emergence of a 'New Cross Scene' (NXS) in the early twenty-first century. In combination with the bohemian

Goldsmiths students' critical creativity, the scene had arrived in New Cross. Drawn in by the trendy grit and, most importantly, low property prices, the first laps of gentrification brought the creative classes to the South-East of London.

In 2007, the *Evening Standard* declared New Cross 'officially cool'[149].

Now New Cross finds itself at the crossroads of London's economy and a key protagonist in London's newest act. The convoluted plot points of the city's past are in open display on the New Cross high street, with no little foreshadowing of the gentrifying storyline ahead.

Elegant Victorian townhouses, now standing on top of storefronts, are mixed in with the worst of post-war council housing. White British people make up only 26 per cent of New Cross' population[150]. Food outlets, from *Nouvelle Spice* to the *Ottoman BBQ Restaurant*, represent a smorgasbord of cultures. A total of 40 per cent of children in New Cross live in poverty and the crime rate is 62 per cent higher than the rest of England[151]. The midday poor potter down the streets. Many sit on the pavements.

Colourful banners protrude from irregular lampposts; Goldsmiths is asserting its off-street dominance of the area through a series of slogans:

> *Countless Paths*
> *Many Viewpoints*
> *Untold Opportunities*

Alongside *Infinite Ideas* and beside a burlesque costume store, I've slipped through a kooky coffee shop that extends into an ad-hoc beer garden. Basking in the inexplicable February sun, I'm here to talk music with the American and German thirds of *Torture and the Desert Spiders*. Along with their English drummer, they are the kind of combination that is only likely to show up in global cities like London. Between the infectious laughter and finished sentences, they look and feel very much like a band on the way up.

They came to London from very different places but for the same reasons. Lead singer Carley, swamped by a suit-blazer and dangling orange earrings that somehow match her jean shorts and winter flip flops, hails from New York via college in Nashville. Coming to London, she tells me:

> was just, like, a different colour of industry for me. I think I just wanted something completely different with just a wider reach.
> I think it just gave me, like, a lot more, like, of a breadth, to reach from, because people are actually like in New York, it's a lot of, like, second/third gen people…But here, it's like, 'Oh, no, no,' like, 'I just came over.' You know what I mean?

I do. So, I ask, was it a dream for you to come to London. I cannot stop Carley's enthusiasm:

> It was a dream for me when I was younger, but it didn't happen the way I expected it to. I didn't think that I would be coming over, at this time in my life, uh, probably for another couple years. And then, like, I had a bunch of stuff go down in Nashville, where I was just like, not cool with being there anymore, and I was just, looking for something, and I was like, 'Maybe I'll drop out, maybe I'll just go play music, maybe I'll go work,' uh, 'Maybe I'll go to community college,' and then I was like, 'No, like, I have a desire to actually further this,' and London became the only, like, sane option.

Only an artist could think that moving to London with no money and no contacts could be the sane option. At least she is here as a student, first on an American study abroad programme and now at Goldsmiths.

Guitarist Patrick, cloaked in a ripped black leather jacket and beanie that looks like it would be a permanent feature on his compact frame, did not have that security. Patrick is German, from Munich specifically, and was working as a stagehand in his home city. He was struggling to find bandmates that were as committed to music as he was. So, he tells us with a twinkle:

I want to have, like, a time, as long as I'm young and naïve, where I just, like, focus on that for, I don't know, like 2 or 3 years, just try it, and if that doesn't work, I'll just, like, completely accept everything...

Patrick was looking for a place with a vibrant music scene. He thought about Berlin but although it was cool, 'if there's a scene, then it's *only* for electronic music'. So, he finished his apprenticeship and came to check out London in August 2018. In the first month he was trying to absorb everything, including the expense, and not get too annoyed by too much going on around him. Now, though, he has found his groove.

The city has always sucked in more than its share of the country's youth. In part, this is what makes it cool. In 1966, *Time* had argued that, 'Youth is the word and the deed in London,' as nearly 30 per cent of London's population is between 15 and 34[152]. Today that figure is 34 per cent in Inner London[153] compared to 26 per cent in the UK itself. To be young in London is to have the energy to fight the city, to take it on and to make your mark. Or at least that is the plan for Carley and Patrick.

What is difficult to get used to is what Halasz celebrated in *Time* in 1966: the city leaves you space to be yourself. But that means, Patrick tells me, that:

because of it being so fast-paced, and everyone is doing their own thing, there's basically no one, especially when you're, like, coming alone here...so you're completely responsible for yourself, and for the outcome of your doings, basically. This freedom can be good, like, when you're aware of it, you can use that as a motivation, basically, or it can be bad, I think we both find a way to get inspired by it, and do stuff.

Carley bounces in (as they both do seamlessly throughout our interview) to tell me London is a place that gives musicians the opportunity to make it, 'but it takes a lot more than basically anywhere else in the world'. They laugh as she describes London as being somewhere between a 'children's playground for musicians and a prison yard workout area'.

London has some magical, almost whimsical spots and underground venues and, she tell us, in London the 'art is so much more than we can even imagine, because here I am, in a place that I've never heard of, with people I've never seen before, and it's, like, blowing my mind', even if the amount of talent and work ethic it takes to make it in this scene feels overwhelming at times. This is a big pond and, like so many artists, they want to be a different kind of fish.

These funky fish took a while to find each other. Patrick had been doing some studio sessions but was finding it difficult to get together with anyone for anything more serious than a jam. Carley had been doing some busking and some gigs on her own, hustling through London Facebook music groups. When they found each other through the sire, she recalls, 'We were both so hungry to make something at that point. Like we were both exhausted and needed something.' There was a feeling that time was running out and from October to December there was not a day that they were not writing, they tell me simultaneously.

The band, they look at each other and tell me, 'transcends style'. Maybe some garage, some punk, some pop. Sometimes. Or maybe it is more psychedelic, or indie. But definitely heavy psych, blues. With a strong British influence. I could not be more lost but they are in their element.

Whatever the genre, they are getting tight and are on the hunt for gigs. Carley unapologetically grins when she tells us that she is a 'hound', hanging around on Facebook groups like *London Musicians* and *London Gigs*, jumping on any opportunities that get posted. Where once musicians were booked through tight networks that limited supply, these platforms now allow for a democratic free for all, much to the frustration of some of the veteran musicians in the groups. And, as a music business major, Carley says she knows the difference between taking a gig now and waiting 5 minutes to talk with your agent, or with your bandmates. The band now have an in with a promoter too and that has allowed them to get six gigs booked. Or maybe seven. There is definitely a debut single going out on all platforms in a week.

This is what London allows them to do. Unlike Munich or Nashville, where they tell me it was either playing big gigs or just for friends, there is a lot of aspirational middle ground here. With London's pub scene, they could play 7 days a week, 'if you are willing to take a dirty gig'.

And if you are willing to do it for free. Or for drink tickets.

As exciting as London's scene is, and as ambitious as *Torture and the Desert Spiders* are, playing for almost nothing or, at best a percentage of the bar after a 40-minute set, is the norm. In London, up-and-coming bands will be playing four shows a week, rehearsing twice a week and funding their recording sessions, all for free drinks and scraps of cash. Even in 'bougie' venues where 'everyone looks like it's Gossip Girl', competition among bands is so intense that only the stars really get paid.

So many come to London as a top talent in their local scene – Carley tells me that her roommate is a former winner of *The Voice: Romania* – and find themselves at the bottom again, despite their Instagram following and steady gigs. As Carley reflects in a brief moment of cynicism, 'Everyone is successful in London and, because of that, nobody is successful.' Getting booked is the prize, not getting paid. For now.

This is a life of musical passions and prosaic ways to earn a living.

Carley lives as a student but also busks when she is short of cash, which she almost always is. In Islington, she tells us, she could make up to £60 for an hour. It's much harder in New Cross, though. Patrick just found himself getting kicked out when he tried. Instead, he works as a fry-guy at McDonald's. No, 'the best fry guy in London,' they laugh in unison.

Patrick was back working as a roadie soon after he arrived in London. After a few weeks he told himself, 'Okay, this is way too time-consuming. I work on weekends and stuff like that. I'm not here for that.' So he took the easiest option he could, a place where he could work without thinking, come in when he likes and not get fired for turning up late or leaving early. So he became the fry-guy at McDonald's in Mile End.

Exhausted as he is after a shift over the oil, Patrick can't imagine how he would manage with a real job, where he can't just 'fuck off' whenever he wants to. It would be nice to earn more than £800 a month when you are the best fry-guy in London, though. But the exhaustion and struggle is all part of the experience. Sometimes, when it gets a bit much, he wonders whether it was worth leaving his job and his friends, family and dog in Munich. He has to remind himself that he signed up for this. He is here to make music and if he has to live like this, so be it.

They look after each other, though, Carley tells me. If 'one of us has money, it's all our money'. So they share meals and drinks whenever they can. Sometimes that comes out of Carley's busking jar, except when it runs out, like it did last year when she had no food for a couple of days before she went home for Christmas.

Despite the occasional emptiness of busking jars and the smell of fries, London is definitely the place for them, even if it is only a temporary moment in their musical lives. Carley's student exchange is due to finish in July and the fate of Germans in the UK after Brexit is still to be decided. They are committed to pushing forward, though, together. London may no longer be the most subversive scene – Patrick is still trying to find those places like in Munich where they had a 'psychedelic community doing gigs somewhere in the forest' and Carley finds Goldsmiths' fabled arts scene to be pretentious and overwhelming – but it is a place that offers opportunity, if you are prepared to hustle, to work yourself to exhaustion, to play at dirty pubs and to do it all for free.

It's all part of the London dream and Carley and Patrick are the ultimate London dreamers.

Section 2

Cool Capital

Chapter 5

Transformation on the Thames

For almost 2,000 years the Thames had been at the heart of London's existence[154]. From the time that it was bridged by the Romans and used to transport *Londinium's* 'abundance of its provisions' [155], London's economy has been orientated around the river that provided its connection with the world. As such, the use of the Thames and the riverfront has stood as a qualitative and quantitative barometer for London's economy, from Roman arrivals and early imperial explorations to Victorian industrialism and the troubled transition to a post-industrial economy.

Following the Romans, in Medieval London wharves and quays were built between London Bridge and the Tower of London. The first substantial (naval) yards were in Deptford and Woolwich in the sixteenth century. At this time most Londoners, whether transporting goods, casually fishing or desperately mud larking, earned a living from the Thames[156].

With the the simultaneous, and not unrelated, expansion of trade and frequency of war in the formative years of the British Empire came the mass expansion of naval and private yards for warships and merchants alike. As the empire inflated, so too did the docks. In Blackwell, the East India Docks were built in 1802 to support the East India Company, which commandeered a private army of 260,000 men[157], ruled 90 million people and controlled half of the world's trade at the height of its rule at the beginning of the nineteenth century[158].

The West India Docks, which opened in 1803, handled products stained by a horror that the British seem unable to fully acknowledge: industrialised slavery. The profits and products of the triangular trade between the UK, Africa and the

Caribbean that transported three million enslaved people from 1690 to 1807[159] were a catalyst for London's development into an industrial powerhouse.

These triangular journeys tended to start and end in London. Slave ships were constructed in London docks and sailed out of the Thames, although this industry later moved on to Bristol and then to Liverpool. Like the East India Company, these expeditions were financed out of London. The surpluses of imperial accumulation returned to London. Coffee, sugar and tobacco were refined and redistributed in London's docks.

The buoyant industry of empire set in motion the development of the infrastructure for London's buoyant transformation into the first city of capital. Although much of the industry of industrialisation (and the subsequent development of an industrial working class) smouldered in the North of the country, it was on the docks stimulated by imperial expansion that London and Londoners met the industrial revolution.

Industrial London was a transformed and transformative city but it made few goods of its own. Instead, London received, processed and distributed the products of the world. This trade meant that London had the busiest port in the world from the beginning of the eighteenth century, acting as the 'warehouse of empire' and the 'workshop of the world'[160]. In 1700, 6,900 ships were recorded as entering London's port. By 1795 it had grown to 14,800, with the value of goods tripling. In 1790, London handled 70 per cent of British imports and over half of all exports[161]. In turn, a vast maritime economy developed, including the UK's biggest shipbuilding centre and a hundred sugar refineries[162], which handled almost three-quarters of the sugar imported into Britain by 1750[163].

London's docks and quays took on all the resources the empire could offer, with watermen and dockers, porters and stevedores handing '...coals from Newcastle, canned and refrigerated food from Australasia, precious gems from Africa and tea from India'[164]. The mass importation of goods marked a transformation of a previously feudal and often isolated economy. Englanders no longer needed to consume only what Englanders could produce, which was wonderful for those raised on flavourless meat and potatoes. It was also a revelation for those with the means to absorb and re-invest the financial surplus generated from production and taxation at the edges of empire. By the time Queen Victoria took the throne, London was awash in the fruits of empire, all of them moving through the docks.

Victorian London was expanding rapidly, as were the opportunities for work on the docks. Like many of these opportunities for survival in the Victorian city, work on the docks was particularly brutal and irregular. In *London Labour and the London Poor*[165], which Robert Fairhurst called the 'Greatest Victorian novel written'[166], Victorian researcher and reformer Henry Mayhew reported the desperation on the docks:

As the foreman calls from a book the names, some men jump upon the backs of the others, so as to lift themselves high above the rest, and attract the attention of him who hires them. All are shouting... Indeed, it is a sight to sadden the most callous, to see thousands of men struggling for only one day's hire...To look in the faces of that hungry crowd, is to see a sight that must ever be remembered[167].

Their struggles, which Henry Mayhew called 'the riot, the struggle, and the scramble for a living', are part of the story of London, one in which the accumulation of great wealth is matched by the misery of those desperate enough to produce it. And still, they came. Working in London, no matter the conditions, is always better than not working.

After World War II, however, London's economy and population declined rapidly. Manufacturers found poorer bodies to exploit. The decline of industry in London meant the decline of the docks, although a range of other factors also contributed to their eventual fall. The independence of colonies fundamentally changed trading patterns, often meaning that manufacturing took place off-shore, and forced Britain to look to Europe. Here ports like Dunkirk, Hamburg, Rotterdam and Southampton syphoned off business from London.

Containerisation was the final blow, forcing vessels to the deeper water in Tilbury that was able to handle these containers. The East India Dock closed in 1967. London and St Katherine's in 1968. The West India Docks went in 1976 and the Royal Docks in 1981. The Docklands, and the industries and workers who relied on them, were derelict, left to the indignities of an 'Enterprise Zone' and the London Docklands Corporation.

Wharves, factories and power stations sat unused, seemingly unaware that they were peak real estate. Once proud warehousing lay empty, something London's students would soon discover to their advantage. London, warehouse of the world and workshop of the empire, was no more.

This was not the end of London's story.

Largely kept alive by the unlikely combination of Thatcher's 'Big Bang' of financial deregulation in the City and international migration, it would re-emerge as a (but not *the*) global city in the 1990s; from 1997-2007, London's economy grew at an annual rate of 4 per cent, rivalling the economies of the East Asian 'Tigers'[168].

Like its rise and decline, London's recovery could be seen on the water. Capital always finds its way back to the water. In particular, London's traumatic transition out of industrialism can be seen in the fate of two of its power stations: Bankside and Battersea.

The Power of London

Both the Bankside and the Battersea stations were a product of London's historical industrial dominance. Bankside first produced electricity in 1891, generating up to 300 MW watts of coal-power. Battersea became one of the first stations of a unified national electricity system in the 1930s, just as London's population was reaching its peak. When construction of a second station at Battersea finished in 1955, the sites' total capacity was 509 megawatts and it stood as a 'temple of power' on the Western curve of the South Bank. The largest power station in the country[169], it produced 20 per cent of London's electricity supply[170].

By 1983, both Bankside and Battersea had been decommissioned. They were two of many across the country[171], defeated by new energy sources, falling output and increased operational costs[172]. Industry was flowing out of the industrialised cities of capitalism and the power plants, warehouses and factories that sat upon its rivers and waterfronts were quickly becoming relics of a different era, as were those who worked in them.

There was little appetite, however, to tear down these waterfront icons. There was also little idea of what to do with them or those they employed. The stations, like the city, were the subject of many failed post-war imaginations.

Battersea, saved by a Grade II listing in 1980, escaped a horrifying existence as either a Michael Jackson envisaged 'fantasy centre' or the new home of Chelsea Football Club. It would not become an urban park or a biomass plant[173]. Numerous housing proposals fell through until one stuck and the station was sold to Malaysian developers in 2012 for £400 million. What the developers had planned was a development frustratingly familiar to all Londoners: luxury apartments.

Of the first 866 apartments in the development, 824 were sold off-plan to foreign investors[174]. Sure, this £9 billion redevelopment, which will include Apple's new London headquarters, will have affordable homes. It is just that in 2017 the new Malaysian investors announced that the number of 'affordable homes' would be slashed by 40 per cent to 386 out of a total of 4,000[175].

As a final blow, an unforeseen need to lay a giant sewer has meant that these homes for first-time buyers were shifted to an area half a mile away from the luxury development, sitting on an old industrial estate beside busy railway lines[176].

The redevelopment of Battersea Power Station stands as a monument to the folly of our post-industrial age and the separation of the success of London from the success of Londoners. It is an economy full of contradictions, whereby the richest tenth earns 270 times that of the poorest tenth[177]. London has more billionaires than any other city in the world[178], but 37 per cent of children in London live in poverty[179]. As is the case at Battersea, many of the traditional English upper-class might have been priced out of central London but a global elite has taken their gilded presence, one that is often hidden from the indecency of public life by iron gates and privatised services.

The transformation of Bankside Station tells a different story of London's transitioning economy, one both cooler, more successful and just as miserable as Battersea. Just as with Battersea, the redevelopment of Bankside was stalled while London worked out what kind of city it wanted to be. For 10 years a series of proposals ranging from an industrial museum to an opera house were rejected before a proposal from the Tate to expand across the river was accepted. Anachronistically, London was the only major capital city without a contemporary art museum. The Tate proposed to not only fill this gap but to redevelop the area, just as the Royal Festival Hall had done on the South Bank some 30 years earlier as part of the Festival of Britain[180].

Compared to the crass greed of the continually troubled Battersea development[181], the emergence of the Tate Modern has been a triumph of the new London. Almost six million people visited in 2016, making it Britain's third most popular tourist attraction[182]. The Tate claims that the Tate Modern adds £100 million to London's economy each year[183], a measure of both its financial worth and the changing value of artistic expression.

Even the Queen suspected this success, she was sceptical of this new London. While she gave a (relatively) rousing endorsement of the virtues of the British Museum earlier in the year, the Queen's only words on opening the Tate Modern were 'I declare the Tate Modern open'. The Duke of Edinburgh had made it very clear that he was not coming.

Londoners are not so dismissive of the new and bold, even if cynicism is built into the city's bones. In its opening year, the Tate Modern attracted over five million visitors. Even the tabloid *The Sun* newspaper, having got on board with the New Labour project, proclaimed that 'Now that White Van Man has approved London's new Tate Gallery, it has the official blessing of the people [184].

In many ways, the transformation of Bankside Station into the Tate Modern is London at its best. Rather than toss history away or cling to an already bolted past, the redevelopment has reinvigorated a derelict space without starting again. The gallery has also been able to connect that which had endured from London's glorious past with those murkier bits of its decline. Most notably, the creation of the Tate Modern facilitated a new, funky, connection between the North and South banks of the Thames: the Millennium Bridge, the first river crossing in central London since Tower Bridge in 1894. Like much of London's re-emergence, it got off to a wobbly start. Specifically, it was forced to close 3 days after its June 2000 opening because of alarming swaying caused by the (seemingly unforeseen) 'synchronised footfall' of the 160,000 people who crossed the bridge during its opening weekend[185].

After extensive testing involving 2,000 volunteers, the bridge re-opened after 18 months. It provided a suitably creative link between the old London and the new. Or, more accurately, the old London and the newest iteration of the old London. Connecting St Paul's Cathedral to the Tate Modern, the Millennium Bridge carries you on a journey across London's history.

It is the possibility of this link that attracted then Tate director Nicholas Serota to the then derelict site[186]. When he was showing the potential site to Tate trustees Serota insisted on beginning their tour at St Paul's, rather than travel through the deeply deprived Southwark streets. At this time there was no link to bridge the gap between the remaining glamour of the northern side of the Thames and the almost abandoned Southern bank. The Millennium Bridge would make this connection. During a 350-metre walk, pedestrians are taken above the miraculously alive brown waters of the Thames, still home to numerous bobbing vessels engaged in work invisible to most Londoners. Those looking behind them as they make their way to Tate Modern can see the nicknamed financial buildings of the City, from the Cheese Grater to the Walkie Talkie. In front of them to the East is the lonely Shard on the South side of the river.

These wannabe iconic buildings house London's powerhouse financial institutions. Where they once funded imperial adventures and industrial endeavours, they are now part of the city's post-industrial future. For many of these institutions, that means financial trading for the sake of financial trading. Profits for the sake of profits. Those daring to look down at the Millennium Bridge itself, if they stare closely enough, will find a different form of post-industrial London in an unlikely form: chewing gum.

Using a blowtorch, acrylic paint and lacquer, artist Ben Wilson has transformed 10,000 pieces of chewing gum into colourful abstractions of London scenes and implanted them into the bridge's grates, turning the bridge into a 'gallery and your simple walk...into an art trail' [187]. Where London's foreign exchange market turns over £2.5 trillion daily[188], Wilson's work produces no revenue. Instead, it is a 'subtly subversive intervention in a public space' that is both 'whimsical' and 'cheeky'.

This sense of supported subversion – Wilson has been

arrested multiple times, but the authorities have taken no punitive measures to stop him – is a vital part of the image of cool upon which London trades. While Wilson makes no money directly from this work, the gum upon which tourists tread is all part of the fantasy of a cool city. In turn, this fantasy enables the success of not only the institutions that come at the end of the Millennium Bridge – a reconstruction of Shakespeare's Global Theatre and the Tate Modern – but a host of tech and communications ventures. It also positions London's financial industry as somehow funkier than its competitors.

Thus the key to the revival of London's unused power stations, and the city itself, was not technological advancement or industrial might. It was a cultural change that was at once a response to stifling post-war normativity and a crisis in capitalism, which needed new markets and a new type of consumer. Here creativity and cool shifted from cultural practices to profitable, commodified, cultural practices.

The redevelopment of Bankside Station and the commodified South Bank is indicative of this change. The Southern side of the Thames has been an entertainment district from medieval times. Outside the reach of the City of London, this unregulated space across the river featured prostitution, bear-baiting and theatre (hence the location of The Globe Theatre). What is new is the wealth it generates and represents. Charles Booth had once said of Bankside:

> there is in this round a set of courts and small streets which for number, viciousness, poverty and crowding is unrivalled in anything I have hitherto seen in London...the inhabitants are...the dregs of the population[189]

Now, Bankside is part of the heavily commercialised South Bank, an area '...buzzing with activity and exciting events to keep you busy' which proclaims itself 'London's cultural district, home to national centres for arts, film and performance'[190]. The South Bank is not just a place for culture and excitement. Or, at least, for culture and excitement for their own sake. In London, creativity, culture (along with finance and the service sectors that support them) is the economy: the creative industries within which the South Bank is part add £42 billion to the capital's economy and account for 882,900 jobs[191]. Moreover, since 2009 the GVA of London's creative industries increased by 38.2 per cent in nominal terms.

In 1976, Harvard sociologist Daniel Bell called this the post-industrial society[192]. More pejoratively, Slovenian philosopher Slavoj Žižek has come to critique 'cultural capitalism'[193], an idea that stems from literary theorist Fredric Jameson's conception of 'the cultural logic of late capitalism'[194]. In the chapters that follow I'll bring these ideas together under the term 'cool capitalism', which owes itself to the work of Thomas Frank[195] and Jim McGuigan[196]. Whatever the term, underneath this creative and cool economy lies the exploitation of dreaming workers, from aspiring creatives to trod upon service workers. I'm going back to New Cross, one of its more unlikely homes, where I'm meeting Margaret to discuss this underside of London's cool economy.

Taking on the Tate

If this Southern suburb is at the cool edge of a gentrifying wave billowing over London, the tide marker is the high-street pubs. I'm waiting here at one of these pubs, which might be accurately described as dark and dingy but is actually a chic gastro-pub. Silly me.

Outside, Goldsmiths, an institution advertising itself as 'a creative powerhouse, a thought-provoking place', [197] has hung a blue banner from a lamp post. It says only 'Critical Thinkers'. The pub's Instagrammable flower display, seemingly necessary to continue to attract the young and the affluent,[198] stands in contrast to the less grammable homeless women silently begging outside the adjacent station.

Inside, day-time drinkers do not mix with estate agent types nursing a coke before their next engagement. Somehow the floors are both sticky and carpeted. The coming of Summertime, more in theory than practice on this grey June Tuesday, has chased away the student population. I'm perched at a lonely corner table, nursing an ill-advised pub coffee and waiting to meet the redoubtable Margaret to learn more about London's transformation from industrial grim to gritty cool.

Few know the contradictions and challenges of London's post-industrial economy like Margaret. As the cultural sector industrial officer for the Public and Commercial Services Union (PCS), she sees the pressures on museum and gallery staff across the city. Especially those in lower-paid roles and particularly those working at the Tate.

Powering through a coke at our table, Margaret strikes a strong, steely presence. She needs it. The PCS had been in dispute with the Tate for some time. In May 2016 there had been friction after the Tate had outsourced roles to the private firm Securitas[199], who then de-recognised PCS and imposed zero-hours contracts on some staff.[200] In September 2016, PCS members voted overwhelmingly to reject a meagre pay offer[201].

This tension between the Tate and its members was thrust into the spotlight in late April 2017, when a notice was posted on the staff rooms of both the Tate Britain and the Tate Modern. It read:

As you know, we are making plans to say goodbye to Nick in a way that is fitting to mark the immense achievements of his 27 years at Tate. We have posted a note on Tatenet about the staff party on 25 May – everyone is invited. At the party we would like to surprise Nick with a leaving gift from current and former members of staff. We have thought long and hard about what to get, and decided to put money towards a sailing boat. Nick loves sailing, and this would be a lasting and very special reminder of the high regard which I know so many of us have for Nick and his contribution to Tate[202].

When she first heard about this note, Margaret thought it was a joke. Surely, no one could be as brazen and as lacking in self-awareness? After all, this is one of London's premier cultural destinations, one full of sophisticated minds and advanced degrees.

She was not alone.

A worker at the Tate employed by Securitas spoke to *The Guardian* of his disgust, claiming:

There was a mixture of shock and laughter. The chasm that exists between upper management and the staff on the ground is just farcical and this just made it clearer than ever. For us, Serota's legacy among staff is one of privatisation and union busting and turning the Tate into Westfield with pictures.

Having heard the frustrations of those she represented, Margaret was taken aback by the backlash she received from the Tate. With a sharp mirth that merges perfectly into her Scottish accent, she remembers with some determination that they 'went mad at [her] for the quote in *The Guardian*'.

She had said:

The staff at Tate are underpaid and overworked, and haven't had appropriate pay rises, and this just demonstrates how divorced from reality the management at Tate are. It seems to me they've made a big error of judgment.
Our members are on zero-hours contracts, they are struggling to pay the bills each month, so to ask them to donate towards a boat – well, I can tell you the staff are not happy at all. It's really rubbed people up the wrong way.

This was not the kind of reaction those who 'thought long and hard' about how to express the high regard staff have for Nick thought they would receive.

The 'Nick' in the note, is our Sir Nicholas Serota, the Director of the Tate, an institution that includes the Tate Britain, Tate Liverpool, Tate St Ives and, of course, the Tate Modern. Serota had been the subject of a number of glowing profiles from the 2012 *Modern Man* in the *New Yorker*[203] to retirement testimonials, *Modern Master: How Nick Serota's Tate Skyrocketed to Success*[204] and How *Nicholas Serota's Tate Changed Britain*[205], in *The Guardian*.

Margaret was fighting for those who have experienced a different kind of legacy from Serota's rule, a legacy that has more to do with the logic of a cooler mode of capitalism than Serota himself. With indignant frustration she tells me of the culture of privatisation that has created lower-paid and precarious work. Real wages were falling and some working at the Tate were being forced to take on multiple jobs. PCS members had been referred to food banks. Some had reported getting off in Zone 2 after a journey from Zone 6 and walking the rest of the way to work because they cannot afford to enter Zone 1. The note went up a week after a long-standing additional 10 per cent discount at the subsidised staff canteen was revoked[206].

Of course, much of this was not the Tate's doing; it was their sub-contractors. If the non-profit cultural institutions do not feel able to properly exploit their employees, the drive to reduce 'costs' has led them to engage private companies who are happy to find more sources of profit.

Neither privatisation and precarious work nor the ongoing union dispute featured in the glowing reflections on Serota's legacy. It is the consumption of the arts that is highlighted, not the messy bits of its production. This story of cultural work in London is missing from the narrative of the London dream, even if PCS members know it well. The only discussion of pay in the reviews of Serota's legacy was limited to why he had not taken up higher paid roles in the United States[207]. Serota's response reflected the values celebrated by his colleagues.

I am not an incredible patriot, but somehow working here means more than doing it somewhere like Chicago. Making a great museum in Chicago is an academic exercise. Doing it in London is about changing society.[208]

He and the Tate were certainly part of a changing society. On the outside things had been going well at the Tate Modern. A significant extension had opened, attracting one million visitors in the first 4 weeks[209] and visitors were at record numbers. For consumers of the contemporary art experience, the Tate was thriving. For workers at the opposite end of the scale from Serota, things were very different. They are across London.

The Tate, Margaret asserts, has 'got really high turnover with a lot of those types of roles, because people just can't afford to do it anymore'. The scandal of it all is that:

most of our members working at Tate have got an interest in the arts and it's quite difficult to get a job actually at the Tate. So it's not only the zero-hour gallery assistants that are being exploited, but now have members who are joining PCS now, because they want to be involved in something and they're basically telling us that in order to gain the experience and the prestige, so that they can develop their career, quite often they're taking a job at the Tate and they're on like £24,000 a year - which is nothing.

Such is life in the arts in London. The city is full of culture, of creativity and of cool, for those consuming it. For those on the other side of the velvet rope, life is tougher – even if they are in London for the same reasons as those they serve.

The Tale of a New City

The story of the transformation of the Thames and the repurposing of two of London's iconic power stations represents the triumph and tragedy of London's economy. This is a story of the separation of the accumulation of capital from labour through financial and real estate speculation. It is one of a service-led, creative, economy taking the place of an industrial one banished to parts of the world where more vulnerable workers were now available to be exploited. It is an economy serviced by Londoners working in conditions increasingly similar to those poorer parts of the world. They are also increasingly similar to conditions endured by Victorian Londoners

Twenty-first century London has an economy that allows both record levels of employment[210] but net incomes for its poorest 10 per cent of Londoners to drop by 10 per cent. It is one with surging capital and increasingly vulnerable workers, creating conditions wherein, as the London School of Economics has reported, despite London recovering from the great recession more quickly than the rest of the country, 'London's economic success does not seem to translate into lower poverty or reduced inequality.'[211]

And still, they come. They always have. Now though, they were coming to an entirely different city.

Young people might be leaving London in droves[212] – and Margaret admits that she has given it some thought – but they are still arriving in officially cool places like New Cross[213]. They come dreaming of a London life. A life where, according to *Time Out* magazine, the official guide to such things:

Fresh-faced students down pints next to New Cross natives, jerk joints nestle next to artisanal coffee shops and laughs from eccentric comedy nights mingle with neighbouring metal gigs. Rowdyism still reigns[214].

This is also a New Cross life where the average rent is 45 per cent higher than the rest of the country. Every time a pub goes gastro or a fried chicken outlet becomes an artisan café, those rents go even higher.

As I leave the pub and trot across to New Cross Gate station, one thought sticks in my mind. It is one that often finds its way into my inner monologue, most often on tube platforms and on grey days. I'm sure that I'm not the only Londoner who finds their consciousness attacked by such a question. Why do we put up with the city?

Because London is still the place to be. It always has been. What the American author Henry James said of London in 1881 is true of London today:

> It is difficult to speak adequately or justly of London. It is not a
> pleasant place; it is not agreeable, or cheerful, or easy, or exempt
> from reproach. It is only magnificent. You can draw up a tremendous
> list of reasons why it should be insupportable. The fogs, the smoke,
> the dirt, the darkness, the wet, the distances, the ugliness, the brutal
> size of the place, the horrible numerosity of society, the manner in
> which this senseless bigness is fatal to amenity, to convenience, to
> conversation, to good manners – all this and much more you may
> expatiate upon. You may call it dreary, heavy, stupid, dull, inhuman,
> vulgar at heart and tiresome in form. [...] But these are occasional
> moods; and for one who takes it as I take it, London is on the whole
> the most possible form of life. [...] It is the biggest aggregation of
> human life – the most complete compendium of the world. [215]

It is this sense that everything is possible in London that drives people to London, searching for dream jobs and cool experiences. Or maybe just a chance to make their way in the world. All of these possibilities are in existence in London's East End, where those urban Richard Florida has called the creative classes have flocked. It is no coincidence that London's tech economy followed. In the next section we will explore the development of this tech economy along with the lives of those chasing a version of the London dream that is animated by a cooler kind of capitalism.

Chapter 6

Producing Cool

Silicon Roundabout started as a very British joke.

When the now-defunct travel social networking company Dopplr moved from above a pub in Hoxton to 100 City Road beside Old Street Roundabout in March 2008, they found not only more space but a burgeoning social scene[216]. Rooftop barbeques, pubs and parties were the settings for stories of success and failure among an ambitious community of online start-ups.

For Dopplr's then Chief Technology Officer Matt Biddulph, this ad-hoc community forged around an East End roundabout felt like the appropriately bleak British equivalent of the utopian vibe of Silicon Valley[217]. His July 2008 tweet gave the name life:

'Silicon Roundabout': the ever-growing community of fun startups in London's Old Street area[218]

While Biddulph, and those around the roundabout, were in on the joke, earnest journalistic interest meant that the name stuck[219]. Silicon Roundabout was now 'a thing'. It attracted more entrepreneurial dreamers and those who would profit from them. It also caught the attention of a government desperate to reinvigorate Britain's economy in the midst of the great recession. Silicon Roundabout is the holy grail of post-industrial administrations: high-tech manufacturing in derelict industrial areas. All that was in the way was the poor people who were occupying these spaces.

By 2010, then Prime Minister David Cameron was announcing 'the government's ambition for London's East End to become a world-leading technology city to rival Silicon Valley'[220]. Tech City UK was born. It would not last[221]. More specifically, London as a tech centre has leapt forward but the name 'Tech City' was far too earnest, and far too associated with the Tory government. Indeed, Biddulph insists that the official use of Tech City has helped to cement his nickname, arguing that 'the government comes in and calls it Tech City, but it's our Silicon Roundabout'[222].

It is not just theirs anymore. A total of 32,000 businesses were created in the postcode EC1V – the area North of the City of London and at the South end of Islington, including the tube stations of Angel and Old Street – from March 2012 to March 2014[223], three times as many as any part of the UK and a record for any postcode in the UK[224]. What started as an ambitious community of disruptive 'creators' has become mainstream. This creative-tech economy is also big business, even if it is still made up of small parts. And even if those parts are increasingly being forced out of Silicon Roundabout.

Still, the Roundabout exists as an idea if not a place. This idea has come to be known as the flat white economy, a fusion of culture and technology which has confirmed London's status as a post-industrial powerhouse. Coined by Rob Harbron, then an economist at the Centre for Business and Economics Research (CEBR), and popularised by his former colleague Douglas McWilliams in his book of the same name[225], the idea of the flat white economy was born from an unlikely source: rail data.

Charged with the exciting task of forecasting rail demand, CEBR noticed an extraordinary rise in passenger numbers at the Old Street station. Somewhat coincidently, their office was only a 5-minute walk from the station. Faced with this data about their surroundings, McWilliams and colleagues were forced to look outside. Where these economists might once have walked past artists and junkies, they were now confronted with 'advanced techie geeks and marketing people to creative types'[226]. The coffee preference of these hipsters was also clear: the New Zealand[227] derived flat white style of coffee.

The economy created by these flat white drinkers, or at least those with digital ambitions, adds £42 billion to the capital's economy and accounts for 882,900 jobs[228]. And the importance of London's 'creative industries' is only growing. Since 2009 the value of these industries has increased by more than a third and the number of tech jobs has grown by 60 per cent since 1996.

London has a third of all jobs in the 'Information and Communication' sector and a remarkable 80 per cent of jobs in 'Programming and Broadcasting' activities. Completing these flat white economy jobs is those in 'Professional, Scientific and Real Estate' activities, which is the largest sector in London with 816,000 jobs[229].

McWilliams argues that it is the creativity of these tech geeks, and their entrepreneurial spirit, that are the heart of the flat white economy and the key to London reinvention[230]. Specifically, it is not that these workers are able to create new information. It is that their creativity has facilitated a disruption of existing practices. Subverting cultural and market norms is big business.

Thus, while Silicon Roundabout and the flat white economy are nominally about technological advancements and big data, it is people and culture that are at its core. It is this combination of culture, creativity and tech wealth that have made EC1V and its associated off-shoots in Shoreditch, Hackney and Dalston a hub for young people, particularly new UK graduates and Europeans escaping crippling youth unemployment on the continent. For young people with ambition and too much heart to have a life in the city, this was the place to be, the locus of their London dream. This critical mass of young, talented, creative and fun young people draws in further young people and only serves to increase the sense that this is the place to be.

And it is the image of a cool, creative and open city that London promotes; this is London's front stage. In his forward to London's 2018 draft culture strategy, *Culture for All Londoners*, Mayor Sadiq Khan exclaimed, 'Culture is our city's DNA, binding us all together - both in times of crisis and in times of celebration. Culture is what makes the daytime thrive and the night-time come alive.'[231]

What Khan calls the capital's 'Creative Spirit' is certainly admirable, as is his earlier assertion in the 2017 *London Plan* that 'Culture also plays a vital role in bringing people from all backgrounds together and I want every Londoner to have the opportunity to access culture on their doorstep. Without culture, London would lose its spirit and soul[232].'

These cultural strategies would not exist, or at least would not be such a prominent part of urban planning, if it were not for urbanist theorist Richard Florida and his celebration of what he calls the creative classes, those urban dreamers capable of rebuilding cities through only their sense of cool and desire to live life differently, together.

Selling the Creative Classes

Florida's 2002 classic *Rise of the Creative Classes* starts with the ambition and clarity that has defined his career:

> *This book describes the emergence of a social class. If you are a scientist or engineer, an architect or a designer, a writer, artist, or musician, or if your creativity is a key factor in your work in business, education, health care, law, or some other profession, you are a member. With 38 million members [in the US], more than 30 per cent of the nation's workforce, the Creative Class has shaped and will continue to shape deep and profound shifts in the ways we work, in our values and desires, and in the very fabric of our everyday lives[233].*

In this millennial vision, he argues that the most significant change to post-war societies has not just been the rise of an immaterial knowledge economy but the importance of creativity and individual expression. Moreover, because 'creativity is the driving force of economic growth' Florida argues that the creative class, those 'whose economic function is to create new ideas, new technology and new creative content'[234], have become the most influential class.

Moreover, the success of cities is dependent on creating conditions that were attractive for the creative classes, those '... whose economic function is to create new ideas, new technology, and new creative content'[235].

It is this idea upon which Florida's lucrative career has been based: that the economic development of economically developed cities is dependent upon attracting the creative classes. In turn, the creative class are attracted by the fantasy of a cool, cosmopolitan urban existence. Consequently, cities looking to escape from post-industrial economic purgatory should throw away their plans for an industrial park. Shelve that Olympic bid and stop bidding for an Amazon warehouse. Leave the Victorian-era working conditions for the distribution warehouses in the provinces that will never be cool[236].

It is because of Florida, or at least Florida's 'discovery', articulation and commodification of urban creativity, that cities like London put so much emphasis on developing a creative strategy. It is also this need for creative planning that allowed Florida to become an academic rock star who was capable of pulling in $35,000 for speaking gigs[237] soon after the 2002 publication of *The Rise of the Creative Class*[238].

Florida, as head of his Creative Class Group (CCG), is himself creative in the management of his brand of urban renewal strategy. The CCG website has a section of 'Praise' that contains no less than 205 individual quotes. Some could not be more laudatory. Eric Garcetti, Mayor of Los Angeles from 2013, is listed as claiming that 'Richard Florida is the greatest American urbanist of our time.'

If you are cynical, including quotes like 'Your session was just outstanding' and 'Richard Florida, an expert on social and economic trends' on the Praise page might suggest that these are just the 205 nice things that have ever been said about Richard Florida.

This cynicism has no place in the creative economy. Florida, currently 'University Professor in the University of Toronto's School of Cities and Rotman School of Management, and a distinguished fellow at New York University's Schack Institute of Real Estate', is an established and influential figure. His trademark black t-shirts might even assert a cache of charismatic cool, even if only by the low standards of academia[239].

Florida is also an immensely divisive figure, even among the creative classes who are so celebrated in his work. *Guardian* architecture critic Oliver Wainwright, for example, claims that:

Florida's formula has proven to benefit the already rich, mostly white middle class; fuel rampant property speculation; displace the bohemians he so fetishised; and see the problems that once plagued the inner cities simply move out to the suburbs[240].

There is even a parody Twitter account, the bio of which describes @dick_florida as a 'fadical urbanist' and 'social entre-manure' with a dead hyperlink to www.saveyourcitywithjustonetrick. com. There are no more unpopular academics than those who make money out of their popularity outside of academia. Gentrification is not all that popular either, except in practice.

Ever aware of emerging trends, Florida does not seem immune to this turn. His latest work, *The New Urban Crisis: How Our Cities Are Increasing Inequality, Deepening Segregation, and Failing the Middle Class - and What We Can Do About It*, the result of a period of 'rethinking and introspection, of personal and intellectual transformation' [241] after seeing the rise of inequality and homogeneity in some of the places he had championed, seems to be an attack on the consequences of his ideas. Still, as he insists to Wainwright, 'I will not apologise. I do not regret anything,' [242] even if he admits that he found the unequal consequences of the urban transformations that he had sold 'deeply disturbing' [243].

Yet, although critics have dismissed Florida as 'part of the problem, rather than the solution' [244], neither Florida nor his ideas should be ignored. Though it is the 'new' class of creative workers that get the title billing, what Florida identifies is really a structural shift in the mythology of advanced urban capitalism, one embodied in the changing attitudes of the young people flocking back to the (cool) cities of the 1990s. As he recounts in a revisited edition of the text, 'Our world, it seemed to me, was changing as dramatically as it had since the early days of the industrial revolution.' [245]

Of course, during this cool revival of the post-industrial city, financial markets only expanded and became more detached from material reality. Industrial production, often supplying the consumption of the creative classes, was displaced outside of the Western world rather than becoming a relic of capital. Capitalism did not become cleaner, it was just that the muckier bits were now conducted far from those who thought it was cool to consume. Or those who consumed without thinking.

Nonetheless, it was the creative-led revival of urban spaces that was capturing the attention of enterprising scholars. So it should have. Despite the cynicism about Florida himself, a new economic mythology was emerging, one much edgier than its predecessors. Where Max Weber's Protestant ethic of thrift and hard work drove the early stages of capitalism, it is the exploitation of workers' creativity and subversive impulses that propel the accumulation of contemporary capital.

These are not Florida's words, of course; Marxism is not especially marketable. Instead, Florida writes that, 'Capitalism has expanded its reach to capture the talents of heretofore excluded groups of eccentrics and nonconformists.' [246] This transformation entails, '…the rise of creativity as a fundamental economic driver, and the rise of a new social class, the creative class' [247].

The crux of Florida's theory of urban development is that in chasing cool to city centres, the creative classes provide a talented and tolerant workforce required by cutting-edge employers. The desires of this creative class, Florida argues, now supersede those of big corporations. Rather than people moving for jobs, people are moving for culture. Instead of workers having to get on their bikes to chase jobs, businesses were moving to find the right kind of people. Rent might be cheaper in Watford but that is of no benefit to your start-up if no one wants to live there. Instead, Florida insists, businesses are seeking places that attracted the young, the creative and the talented.

Consequently, he reports that economic growth was 'occurring in places that were tolerant, diverse, and open to creativity – because these were places where creatives of *all* types wanted to live'[248]. Businesses 'no longer call all the shots', Florida claims, and cities need a *people climate*[249] as much as they need a business climate. As such, Florida argues that cities must chase his patented[250] 3Ts: talent, tolerance and technology. Tacitly accepting the (free) work of street-artists like Ben Wilson on the Millennium Bridge will attract the right kind of workers far more than any tax-free tech hub. In turn, these creatives will stimulate a service economy that has delivery riders buzzing around the city in employment that would be deemed as precarious as any, if they actually had employment contracts[251]. But I digress; there will be more on the service class later.

Booming post-industrial cities are about creating the conditions for a thriving LGBT+ community, pedestrian-friendly streets and a cool music scene more than big-box retail with ample parking. London, with its 17,000 music performances and 250 festivals a year, and more live comedy than anywhere else in the world (according to the Mayor of London), certainly fits this bill[252].

Thus, cities should not specifically seek to make spaces enticing to the long-desired upper-income families. Instead, younger single people, with their capacity to think differently and, perhaps more importantly, work longer for less, add just as much to the economy[253]. Thriving creatives cities are as much about Tinder as they are toy stores. Or, put somewhat more creepily by Florida, a 'thick mating market'[254].

And yet, Florida's people climate feels suspiciously like the kind of environment in which business might well thrive. Indeed, this is the core of the Floridian strategy; cities designed for businesses because they are designed to attract the type of workers businesses need. This new edge of capitalism was what then Major of London Boris Johnson, in his pre-Brexit liberal guise, was trying to express in the garbled exuberance of his speech to the Conservative Party Conference when he claimed that:

> London acquired a deserved reputation as the greatest city on earth, a great jiving funkapolitan melting-pot, where, provided you did nothing to damage the interests of others and provided you obeyed the law, you could make of your life pretty much what you wanted. And that's why we lead in all those creative and cultural sectors and that's why we have the best universities. Because the best minds from across the world are meeting in some of the best pubs and bars and nightclubs, like subatomic particles colliding in a cyclotron. And they are producing those flashes of innovation that are essential for long term economic success[255].

And so, the talented and tolerant come to London to live their dreams: the creative class make up 41.6 per cent of London's workforce[256]. They are not only the driving force of London's economy but it is the creative class and the experiences they consume that are the new face of the London dream. As a result, for companies, this is the place they have to be. In 2011, Nick Beck, managing director of the Tug Agency, explained that, 'I really think Shoreditch is what Soho was 20-years ago.' For Beck, however, the benefits were not so personal. Instead, 'from [his] point of view, having a cool office in Shoreditch has been a big selling point when we've been looking to hire, young, dynamic staff'[257].

Thus, while many entrepreneurs wanted to be part of the scene, businesses needed to come to Silicon Roundabout because they were in close proximity – often measured in cycling distance – from the cool young people they sought to employ. They also came because office space for tech companies with relatively high numbers of low-paid employees was far more cost effective[258].

Most of all, they came to the East End because other tech businesses were already there, in turn chasing spaces made cool by artists and their bohemian edge. These tech companies are not competing retail outlets establishing a territory. Companies in the flat white economy are reliant upon access to a networking culture and the workers who move within it. Perhaps ironically, the very digital technology that was thought to bring about the death of place is now an industry that is reliant on physical clustering and conglomeration.

Conglomerations of Creatives

Technological advancements mean the creative classes could stay in the provinces, enjoying the benefits of cheaper house prices and the countryside. Increasingly, they do. But for much of the twenty-first century they have come to London to consume and enjoy the city. They have also had to come to London to take advantage of the networking opportunities necessary to get work.

Sometimes they are one and the same. Socialising becomes work, if you want to play the game. In the flat white economy, the gap between work and consumption, pleasure and labour has never been narrower. For many professionals in London, work becomes all-consuming and becomes your social life out of necessity. In a city of so many migrants, the workplace (and the house share) provides an instant stock of like-minded young people. For many of the most privileged new Londoners, other than old university besties and acquaintances, work friends are their first friends.

Workplaces are keen to capitalise on these bonds, seeking to eliminate any excuse employees have for leaving. Cafes, gyms, nap-pods and slides are all features of big-tech offices. Employers are capitalising on this environment by attempting to create a workplace culture in which what the employee might see as a procrastinating chat is actually, for Google, a 'casual collision' or 'creative encounter'[259]. Why ever leave if your workplace is also your leisure space?

Flexible hours are the norm, although whether workers reap the benefits is generally bypassed: flexible contracts are just as common, especially in start-ups. We are at work and not at work at the same time. Always working and never working. It is no wonder that Londoners work the longest hours in the UK[260].

It is not just that I can (and, sadly, do) access my email at any time. Or that university career services and social networking sites like LinkedIn are encouraging people to develop their personal brand. It is that every interaction is potentially a business interaction, as the original Silicon Roundabout members knew very well. The flat white economy, with its more fluid – or precarious – forms of employment is reliant on networks and cultural capital. This not only means these professionals are always potentially at work but that those outside of these dominant networks find it difficult to make their way in.

The mixing of work and play is not restricted to big corporate employers. Start-ups and other small businesses mix in 'co-working' spaces, paying for individual desks and enjoying the benefits of competitive co-operation, otherwise known as networking. This flexible work, and flexible employment, flips the dynamic seen in big-tech corporations but with the same result. Whereas at Google the office becomes a place of community and leisure, for freelancers in the gig economy, the home and places of leisure become places of work.

Work as play. Play as work. Sounds like a dream gig. It is, for some.

Chapter 7

Working the Dream

Silicon Roundabout may be the apex of post-industrial London but there is nothing glamorous about leaving the Old Street station. My students are always bemused when I tell them they are in Britain's equivalent to Silicon Valley; it is all far too grey. But, if you look closely, the signs of a hipster economy are all around us. There is the Shoreditch Grind coffee shop[261]. A colourful oversized polyurethane mushroom, a familiar curio around the hip parts of the East End thanks to street-artist Christian Nagel, pokes out from a rooftop. Beside me is the Nightjar, a 'Speakeasy-style subterranean bar with live jazz and blues, for cocktails and rare spirits'. We have come a long way, and not very far at all, from Victorian gin palaces.

A little further down Old Street on the way to the City is a co-working space that 'has cultivated an innovation ecosystem of remarkable sector-focused coworking spaces for entrepreneurs, innovators, and creatives' in a once abandoned warehouse. Outside, a fleet of bicycles worthy of a college town are locked to purpose-built stands. A ping-pong bar advertises specials and the upcoming football fixtures. Inside, an open-plan office, fit with meeting rooms, event spaces and a café/bar leads me to Robbie, a marketing executive at a digital agency specialising in the craft beer industry.

And we have not even reached peak hipster, as we soon move on to one of those funky bars that brings together creatives, who are then overwhelmed by City types. Here, over an incomprehensively expensive gluten-free beer, Robbie is recalling his journey to the Silicon Roundabout[262].

With his tidy neck-beard, the craft beer podcast and the bicycle tied to the rack outside, Robbie certainly fits in the stereotype of

Richard Florida's creative classes. The Instagram account he has
for his dog adds to the stereotype. His affection for London is
exactly what Florida would expect out of the creative classes:

*what I love about London is how diverse it is. There are so many
different sides to the city that offer a multitude of opportunities,
professional or cultural. Think of anything you want to do, and you
can do it in London.*

Like much of London's creative sector, Robbie is young, male
and white; over three-quarters of all creative industry jobs in
London are held by white folk and two-thirds by men[263]. But he
is no digital-bro stereotype. Robbie is articulate, intelligent and
socially liberal. His distaste for some of the behaviour around us
is clear. He is also a man who knew where he wanted to go: into
beer, in a creative way.

Robbie has been in London for 6 years, although his first salvo
was 10 years ago. He is officially British now although, like me,
Robbie is a BIPO (British in Passport Only). Instead, his identity
is still in Cape Town, South Africa, where he left for London as
a 17-year old on a 2-year working holiday visa.

Robbie early days in London were funded by working in a
Soho bar, which was 'really, really cool, you know, just being 18
years old, free, partying'. He had wanted to be an actor, which he
had been at school. Spending so much time in Soho, surrounded
by failed actors, taught Robbie some valuable lessons. He had
been to a couple of auditions and had even been on screen as
an extra, but he felt that he was not in the right place and he
returned home to go to university.

The university application process emphasised his creative
attributes and he took a practical approach, completing a degree
in copywriting. But Robbie still dreamt of London, even if the
appeal was more about travel and partying than using his degree.
He wound up in the South of France, staying in a campsite and

running out of money like so many migrants around the world. Except that most of these migrants are not trying to find work in an industry as glamorous as superyachts. London called; with his last £50, he caught a flight back to the city and his sister's couch.

Robbie 'wasn't done' with the city. He wanted to write, to be creative. And then there was beer. There was always beer.

Unfortunately, like many graduates, Robbie had not actually done any of the copywriting he had trained for. What he had done was work in bars. London always needs more hospitality staff and Robbie was soon back at his Soho haunt before being enlisted into their management academy where there was an opportunity to go into marketing. This was not the superyacht life that Robbie had originally planned.

It was horrendous, I mean, I was like, minimum wage, living in a shithole in Stratford. It wasn't the most glamorous life.

Robbie was always running on empty, working in a 1,000-capacity venue serving 'city wankers'. One Tuesday night a group of these wankers trashed the place. He was done. He needed to get out of hospitality, which is pretty much what everyone in hospitality says. Robbie's break was a brewery in Bedford that did not understand what was going on in London and did not understand the burgeoning craft beer market. Robbie did. It certainly helped, in Robbie words, that the person who did the interview:

went to all-boys school, was a massive cricket fan, massive rugby fan, went to boarding school, and so I just had a lot in common with him. We had the interview in a pub on the rivers in Blackfriars and after about 20 minutes, we just had a beer, and we just chatted shit for another 45 mins.

Unsurprisingly, he got the job. For a beer enthusiast, Robbie should have been in his element. Instead, he found himself doing sales work, equally frustrated by driving around London's suburban pubs or filing reports from home. There was no outlet for his creativity and any horizontal move into the marketing team was thwarted by his own success as a salesperson. Robbie's goal of working in beer brand marketing seemed far away. Even still, he was building contacts and that is what matters in niche industries. And what is more niche, and more cool, than the craft beer market?

Robbie was determined to get where he wanted to be. Some cold outreach emails and a couple of well-placed calls and he was soon impressing an agency with his passionate presentation on beer. They were looking to move from being a generalist web developer to specialising in building websites for craft breweries and needed a marketer with contacts in the craft industry to write copy. This was it, although it required a significant pay cut. Robbie was soon riding his bike to Old Street and the promised land in the heart of London's cool economy.

They were originally in Watford, which is not quite the dream. Or the place for a digital agency specialising in craft beer. Just as hedge funds have to have a Mayfair postcode[264], even if much of the business is undertaken elsewhere, cool companies need a presence in the East End. With only two full-time employees, Robbie's agency was dependent on freelancers, and that means networking. And, Robbie tells me, the perception is that Shoreditch and Hackney are the places to be for both breweries and digital agencies. It's tough for clients and potential colleagues (temporary or otherwise) to take you seriously if you are not here. As a result, it is also the place to be if you want freelancers.

His agency knew, Robbie says:

that we needed to be in London, because in Watford, it's difficult to

attract talent. So, [we were] struggling to hold on to people, because Old Street roundabout, Silicon Roundabout, effectively is known as the tech city of London. If you're in anything digital, you need to be in this place.
If you want to recruit freelancers, then you need to travel into London. If you want to meet people. You have to network. The best networking opportunities are always in London.
And that's just how it works.

As much as platforms like PeoplePerHour and Upwork make it easy to connect with people, 'you've got to have a relationship with your contractors, otherwise, you are just gambling', Robbie tells me. Perhaps this is how it has always worked in London. As much as the East End has changed, the logic of production has stayed remarkably consistent. While manufacturing made up a significant part of Victorian London, the mass factories and mills that came to symbolise the horrors of the industrial revolution in England were not the dominant presence in London[265]. Instead, manufacturing in London tended to focus on the reprocessing of goods with an extreme division of labour. Here, as Jerry White tells it:

more often than not, the neighbourhood became the factory. And factory discipline was unnecessary where an endless labour supply had to work long hours to gain a living and as often as not had to find its own heat and light in a workroom that was also home[266]

Just South of Silicon Roundabout around Curtain Road, it was the furniture industry that was the neighbourhood factory by the twentieth century. Each part of the manufacturing processes, from carving to the upholstery, would take place within a 5-minute area[267]. Parts would be wheeled from home workshop to home workshop, reliant upon efficient communication and trusted networks.

This kind of extreme sub-division of labour is the basis for the gig economy that silently dominates much of the flat white economy. Around 35 per cent of those in the flat white economy are self-employed (compared to 15 per cent in the general population)[268], engaging what professionals call freelancing and the new working class know as the gig economy. They move from contract to contract, often by the hour or single task, as exploitable micro-entrepreneurs.

Some may inhabit co-working spaces with other micro businesses: the Creative Industries Federation reports that 95 per cent of creative industry businesses have less than ten employees[269]. For others, their MacBook and portable charger are all they need as they choose a different co-working office to ride to every day. The coffee shop, rapidly taking the place of the pub as a meeting place in the European style, is symbolic of this shift; walk into any café worth its foam in East London and you will see laptops glowing as young(ish) people, both hip and earnest, use this space to both work and to socialise.

This gig economy creates conditions of maximum flexibility, allowing companies like Robbie's to hire piece-meal whenever they desire it and move on if they want something different for the next job. For example, when it comes to:

> *the big content pieces that we write for ourselves, I write them first,*
> *I just write them really quickly, and send them off. We've got a*
> *copywriter on a retainer basis, so she will have a look at that, and*
> *then send it back to us. If she doesn't have time, then I can send it off*
> *to Upwork, or I can send it off to PeoplePerHour.*

For those highly skilled programmers in high demand, this allows wonderful flexibility. For others who might once have had the privilege of secure employment, it only increases their vulnerability.

Robbie is thinking about doing some of this work himself,

although definitely not for his agency. Not only did the cost of staying in the UK set him back, but he is also getting increasingly frustrated with his job, which is 'becoming less and less enjoyable because it has to be more sales-orientated now...I might be entering the job market again.' Even in a cool, co-working space, when you are sitting right next to the owner of the company, it is 'not exactly the most conductive environment to be creative in'. And so, the idea of freelancing feels pretty good, even if it is a step away from the dream of working in marketing for a brewery.

Hannah has made a different decision. And, for her, digital freelancing provided a lifeline out of London.

Gendered Gigs

I've never met Hannah, at least not properly, but she sure is an efficient transcriber[270]. We've come in contact in the new-fashioned way: through a freelancing platform that I'm keen to experience for research more than for economy. We soon move our interactions away from this exploitative website while remaining in the online sphere. Who needs a noisy pub when you have email?

Hannah writes that she dreamt of London but these dreams, like many others, were of necessity rather than unabashed desire. She moved:

...straight after graduating from the University of Southampton, but it was a very last-minute decision. Having grown up in a very rural village, I knew if I wanted to jump straight onto the career ladder then I needed to move out.

She started with an unpaid summer internship in the curator's office of a major London attraction, 'then, before I knew it, I'd decided to stay, almost by accident. I guess I was after opportunity and I wanted to be near my friends, it snowballed over time.'

Hannah had come to London with dreams of a career in the arts. And yet, despite her internship and having achieved top marks in English literature and history, she was not qualified for a curator's job. Even entry-level roles at places like the Tate Modern required a PhD. Instead, she started looking for work in roles at the media and communications side of the flat white economy. She cast the net widely, searching for opportunities in the publishing sector and for other public history roles. Or anything in culture and the arts.

Unfortunately:

literally, no one would have me, I couldn't even get an interview for entry level jobs. I was constantly typecast into PA and receptionist roles by recruiters and eventually, desperation drove me to accept, where I constantly flitted between different companies. I'm blonde, educated and I am well-spoken...the only other friends who faced this problem trying to get employment fit into that exact category. People refused to take me seriously. My education was seen as a shiny accessory, not an indication of the hard work I was capable of. Despite consistently pushing forward my interests, the only interviews (and therefore jobs) I got were in Finance, Property etc.
After a while, I just couldn't do office-based jobs anymore. So I took on a live-out nanny role, which freed up my time to work on my writing portfolio and work towards an MA in Early Modern History

It is not that Hannah expected to start at the top. Instead, 'what was frustrating is the total lack of time people will give your capabilities. I faced the assumption that I wasn't as bright, or was a doormat a lot because of my appearance and my age (and dare I say it, at times gender).'

Nonetheless, Hannah was surviving. She had friends and enjoyed 'the freedom of being able to get up and go somewhere, whenever I liked'. Rent was extortionate and there are a lot of pressures to socialise as much as possible, which Hannah 'found extremely mentally and financially draining. I also hated the competitive atmosphere, all of a sudden it was all about displays of wealth and displays of fun - who's having the most fun!'

Then there was the façade of London's professional drug problem; weekday use of cocaine is higher in London than anywhere else in Europe[271]. Recreational drugs were a celebrated part of London's dual resurgence in the 1960s and then the 1990s. What goes unspoken is not only the seeming necessity of these drugs, specifically cocaine, for surviving in London but its link to gang violence[272].

With this façade of fun all around us, it is no wonder that Londoners report lower life satisfaction than the rest of the country[273]. Hackney, possibly the coolest part of London, is also the least happy place in London[274]. Peter Ackroyd claims that this was a paradox of Victorian London, 'there is an appearance of energy and vitality in the mass, but the characteristic individual mood is one of anxiety and despondency'[275].

This sense of alienation has been around for as long as London, and urban life, has existed; the overwhelming stimuli of urban life leads to a sense of alienation and protective isolation. Just as every Londoner knows how to put their headphones on or lose themselves in their phone to avoid the unbearable proximity to others on the tube, the early inhabitants of the mega-metropolis in the nineteenth century learnt to develop the hardness to battle the crowds.

But not all alienation is made equal and not all experiences of public space are the same. Like many women in London, Hannah was confronted by a form of discrimination experienced by more than half of London's population: sexual harassment. It led to the final straw when Hannah was:

working in the property sector, it was me and five men in the small high-end property office in Pimlico. Lewd comments about my sex-

life, suggestions I was overweight, comments that I shouldn't be eating certain things, constant comments that I wasn't intelligent were the norm and I eventually quit after the Managing Director asked me to polish his shoes and kneel in front of him (in a suggestive manner) in front of the whole team, who couldn't stop laughing. It was around this time I was diagnosed with mental health issues and I definitely think that my working life played into it, I had a lot of panic attacks on my way to work.

Sadly, she is far from alone in this experience. Not only do half of all women report being sexually harassed at work[276] but London has the highest gender pay gap in the UK[277]. Women hold the majority of low-paid jobs in London[278]. Historically, this has occurred because women have taken on part-time roles to account for care-giving activities. Although this is still the case, there was an 87 per cent increase in the number of low-paid women in full-time jobs between 2011 and 2016[279].

In the creative sector within which Hannah sought to work, the gender pay gap stands at 28 per cent[280]. For much of Hannah's time in London, this discrimination felt like a faceless force holding her back. In those fatal moments in Pimlico, it felt very personal. Her London dream was over.

This Is the End

When her time in London ended, it ended quickly. Even over email, her emotional journey comes through clearly:

I'll be honest, I had a breakdown and I decided that it was no longer safe for me to be there and to be away from family. For the majority of the time I lived in London, I lived with very good friends, but I'd recently (due to a rent hike) had to move in with two acquaintances from Uni. They spent a lot of the time out of the house and I was becoming quite isolated. I was working two jobs, whilst simultaneously studying and battling a serious mental illness. All

*of a sudden something clicked that it didn't have to be like this. I
realised that the culture on my doorstep and my constantly busy
friends weren't enough to keep me somewhere that was damaging my
health.*
*I also really missed the countryside, so that was a more cheerful
reason to leave.*

How does she feel about leaving?

*I think London is like a very bad boyfriend, you convince yourself
that you love him so you should stay. You cling on to the brunches
and the galleries and the snippets of fun, and you think it's going
to get better...but it just doesn't. Then once the facade has gone,
you cannot wait to leave. I left London (for good) within 4 hours
of making the decision one Sunday morning. I literally packed a
suitcase, grabbed my dog and got on a train. If you'd have asked me
that Saturday if I'd move home, I'd have told you not to be ridiculous,
of course, I'm going to stay!*
*I miss my friends a lot, but I do still see them. I don't feel any regret
to be honest. I miss Tooting Bec Lido and I miss curing a hangover
with a walk around the V&A and I miss the food markets. I feel very
empowered in my decision in some ways, I think a lot of my social
group all feel the same but are better at burying those feelings at
the back of their heads. I wouldn't be at all surprised to see people
disperse in a few years' time. I think it was brave to admit it wasn't
for me so early on.*

Ironically, it is only now that Hannah is truly working in the
flat white economy. From the countryside, she works through
online platforms to find transcription and copywriting work,
often finding herself engaged by companies like Robbie's. Now,
she can create her own schedule and can avoid toxic office
environments. The platforms are great for finding clients but
their 20 per cent slice stings. So do the pay rates. Hannah might

be out of the city but now she is competing against the world.

Platforms like peopleperhour.com, upwork.com and freelancer.com facilitate open competition for projects across the country, just without any of the benefits of regular employment. Or the protection of a minimum wage. This pure labour competition is the dream of capital but a nightmare for many. Amazon's Mechanical Turk, like so much else that Amazon does, provides the logical end to this exploitation of the online vulnerable. Here workers search for 'HITS' (Human Intelligence Tasks) from requesters, such as personality surveys and transcription services, for as little as £0.01. Fortunately, they can be done from anywhere in the world. This is not quite what American political commentator and globalisation celebratist Thomas Friedman had in mind when he celebrated the coming of a 'flat earth'[281].

There is an extra kicker for Hannah: women engaged in creative freelance work are paid a third less than male freelancers[282].

And so, along with 35,000 other 22-29 year-olds, who leave London each year[283], Hannah is now gone. She came to find her dream job and found that cool consumption in London was easily paired with the misery of production.

Robbie has made a different choice, although his dreams have become more complicated, and more pragmatic:

I think economically it makes sense for me to stay here based on the diversity of opportunities. If my career crashed, it's easier to pick myself up here than in South Africa. So I guess economic security. Saying that we're about to go through some economic turmoil so we'll see how I feel in a year. Aside from the economic benefits, I think I've spent the last 7 years building a life here, and that's not easy to walk away from. The friends I've made and lifestyle that I've grown used to aren't things I can take with me.

London lives are complicated. They are messy. Often they are thrown out by forces well outside of our control. And still, the hip and the nerdy alike come to London, even if they are leaving in equal number. Rents continue to rise. Buying a house in central London is not even in the realms of fantasy. The cost of living is punishing. And yet, economic mobility is higher in London than anywhere else in the UK; 20 of the top 23 local authorities for social mobility are in London[284].

London remains a leading tech hub and is still cool, creative and cultured. If you are young, creative and talented, London is still the place to be and a place where there is always something to do, even if you do not immediately end up working where you want to be. Living in London is not all about work. It might not even be about work. It is about living in a place where there is always something to do, despite the cost.

Chapter 8

#Cool #London

Tessa is sure that she is a Londoner, even if she does not live here. Instead, she travels in from leafy Surrey, paying £12 a day in rail fares to come into places like Soho and experience the city. But not just for herself; Tessa posts her experiences to her 26.7k followers and makes a living from doing so. Almost.

She has suggested that we meet for coffee in Soho to help me understand the strange world of influencing. It should be no surprise that Tessa loves it here nor that it is a regular character in her stories. Soho has long been a hub of cool in London. Taking its name from a hunting cry, Soho was once the farmed edge of Western London. But it did not follow the usual pattern of development. The area was claimed in 1536 as a Royal Park for King Henry VIII and it should have gone the way of Bloomsbury or Marylebone and become a grand estate with wealth growing at its fringes. Instead, neighbouring Mayfair took all the prestige and Soho became defined by diversity and makeshift forms of life as waves of European migrants packed its tight alleys.

French, Greek and Italian restaurants opened. Political exiles took sanctuary. In World War II Soho became a haven for those escaping the pressures of the war, even if just for one night. Music thrived here, especially jazz. The Hand Jive was invented at the Cat's Whiskers Coffee Bar in Soho, a few feet from the Grind. Like so much of Soho life, it was an improvisation forced by the twin pressures of overcrowding and the overwhelming need to embrace the possibilities of a London existence.

As Richard Florida would insist, this is an ideal environment to attract the creative classes. As a result of their influx, Soho is rapidly catching up with the wealth of its surrounding neighbourhoods. What now strikes visitors to the area is not its diversity but the density of cranes and the flurries of fluro-vested workmen. If you pause at lunch time, however, you will be overtaken by a stream of creative and media types heading to markets, European eateries and coffee bars. Or just Pret. They move in packs, almost always pale and male, casually shirted with a hint of style and likely a covering of facial hair.

They are part of what a report for the City of Westminster called the 'World's Creative Hub' [285]. It is certainly London's creative centre, as long as you exclude artists of almost any type. Where Silicon Roundabout is the base for tech jobs, 20 per cent of London's creative industry jobs are in tight confines of Soho. The streets from Piccadilly Circus to Tottenham Court Road house the largest concentration of motion potion production and distribution companies in the city so that, the report claims, an entire film production chain is available within one square mile. But it is not these employees who are increasing property prices: it is the investors who chase them. No one who works at this end of the film industry really lives here; at four jobs for every resident, Soho is the most employment dense area in the country (with the exception of the City of London).

These creative class employees are waiting outside the door at the ever so hip Soho Grind, where Tessa and I have agreed to meet. Inside, a neon sign shows the way to the basement. It reads, *French Lessons Downstairs*, a wink to Soho's starring role in the witty subversion of London's theoretically censored red-light district.

Tessa loves it here, especially the oddly deserted downstairs and the retro walls, which are perfect for a post. This is Tessa's London existence, although it has not always been. After beginning her millennial life in Kilburn in North-West London, Tessa moved to Leeds for university, completing a BA in Creative Design. But she was always going to move back to London, as she had only gone to Leeds to 'get as far away from my parents as I could'. Tessa's return journey is part of a distinct migratory pattern of young people in England that accounts for a fifth of all internal migration within England and Wales.

This cycle has London as its hub. The first step is out of the capital, which loses 50,000 students (net) to smaller cities and provincial universities across the country. The capital's 49 higher education institutions do not suffer too much, as 100,000 overseas students – most paying much higher fees than local students – take their place[286].

Following their time spent in the cocoon of university, students spring back to London after graduation. Following a pattern established in the nineteenth century, ambitious young men and women travel on Victorian-era train lines to take their chance in the big city. Not only do three-quarters of those who left London return but they flock in from other centres. In a city that houses 15 per cent of the country's population, 6 months after graduation almost a quarter of new graduates have jobs in London. A total of 38 per cent of those with degrees classified as 2:1 or higher from Russell Group universities came to London. Remarkably, more than half Oxbridge students[287] with good degrees were employed in London 6 months after they graduated[288].

And so it seemed inevitable that Tessa was going to move back to London. She just did not know what she was going to do with herself when she got here. Visual merchandising for Top Shop in Oxford Circus was the result. At first, she was 'absolutely in love with it' but the hours were tough; to avoid customers, they worked from 10pm to 5am. It all became a bit chaotic, a bit stressful. A bit too much. When Tessa broke up with her fiancé, she escaped London in search of a simpler life and ended up living on a small island in South-East Asia for 5 years having 'the most incredible time'. She had set up a charity teaching English to kids but, as meaningful as it was, London called.

She needed to go back. She just needed to work out how to live the London life she wanted. As a creative person, Tessa tells me, she had struggled when she was 'not being fulfilled in roles that, kind of, didn't scream out to me, and didn't allow me to be creative 100 per cent of the time, I get bored with, and I can't put my all in to it…I get frustrated'.

But, even from Surrey, Tessa:

> *was seeing things that I never saw before, even more so, moving out of London, and actually coming in to see places, and discover places, and actually, I loved finding new places, and exciting places, that I can go visit, shoot, and whatever I wanna do. I think it's just the best city in the world so I've fallen in love with it all over again.*

At the same time as this love affair was reigniting, a new world was expanding: the world of Instagram. Not that Instagram was new. By 2017, when Tessa started getting serious with the platform it had been around for 7 years and had 500 million daily active users. What had developed was micro- and nano-influencing and the possibility of making a living without a celebrity-sized following.

The stars of the smallest of screens can earn up to US$50,000 for a single post to their millions of followers. But, despite their reach, celebrity status can create a sense of distance. According to *The StartUp*, engagement, that vital characteristic of social involvement measured by Likes and Comments, peaks at 1,000 followers (think of your popular Insta friend) and drops off strongly at 100,000 (that overenthusiastic Insta-model with #goals) [289].

Consequently, if you want your campaign to influence a specific group of potential customers, then smaller scale users are for you. 'The Game', as Sidney Pierucci, in *The StartUp* insists, 'isn't just getting eyeballs; but getting eyeballs that care!' [290] There is no value in paying Kylie Jenner US$1,000,000 to promote your Shoreditch coffee joint. What you need is someone who has influence in the Shoreditch scene. Having 30,000 followers in East London is better than 100,000 around the world. Once again, location matters, even in the digital world.

Tessa was ahead of the curve. She saw a niche in the market and her London-themed account quickly grew out of her renewed passion for the city. Discovering the possibilities in influencing was the 'best thing ever' as it gave her the possibility of 'actually living a fulfilling life'. This is a life where Tessa can be her best creative self. And, she can do it independently, a micro-entrepreneur creating a brand and managing her destiny. This is the millennial dream: a complete fusion of work and play. Plus the instant gratification of watching the likes and shares tally up.

It is a passion for London that Tessa wants to convey to her followers: authentic, creative and fun. Just 'an average person who likes to create and who lives to do things out of the box'. With a lot of hashtags. She won't work with brands unless she really wants to or believes in their message. Tessa tells me proudly of a campaign for food waste. Flowers and anything kind of floral are big for her as well. What Tessa needs are campaigns that allow her to connect with her followers and to establish trust so that her 'audience will actually listen to what I'm going to say'. It's not about the numbers, of course. It's about doing something that 'people can look at and say, *Wow, that's different and better*'.

But Tessa is competing with an ever-expanding band of influencers who are trying to be 'as unique as possible'. This is the game of content creation in the attention economy: you are not selling a product, you are selling an experience or a lifestyle in a way that halts scanning eyes and flicking thumbs for long enough to soak in the message. Doing so requires you to create a brand that connects with the audience, without feeling like a brand[291]. You can then sell on your audience's attention to advertisers; micro-influencers like Tessa are valued by advertisers because their personal investment in their recommendations is obvious to their followers.

It is important, then, that Tessa's audience is mostly from

London, although she has 'some amazing followers from America'. With a sparkle, she tells me that they message to tell her 'how amazing it is to see all these pictures of London, and they wanna visit'.

Sounds wonderful. But it is not an easy life. In the first instance, as Tessa admits, they 'don't get paid a lot of money' and have to absorb their expenses. While there are a lot of perks, like invitations to events and free products, she finds herself working 7 days a week. And, when your life is your work, there is no way to escape.

Tessa is not alone in this struggle, which is kind of the problem. Instagram superstars, of whom there are obviously only a few, might be approached by brands or PR companies directly. Micro-influencers have to work harder for attention. Luckily, as always, there are platforms that help. Sites like Takumi, TRIBE and indaHash help to manage the relationship between influencers and brands, for a healthy cut.

On TRIBE, campaigns advertise for influencers, posting the content and style they would like, along with a price. It seems like a recipe for insecurity. And precarity. According to TRIBE, an influencer with 25k-50k followers can expect to receive £180-250 per post, if all goes well[292]. Like most forms of micro-entrepreneurship, voluntary or otherwise, the risk is taken on by the worker. You can then create the content but you do not get paid until the campaign buys it off you, Tessa informs me. This means that:

> *You can go through hours of work, and not get anything at the end, and you might just get a generic response saying, 'Oh, we don't want to work with you, because you're not really our style' or something like that.*

This is Uber for creatives. There is no barrier to entry and certainly no minimum wage. Instead, an almost unlimited supply of influencers competes for limited work. Don't like the price? Don't take the job. Someone else certainly will. It certainly is not Tessa's game, but a recent report in *The Atlantic* revealed the rise of 'Fake Influencers' posting what appears to be sponsored content for free in order to increase their professional, and social, credibility[293]. In the creative world, there always seems to be someone who will work for free.

As a result of this downward crush, Tessa supplements the influencing with what she calls 'content-only work', specifically doing photography for the social media accounts of hotels and restaurants.

It is no wonder that a competitive personal environment festers. Tessa earnestly insists that most influencers are lovely and she is keen to tell me of the wonderful circle of like-minded influencers she has found. But, she tells me with widening eyes, 'some of them are mean', especially those who have been around for a while and feel that others are getting on their turf.

But Tessa is inspired and undeterred. She is soon moving back to a house she has been renting out in Queen's Park near Kilburn. From here she can walk to Soho, where her cameraman partner works. It is this that she loves most about the city. She leans in to tell me over her long-finished soy flat white, 'the fact that we have everything...if I walk to London and, you know, wanted a certain food, I probably could find that. I think when you're living near London, you can get anywhere on foot.'

More than that, she loves the way London is developing, Brexit aside.

> it has changed over the years, and I think it's changed to doing more for tourists, doing more for people who are coming to the country... you know, making an effort to welcome people in, and I think it's just beautiful how it's changed and things like, you know, the amount of money they spend on their shop facades and, you know, the new job roles that are coming for creative florists and things like that.

This is the London dream of the creative classes. It is the idea of a city full of new and unique experiences just waiting to be consumed. For Tessa, it's just a bonus that she gets paid for it. Mostly.

Consuming London

This is not your grandfather's capitalism but it is capitalism all the same. Tessa's way of life is part of a marked shift in London's economy from a place of industrial production and distribution to one of ideas and consumption. In particular, as Tessa shows, the consumption of experiences, identities and lifestyles. This rendition of the dream of London as the place to be is now the place where there is 'always something to do'.

The idea of a London as a place of new and shiny things, whether goods, the idea of cosmopolitan civility, or cool experiences, has also been part of London's story. The most privileged from the provinces had long come from the countryside to take in the shiny new things only available in the capital, if only for a day. As Jerry White recounts, in 1703, 'the Number of Shops both in the City and in the Suburbs [is] so great, and indeed so far beyond any foreign City, that it is to Strangers a just Matter of Amazement'[294]. This enticing world drew in those enthralled by the idea of the big city, those dreaming of making their fortunes, and those eager to improve the station. Little has changed.

If London was the place to consume, its products came from all across the burgeoning empire. London was at the vanguard of consumer desire as foreign goods forever changed the way the British ate, drank and furnished their homes. East India merchants traded in household fabrics, porcelain and wood for dye that supplied the markets that gave London its cosmopolitan status. These merchants also made London the greatest spice market in the world, much of it on Mincing Lane in the City. Curries and chillies entered into the national diet. Tea, coming first from China and then India and Ceylon (now Sri Lanka), would become an integral part of English-ness. Men of all classes, from aristocrats to slaves themselves, were engaged in the consumption of tobacco[295]. Hindi words entered the English language. It should be no surprise that 'loot' and 'thug' are two of the most pervasive terms.

London became the 'Emporium of the World'[296], a heaving cornucopian world of splendour and newly discovered collective vice. Goods that were not strictly necessary for human reproduction, from coffee and cotton to sugar and spices, were now available, creating the everyday possibility of consumption for desire not necessity. As the eighteenth century advanced, rumours of the revelatory idea of *shopping*[297] as a leisure pursuit came to dominate foreign and provincial imaginations of a city where 'everything was to be had'[298].

This idea of London as a magical marketplace was not only for the consuming elite but took on, as White describes, '... an almost mythic quality, the living embodiment of London's opportunities, proof that gold really could be scraped from its paving stones'. [299]

While leisure shopping may have been an upper-class pursuit, urban and waged lives meant that products needed to be bought rather than made. This produced the first generation of consumers, buying everything from household textiles and china to beer, butter and fish. Moreover, just as the fashion of tea drinking drifted down from the aristocracy, so the growing middle class attempted to emulate the consumption patterns of their social superiors. Where 'keeping up appearances' was everything in a class-based society, for the first time shop-level consumption offered a way of communicating one's standing on the streets. This was the dream sold by London's shops and they were keen to advertise it on revolutionary window displays and billboards[300].

In this city of mythical luxury, the night was becoming increasingly banished by light, both philosophically and quite practically as oil and then gas lamps lit up the streets. In her *London Journal* of 1840, the French writer and socialist activist Flora Tristan wrote that:

London, magically lit by its millions of gas lights, is resplendent! Its broad streets disappearing into the distance; its shops, where floods of light reveal the myriad of sparkling colours of all the masterpieces conceived of by human industry[301].

Even James Boswell, before he had wondered whether he would lose his zest for London, had noted the 'glare of shops and signs'[302]. By the start of the twentieth century, the 10,000 electric lamps that illuminated the West End and Leicester Square made it 'the most brilliant spot in the Empire'. This light, according to White, allowed 'a veritable carnival of extravagance' with luxury that 'reached an almost excessive point'[303].

These advances further fuelled the productivity of the industrial revolution and, as historian Peter Ackroyd writes, it is not difficult to see the link between 'the great new brightness' and 'the brightness of burgeoning commerce'[304]. And still, modern London was defined by production and for most consumption was an act of necessity. So it was until much of the twentieth century. It was only with the counter-cultural ideas of the Swinging Sixties that consumption became a way to express yourself. This was not just good news for those bored by suburban conformity. It was also the very thing needed to keep capitalism afloat.

Consuming Pleasure

The industrial revolution generated a problem that threatened to bring down the global economy: it was capable of producing too much. Having starved and suffered for much of its history, this might have felt like a nice problem for humanity to have. As Marx had predicated, though, the capacity for industry to produce more than we need was threatening to throw capitalism into an existential crisis, a threat that peaked during the 1970s[305]. Rather than overproduction bringing down the global economy, however, this crisis of overproduction was a spur to the next stage of capitalism.

First, businesses needed to find a way to increase consumer demand. One solution was to find new consumers in different parts of the world. The rise of China and India took care of that. The next was to compel those who already consumed to consume more, both through ensuring what they owned would not just be used but used up, and by stimulating the desire for consumer goods. Not only were we made to want microwaves and whiteware, but they broke down much more often. The easiest way to sell more toasters, or iPhones, is to make sure that we need new ones every few years. These strategies produced a new society – a society of consumers[306] – and cities like London became places of consumption rather than production.

Of course, work and immaterial production are still instrumental to London's success. But work is not necessarily the mythology that brings Londoners to the city, at least those aspiring to be in the creative classes. As Florida's research has shown, attracting creative workers is not so much about the availability of jobs but the availability of certain lifestyles and the experience of cool. Whatever that means, for them[307]. For some, this is clubbing, cocktail bars and cocaine. For others, it is street-art and museum late-nights. London is not particular about how you consume the city, as long as pounds are magically drawn from contactless cards and Instagram posts compel others to join in.

The transition to a consumer society is part of a shift from what sociologists have called a disciplinary society, where conformity and authority were king, to a post-disciplinary environment in which enjoyment and subversion are normative. Today, the place of sin has shifted from enjoying oneself to not enjoying oneself[308]. Here, as French sociologist Pierre Bourdieu writes in his seminal *Distinction*:

...whereas the old morality of duty, based on the opposition between pleasure and good, induces a generalised suspicion of the 'charming and attractive', a fear of pleasure and a relation to the body made up of 'reserve', 'modesty' and 'restraint', and associates every satisfaction of the forbidden impulses with guilt, the new ethical avant-garde urges a morality of pleasure as duty. This doctrine makes it a failure, a threat to self-esteem, not to have fun...pleasure is not only permitted but demanded[309]

Getting married and having children at an early age was the norm in the 1950s. Today, this act would be seen as a waste of opportunities. There is no virtue in delaying gratification. Faced with maximum opportunity we are made to feel guilty if we are not enjoying ourselves as much as we should. As such, thrift is no longer the virtue it once was, although it is a necessity for many. Instead, we are encouraged to spend, consume and enjoy! Realising #YOLO leads to major #FOMO[310]. A housemate's rebuke to a young Londoner is far more likely to be, 'you're in this great city with so much to do, why are you staying at home on a Friday night?' than, 'you spent all your money on cronuts and cocktails, shouldn't you be saving money to buy a house?'[311] Thrift does not feature heavily in the London dreams of the graduates and professionals shifting to the city.

For many millennial Londoners, this would all sound far too superficial. They do not want to spend their money on whiteware, cars and dinning sets. Anyway, accumulating goods is not all that practical in London flats. Those who have fled to the Shires can live that life. Nor is it necessarily about showing off brands, although there are certainly sub-cultures in London where having the latest Birkin bag on your arm is a necessity for membership. Instead, cool consumption is the consumption of ideas and experiences. While tote bags might fill with artesian cheeses at Borough market or vintage frocks in Spitalfields, these purchases are mere tokens of authentic London market *experiences.*

Experiencing London

The London dream, for the creative classes, is about consuming experiences, identities and lifestyles rather than mere objects. People want, as American entrepreneur Case Lawrence claims, 'to do things. They want to have adventures, narrative, and meaning in their day and their activities.' [312] Even when we consume things we are not buying the object itself but consuming what it represents. Buying a rainbow beigel from Brick Lane's Beigel Shop is not about how the rainbow tastes as much as posting #rainbowbeigel #lovelondon #bricklane and waiting for the Likes to tally up.

It is out of these experiences that the London dream is propagated. Today's Time Out magazine taunts me with a list of 24 Dreamy Things to do in London this weekend[313]. I could attend an Oktoberfest event in the Olympic Park, which will no doubt inspire a generation. The Science Museum is offering up *Hooked*, an exhibit on addiction. After that, it is either hanging out with the guinea pigs at the London Harvest festival or soaking up The Joy of Sake. It probably depends on how Oktoberfest went; I'm not young anymore. These choices do not exist in the provinces. They are the stuff of graduating student dreams and influential Instagram feeds. To live your best life in London is to experience everything the city has to offer. And always want more. With every experience, every post and every touch of a card we are buying into the mythology of the city and constructing our sense of self and our community.

But, while the consumption of experiences allows us to construct a community, virtual or otherwise, this is not an economy of conformity; people like Tessa do not want to buy cookie-cutter lives. Instead, living in a place where there is always something to do allows the possibility of seeking an authentic, creative and unique life. Just like everyone else.

Consuming Londoners can choose how to construct their lives. They can throw off the weight of the consuming sheeple and make informed ethical choices and have the pleasure of consuming while doing good. But ethical purchases are still purchases. The vegan market is still a market. A gluten-free cupcake stall has a greater gentrifying influence than an Apple mega-store. Capitalism is still capitalism, even if it is done with good intentions[314].

Now, though, it is capitalism with an edge of cool.

(Last Days of) Cool Capitalism

Cool and economics are not natural dance partners but it is the addition of cool to capitalism that makes London go round. The idea of cool, claims American Art Historian Robert Farris Thompson, can be traced back to Africa and the region of what is now Nigeria. Here he notes, 'coolness is an all-embracing positive attribute which combines notions of composure, silence, vitality, healing and social purification'[315]. When it was forced over the Atlantic, this almost sacred reading of cool 'evolved into a kind of passive resistance to the work ethic through personal style'[316]. This sense of cool was most powerfully evident in black music and style, which came across to London in the form of jazz in the 1960s and facilitated the flow of cool London in the 1960s.

Although the meaning of any word is subject to change, coolness is even more fluid. What is cool for me may not be for you. What was cool in 1960s London need not be now. That is far too vague for academics, though. And so, sociologist David Robins and author Dick Pountain reduced cool to three essential traits: narcissism, ironic detachment and hedonism[317].

This sense of coolness has long been present in London's youth, whether those who sought the glamour of Georgian London, the

Dandies and Flappers of the 1920s, the Mods of the 1960s or the YBA-inspired rave scene and Brit Pop louts of the 1990s. The youth of the global elite going table clubbing in Knightsbridge live in a wholly different city from the grime artists of East and now South London, but they too share Pountain and Robins' cool categories of narcissism, detachment and hedonism.

Such qualities became mainstream, if in a transgressive way, in the 1960s with the birth of a counter-culture movement that sought to throw off the binds of the disciplinary society and the binds of suburbia. But, if counter-culture was an opponent of the establishment, capitalism (or at least those charged with promoting its wares and widgets) was quick to duck the charge. Capital needed new markets as much as the youth wanted to drop out of the grip of the conformity of the 'mass society'.

As a result, Thomas Frank argues in *The Conquest of Cool*, 'what happened in the sixties is that hip became central to the way American capitalism understood itself and explained itself to the public'[318]. Thus, he argues, the 'madness' of the 1960s counter-culture of 'turn on, tune in and drop out' is now baked into our economy through a focus on youth and the idea that new is always better. For Frank, writing as a 32-year-old in 1997, '...the sixties are the beginning of the present, the birthplace of the styles and tastes and values that define our world' and in the 1990s we were witnessing 'the consolidation of a new species of hip consumerism, a cultural perpetual motion regime in which disgust with the falseness, shoddiness and everyday oppressions of consumer society could be enlisted to drive the ever-accelerating wheel of consumption'.

The disgust with the inauthenticity of consumption that is driving consumption is what Jim McGuigan[319] calls 'cool capitalism': the marriage of counter-culture and capitalism. Tessa might call it work. Cool, McGuigan suggests, is the 'front region' of capitalism. It is the processes of producing, buying and serving cool that animates the mythology of London's twenty-first century economy.

We see this relationship between transgression and profitability in the 'pop-up' entrepreneurship that thrives in the experiential global cities[320]. Here the selling points of 'Secret Cinema' experiences or the momentary presence of a London gin bar are both the newness and the temporariness of the experience so that, according to *The Nudge: Popup London*:

> *there'll always be innovative chefs, designers, musicians, bartenders,*
> *artists, actors and more turning up in unexpected locations to*
> *do what they do best: making life more random and enjoyable for*
> *everyone*[321].

'All that is solid melts in thin air' is no longer just a critique of capitalism, it is a marketing strategy. Even political activism has become an opportunity for profit, creating a troubling loop in which radical energies are the fuel for new marketplaces. Naomi Klein's magnificent *No Logo*[322] might have identified the disconcerting presence of advertising and the commodification of public space, driving a desire for alternative occupations of public space exemplified by the rise of street art, but this energy is now also reflected in the 'anti-advertising' advertising campaigns spread across London.

In Florida's words, 'Capitalism has expanded its reach to capture the talents of heretofore excluded groups of eccentrics and non-conformists' taking 'people who would once have been viewed as bizarre mavericks operating at the bohemian fringe and placing them at the very heart of the process of innovation and economic growth'[323]. All that is missing is the subversion.

This commodified subversion and the cool economy it attracts, perpetuates and sells is written on the walls of London's East End, where the transformation of London's economy from prosaic production to cool consumption is complete. East End Londoners might still be miserable, but now they have cupcakes.

Eastern Cool

The East End has always been an idea as much as a specific location. Once, that idea was of a place of community, industry and solidarity. A place capable of absorbing wave after wave of newcomers. A place so densely packed that it was able to harbour the specifically London Cockney dialect. Its enduring mythology is of squalid poverty and scandalous crime, from Jack the Ripper to the Kray twins. It was not for nothing that Marx's great collaborator Fredrich Engels' described the East End in the mid-nineteenth century as '...an ever-spreading pool of stagnant misery and desolation, of starvation when out of work, and degradation, physical and moral, when in work'.

When Charles Booth meticulously mapped London's poverty in 1889[324], he recorded that the worst poverty – that which he deemed 'Lowest class. Vicious, semi-criminal' – was concentrated in the East of the city, particularly around Bethnal Green. This stood in stark contrast to the wealthier enclaves of the West, especially around the Royal palaces, where Booth found widespread evidence of the 'Upper-middle and upper classes. Wealthy.'

The Second World War did not help matters, with much of the damage of the Blitz occurring around the Docklands and East End factories. Unsurprisingly, de-industrialisation affected the industrial East more than the cultural West. The East End of the 1970s and 1980s was not the place to be; in the 1970s cases of depressive illness were three times higher in the East End than the remainder of the UK.

Fortunately, London had another card to fall back on, one much cooler than the toil that used to occur in its warehouses and workshops. London has always been sought out as a cultural destination, one of sophisticated thought, cosmopolitan consumption, creative explorations and visceral pleasures. These civilised virtues were the purview of the city's elite and those privileged visitors seeking the London experience.

London's post-industrial transformation offered culture for mass consumption, if only out of the economic necessity of new markets and new consumers. In the 1960s, cool London was restricted to the West End haunts of Soho and Chelsea's King's Road. By the 1990s, cool had spread to more egalitarian spaces of the East End.

Urban decay gave space for creative expression and the cultural deviance with which it is so often paired. What better place is there for shooting heroin and making the city your canvas than the alleys around a dilapidated factory? The Shoreditch tour guides and PR copywriters of the twentieth century should be more grateful for the unique combination of industrial decline and suburban repression that led to this juxtaposition of surplus spaces and virtuous vices in post-industrial, post-disciplinary London.

The earlier years of the city's post-industrial transformation were not always so culturally sophisticated, however, though they were equally necessary for the transformation of the East End. The Big Bang of financial deregulation in 1986 set off a series of changes that brought not only a new level of financial wealth to the City but the end of gentlemanly capitalism and its associated cultural pursuits. In its place came a 'loadsamoney' culture occupied by that most hated British category; the nouveau riche. As the number of financial jobs exploded – these roles doubled from 170,000 in the 1980s to 350,000 in 2007[325] – so too did a bonus culture.

City bonuses peaked at £14 billion in 2008 and the number of financial workers granted million-pound bonuses jumped from 30 in 2000 to 1,500 in 2007[326]. Much of this obscene wealth was thrown into housing. Much of the rest of it went up the noses of newly-wealthy young people who invested their money and their identity into whatever vice was in fashion. Some of this occurred in the old haunts of the West End. Increasingly, however, the scene was in the East.

The young, creative and talented flooded into the East End to reclaim the industrial spaces their parents (or maybe those of the working classes) had left behind. Endemic poverty enabled affordable housing for those of a creative bent and those whose fantasies of city life did not require sparkling décor. Urban decay gave space for creative expression and the cultural deviance with which it is so often paired. What better place is there for shooting heroin and making the city your canvas than the alleys around a dilapidated factory?

Now, the East End is the home of the creative classes, up-start communities and gritty glamour. From 2001-2011, those employed in the 'cool' professions of culture, media and sport rose by 70 per cent in Hackney and fell by almost 20 per cent in Kensington and Chelsea. When you add in other 2011 Census data like house shares and moped users, Hackney and Islington are clearly the epicentres of cool and the Silicon Roundabout sits right on their junction[327]. And precarious migrants working in the service classes. It is all capitalism. Few of these creative types and investors would argue that the East End is beautiful, at least in a conventionally pretty way. It is cool, though, for now.

The relationship between subversion, deviance and capitalism is on full display on the Ebor Street Wall in Shoreditch, not far from Silicon Roundabout. Where Ebor Street connects to Bethnal Green Road, there once existed a Shepard Fairey mural that exclaimed THIS DECADE ONLY! SHOP LIFTERS WELCOME! in bright red and yellow against a black background. Fairey, best known for his Obama Hope poster, was no stranger to entrepreneurial activity. But, standing opposite the Shoreditch Box Park which claims to be 'Effortlessly fusing the concepts of the modern street food market and the pop-up retail mall'[328], it did convey a kind of political message, ironic as it was coming from Fairey.

One day, however, when giving a tour of the area, my class and I discovered that it was gone, one of many works now consigned to my increasingly historically focused street-art tour. In its place was first a shabby blackness, followed by advertisers a little too earnestly intimidating an improvised message. It was now officially the Ebor Street Wall. Here, for only £2,875 a week, advertisers can reach 'the most fashionable crowd' as 'Shoreditch House brings a steady flow of creative and well-connected professionals to Ebor Street' [329]. These creative class Londoners would not be here if pioneering, and much poorer, creative people had not moved here some 20 years earlier. Likewise, the area would not maintain its coolness, heavily sanitised as it is, without the previous presence of the Fairey mural and the ever-evolving Eine block letters running up the sides of the Northern End of Ebor Street. Now, however, many of the walls in the Shoreditch High Street area have become an ominous grey, marking the dull presence of anti-graffiti without even offering the pretence of irony.

And here we have the contradictions of cool capitalism. With cool comes popularity and with popularity comes commodification and homogeneity. But it is not just about the blandification of the city. Popularity means higher rents and higher prices, which pushes the coolest and the most precarious – who are often one and the same – further away from the city centre.

And so, while the East is still the place to be for companies and fantasies of London, the coolest of Londoners are moving further and further East. Or South. The Last Days of Shoreditch[330] may be over but Bethnal Green and Dalston are newly cool.

And still, like Tessa, they come. Now they are living and playing in places like Brixton, which embodies the triumph and underside of cool capitalism and the London dream.

Chapter 9

The Battle of Brixton, Redux

Arriving in Brixton is a dizzying experience, no matter how often you do it. Being in Brixton crystallises the contradictions of London's new economy.

Climbing the tube station stairs, commuters are confronted by all of London at once. A cacophony of sounds and smells seemingly from no origin and every origin overwhelms the senses. There seems to be no categorisation to those you encounter. Steel drummers mix with hipsters and trolley-lugging grandmothers. The children that Enoch Powell feared would be building Britain's funeral pyre form a pushing line for bright red buses.

Above us, elegant Victorian buildings loom over Caribbean venders hawking everything from lingerie to fresh meat. Homeless men look up from the street. The stalls in Brixton Arcade, hidden today and tomorrow by scaffolding, reveal a history rapidly being usurped. Smells of incense and fish signify the continued presence of Caribbean culture.

The public space in front of the Brixton Tate Library, previously the Tate Gardens, was renamed Windrush Square to mark the fiftieth anniversary of the 1948 arrival of the *HMT Empire Windrush* and its 539 Jamaican passengers into the Tilbury Docks. Beside the Black Cultural Archives, a memorial stands to fallen African and Caribbean soldiers. Locals hang out beside a bust of the Victorian sugar merchant, Henry Tate.

Inside Brixton Village market, a Champagne + Fromage chain store faces Faiz Food, which advertises Latin and Caribbean Groceries. Outside, on Pope's Road, a gleaming Sports Direct sits incongruously in a row with luxury retailer Van Mildert and Dreph's giant mural of Michaeal Johns, a local icon who runs the market toilets[331]. Those who worked at the coal deposit or the Cash and Carry that previously occupied this spot could only imagine consuming the kind of experiences available further down Pope's Road at Pop Brixton.

If there is anything that is constant in Brixton, it's the possibility of transformation. As architecture critic Rowan Moore argues:

London is a city that burns slowly - it renews through consuming itself, through changing its physical and cultural fabric, its buildings, neighbourhoods and traditions, from one thing into another, but without devastating what is already there. Its past is the raw material of its future. It tends to avoid the tabula rasa, the clean slate or scorched earth[332].

Today, those fires are propelled by the seemingly benevolent, even pleasurable, cool and creative forces of capitalism. For those in the position to consume and create, the new Brixton is another locale to live out in their London dreams. Others are just being forced out. Out of their homes, out of Brixton and out of London. Richard Florida calls this the New Urban Crisis. He is right; capitalism is always a form of urban crisis.

Being Brixton
Brixton came to being as a middle-class suburb of the burgeoning Victorian London, with Electronic Avenue the first market street in Britain to be lit by electricity. Brixton was described by Charles Booth in 1902 as home to the 'servant keeping middle-class', although by 1931 the boxes at the Empress Theatre had been replaced by cheaper seats as 'the neighbourhood had become hardly the place for social graces'[333]. Many of the seats were replaced by craters during World War II and, as for most of London, the immediate post-war years were trying.

Brixton, like London, was saved by the arrival of migrants

from around the empire, specifically the young West Indies who would come to be known as the Windrush generation. They came to London because the city had a long-standing place in the Caribbean imagination[334]. The Jamaican author Donald Hinds, who sailed to London aged 21 in 1955, wrote in *Journey to an Illusion: The West Indian in Britain* that, 'I had decided long before I was ten that I would come to London. I cannot be certain at what age the thought first occurred to me.'[335]

They came to Brixton specifically through a series of historical chances. Migrants have traditionally settled near to their point of arrival in London, especially those who came with next to nothing. So it was with the West Indian diaspora, many of whom moved into the suburbs around Paddington, principally North Kensington, Notting Hill and Shepherd's Bush, with some moving from Liverpool Street to Stepney Green in the East End.

Brixton, however, was far from the Southampton boat train terminus at Waterloo. It just happened, however, that the billet for those on the *Empire Windrush* without pre-arrived accommodation was an air-raid shelter on Clapham Common[336]. A labour exchange on Cold Harbour Lane in Brixton brought them a little further West, as did the presence of a small but comforting community of black residents built from pre-war students and African-American serviceman[337]. Naturally, new arrivals, seeking community and finding racist hiring and renting practices, accumulated nearby. Markets and new communities developed, both harking back to home and seeking to make a new life out of battered dreams, cold winters and hostile hosts. And so it was for more than 50 years.

For much of that time, Brixton experienced all the ills of de-industrialising London and few of the glamorous thrills of the Swinging Sixties, even if 'calypso' music was drifting into the London scene and providing the coolest avenue (the other was cricket) for cultural integration[338]. One BBC report on a dance event in Lambeth enthusiastically reported that 'The rhythm of the mamba was doing its bit towards racial unity.'[339]

Such unity was always more choreographed than executed and racial tensions were never far from the surface. Brixton's housing estates were, and still are, some of the worst examples of post-war design. There were few amenities and young people reported feeling trapped. In 1981, 55 per cent of black youths were unemployed[340] and 'ghetto' was evoked all too often, especially during the 1981 Brixton Uprising.

For some residents, though, Brixton was a place of community and excitement unavailable elsewhere in London. Writing of the late 1970s and early 1980s, Brixton-born author Alex Wheatle recalls that, 'People often talk about the police oppression and it was intense in that era. But if you loved reggae music and partying, there was no better place to be than London SW2 and SW9 [341].'

If many Brixtonians only felt at home in their part of South London, many other Londoners did not feel welcome, or perhaps just safe, in Brixton. As a result, unlike its once Caribbean counterpart Notting Hill, there were few signs of gentrification in Brixton during the twentieth century. There would be no Richard Curtis films made here, although *Attack the Block*, Joe Cornish's horror-comedy of street gangs defending themselves against alien invaders, received rave reviews.

Now Brixton is in the process of becoming one of London's fallen suburbs. The story is a familiar one and straight from the Richard Florida school of urban development. The young, adventurous and poor move into a (safely) deprived area to search for and live a bohemian lifestyle. Brixton's music scene was particularly attractive. Rents, both commercial and residential, rise with each wave of progressively wealthy newcomers. At some point, property developers get wind of investment opportunities and the game is up, even if the fun continues for those who have avoided social cleansing. This could not be clearer in Brixton.

It has happened across the city. Where *Time*'s 1996 image of London centred around King's Road and Soho, the former is far too posh to be cool and the building site that is the latter is a monument to the new combination of gentrification and plutocratisation. Hampstead, Islington and Camden have long since fallen. Shoreditch and Hackney are soon to go, if they have not already. Cool capitalism is spreading and Pop Brixton is its apex.

Popping Up

In 2014, Lambeth Council hung a banner over a disused carpark adjacent to Pope's Road. It read:

What should we do with this space? [342]

The community, already faced with rapid change that felt out of their control, was not short of ideas for what to do with this space, which had most recently been used as an ice rink[343]. There was a catch though. The offer was only valid in the 'meanwhile' before it became the apartments and (most likely) big brand retail space designated by the 2009 Brixton Central Masterplan[344].

In April 2014, the council announced that the winning bid was to be a partnership between the Edible Bus Stop group (EBS), who had previously worked on the award-winning transformation of the Landor Road Bus Stop, and Carl Turner Architects (CTA). The partnership, Grow:Brixton, had beaten a proposal from Brixton Tool Kit to work with the local community to lend tools and develop construction skills. A green oasis with a community ethos was promised through an installation of 're-purposed shipping containers [that] provide studios, live/work spaces, workspaces, retail units, workshops, bar/café, performance space and green spaces'[345]. A 5-year lease was granted.

The move was met with some optimism, with one editor on the active Urban75 community forum stating, 'I don't think this project is really directly comparable with the Village. I had a good chat with some of the people involved in the Edible Bus Stop and was rather encouraged.'[346]

Soon after, however, CTA worked to edge out its more community-minded partners. Talking to *Brixton Buzz* journalist Jason Cobb, the EBS claimed that once the application was granted they were reduced to mere 'community gardeners' and had been used to give the application community credibility[347]. After EBS were forced out, the council announced the arrival of Pop Brixton. It was to become a 'community business park for the twenty-first century', according to Lambeth Labour councillor Jack Hopkins[348].

Part of the bidding process was that half the profits would be returned to Lambeth Council in exchange for peppercorn rent. The community ethos of Grow:Brixton was admirable, but were they profitable? Ironically, one of the reasons for the 2017 extension of Pop Brixton's lease was to give the project more time to generate a financial return for the Council[349]. In 2017, Pop Brixton lost £480,000 in 2017 and owed £1.65 million to its creditors[350].

More ironically, Pop Brixton is certainly a community. But it is also sharply divided from the community that surrounds it, a community where half live in areas that are in the top 10 per cent of the most deprived nationally[351]. Lambeth Council reports that only 20 per cent of commercial space in Pop Brixton needs to be 'affordable'[352].

And so, a little more than a year after posting positively about Grow:Brixton on Urban75, the same forum editor replied to a poster remarking that Pop Brixton felt like 'a kind of spaceship that's landed there for all the connection it has with the rest of the area' by stating that it was 'a community project that's aimed at anyone but the actual local community. And the least said about the horticulturally led "green oasis" PR bullshit the better.'[353]

Many of those enjoying Pop Brixton probably spent their working days creating PR bullshit; the top occupations for those living close to Brixton tube station are 'Artistic/Literary/ Media' and 'Marketing and Associated Professions'. By contrast, 'Cleaning' and 'Other Elementary' are the top occupations in Stockwell, one stop and 2 minutes away on the tube[354]. These new Brixtonian professions, roughly in the fields of culture, media and sport, were used by *The Economist* as a proxy for 'coolness'[355]. And, if nothing else, Pop Brixton offers the consumption of a certain type of cool aimed at those occupied by producing cool.

The cool in capitalism hits you as soon as you walk through the shipping container gates into Pop Brixton. This kind of cool is not about mere pleasure but is coated in a sugary social good. Inside the entrance, a blue board announces:

Who we are

This is Pop Brixton. Come and take a look around. Inside you'll find a community of independent, local businesses serving up food, fashion, music and more.

We aren't here to give high street brands another storefront. All our members are independent, most come from Brixton and Lambeth and many of them are start-ups entering their first permanent premises.

So come in and find out more. It's here for you to experience and enjoy. So make yourself at home.

It finishes with a simple but ominous line:

Here until 2020.

To my right is a vintage clothing stall and beside it is Prohibition Ink, a tattooist. If it did not feel so contrived, we would have struck peak hipster. Maybe we have anyway. Next is a New Zealand Wine place selling its wares for around £25 a bottle. The food stalls that compete around the ground floor offer the world in a biodegradable container. I could have Japanese, French, Jamaican, Spanish[356]. Perhaps Italian. This is experiential consumption in the global city. This is the Pop Brixton community, as asserted in the welcome message, which insists:

At the heart of our project is a focus on supporting and engaging the community. So as well as providing space for local businesses, we work hard to get involved in positive projects in the area.
We offer discounted rents to social enterprises and total start-ups who need space to get their business off the ground.
All our members use their time and skills to support local causes, investing at least one hour each week into a Community Investment Scheme.

This utopian ideal is plastered throughout the project. Posters advertise community events. I could join the 'Fun and Friendly' Brixton Guitar Club. Or partake in Pay-What-You-Can Yoga. I take myself upstairs to the community garden, which tells me that I should 'feel free to pick crops which you recognise, but leave some for others who follow'.

Blue plaques comment on the origins of stalls. Outside of Mama's Jerk, for example, the plaque tells us that:

Adrian is the third generation to be using this secret Jerk recipe. It started in Jamaica in his great grandmas house and has been passed down the family and he started mamas jerk as a legacy to his great grand and wanted to share it with as many people as possible, hence the creation of this unit.

There does seem to be a genuine community between stall holders and those who flock to them. This economy of creativity, enjoyment and experiences is created and consumed with good intentions. These pleasurable opportunities mitigate against the misery of some who have come to London to live the dream only to find themselves battered by the winds of the city. For others there is little but misery as they are pushed further and further out of the place they called home.

Despite Brixton being the spiritual home of London's Caribbean community, and only 38 per cent of the population in the Coldharbour Ward where Pop Brixton exists recorded as being part of a white ethnic group[357], I see no black faces enjoying the (street) food-court worth of multicultural fusion and community spaces. It is this homogeneity among all that capitalism has to offer that bothers Lisa.

Making an Impact

If Pop Brixton is cool capitalism in operation, the Impact Hub, a co-working social entrepreneurship space at the rear of Pop Brixton that is a 'membership community for people working on projects for a better Lambeth and beyond'[358], is the ethical ethos that attracts the creative classes. And Lisa, young and sincerely committed to the greater good and a creative life, is the creative class at its Floridan best.

And yet, soon after we start to chat in a small meeting room tucked into Impact Hub, Lisa tells me with reticent earnestness of an article she has just had published in a 'new economy' magazine. She was arguing that:

> co-working spaces seem to, rather than dismantling structures of inequality, kind of add to it and are symbols of gentrification within London.

I'm here to wonder how Impact Hub might be different. So it seems, is Lisa.

Lisa has been in London for 3 years and Impact Hub for a few months. Having graduated from the University of Vienna with a degree in Economics and Business in 2013, and after some time with UN-Habitat in Kenya, Lisa had begun working in an international development role in Sheffield. She loved it.

What, I wondered, was the appeal of Sheffield? Lisa doesn't hesitate:

> *I like the fact that it feels very creative. There are not many jobs around, so I feel like people just start up things. But not in this, like, kind of, nasty, disgusting start-up idea that you see in London, but like they just get active. There's, like, a really creative arts scene, and, lots of amazing musicians that just, like, play in underused spaces. It just felt real and authentic. I really enjoyed it.*

Sounds like a version of London in the 1990s. It was a shame to leave, I suggest. The answer comes equally quickly: 'Yeah. No jobs.'

And so, like so many other young people working in the North of England, Lisa made her way to London. She 'wanted to throw [her]self into this world, and see what happened'. This world was Brixton in particular. Lisa had worked in and around the community development scene for a while but the diversity of Brixton appealed. Now she lives locally, working as the Head of Programmes and Communities at Impact Hub.

Founded in Lisa's native Austria in 2005, Impact Hub has expanded to over 100 cities and boasts of more than 16,000 members, spreading its mission of 'fuel and mobilize amplified innovation'. In addition to Brixton, there are Impact Hubs in Islington, King's Cross and Westminster. Each Impact Hub is:

> *a vibrant community of passionate and entrepreneurial people who share an underlying intention to bring about positive change and act as peers to cross-fertilize and develop their ventures. Second, it is a source of inspiration that provides meaningful content through thought-provoking events, innovation labs, learning spaces, programs and facilitated conversations that support positive impact. Third, an Impact Hub is a physical space that offers a flexible and highly*

functional infrastructure to work, meet, learn and connect. The magic
happens where these three elements connect and are brought to life
through the art of hosting[359].

It must have been an exhausting corporate vision meeting.

Like Pop Brixton, Impact Hub Brixton is a product of Lambeth Council's goodwill and cuts to local authorities by the Conservative government. From 2010 to 2018, Lambeth Council's budget has been cut in half, resulting in spending cuts of over £200 million[360]. As a result, it has been forced to find ways to outsource the social good.

Nonetheless, when it started in 2014 in the basement of Lambeth Town Hall, Impact Hub was funded by the council, which is extremely rare for a co-working space as they tend to be entrepreneurial profit spaces. At that time, Lisa tells me, Impact Hub Brixton was creative, diverse and inclusive.

When, as part of its Your New Town Hall redevelopment, Lambeth Council moved Impact Hub it was contracted to find a home for the Hub. Pop Brixton was in need of tenants and Impact's transition from a community space to a business centre was complete. It also helped that CTA was awarded £100,000 to design and move Impact Hub[361].

Pop Brixton offered below market rents. It was still a significant increase. A source of funding was required to make for a sustainable business model. Impact had always had some for-profit business but the proportion is definitely growing. I ask Lisa, is that something that you are comfortable with?

'No', she laughs bashfully, 'No I'm not. Um. How am I going to go from here?...now I hate that you're recording this.'

I offer to take a break. Her goodwill quickly returns with a slight sigh.

'No, it's not that it's secretive, it's just...'

'A difficult trade-off,' I offer.

'Yes. Yes, it is. And, um, I wonder what we can actually do, what is actually possible, and achievable.'

They might develop a community fund, or charge certain members more. Not necessarily for-profit members, though. Lisa rejects the idea of a black and white distinction. Many people working in the non-profit sector, she tells me, are from a middle-class background and can afford unpaid internships. This is certainly backed up by the research[362]. We must be careful though because:

actually everyone has good intentions. I think, if you're not careful, then you could easily end up with just, like, a bunch of middle-class white people, because, like, they're all nice and comfortable...and they have dreams, and they want to change things.

Before we go, I ask Lisa if she is a Londoner, 'I am. Yeah.'

Is she a proud Londoner?

Now Lisa laughs politely and looks away for a second. 'Yeah. But sometimes I hate it so much.' A qualification for being a Londoner, perhaps. 'I feel like it sucks your soul out, sometimes.' Interesting. Does she feel positive about Brixton's future?

Oh. Good question. Um. I worry, and I find it difficult to feel positive about it. Because, if I think about the fact that I'm getting annoyed at the way the Pop Brixton is run, and the fact that it presents an artificial subcommunity, sort of, in, like, an existing community, and I think, constantly, 'How can we change it? How can we dismantle that?' But the fact is, this is just a meanwhile space, and in 4 years, it's going to be knocked down. Then there's going to be a developer coming in, and all of our discussions about, 'Is this community enough or not?' is worthless, because there is a speed of change that, yeah. You can't really seem to-, yeah, we-, I feel very powerless, in the face of that. So, um, yeah. That worries me.

It worries us all. Her commitment to working for the social good, and awareness of the challenges around it, is admirable. Well-meaning commitment like Lisa's can change lives. But it cannot change the circumstances in which those lives are lived. For all of Impact Hub's earnestness and Pop Brixton's energy, they are only fuelling what they are there to fight. Capitalism can be cool. Capitalism can be cold and brutal. It is still capitalism, whatever form it takes.

Florida brands this the New Urban Crisis.

The Creative Crisis

London, Florida claims, is at the epicentre of his always capitalised New Urban Crisis[363]. The first urban crisis occurred during the 1970s when industry, investment and people were fleeing de-industrialising urban areas. London, as we have seen, was hit hard. The city has been hit hard by this new crisis, just in a much cooler way. Ironically, the crisis has been caused by the very popularity of the city and those creative classes who see London as the place to be.

Here, after selling the value of the class for 16 years, Florida seemed surprised to report that the resulting clustering of the creative classes has produced a 'lopsided, unequal urbanism' whereby, he argues, 'the very same force that drives the growth of our cities and economy broadly also generates the divides that separate us and the contradictions that hold us back'[364].

This New Urban Crisis, Florida suggests, is 'not just a crisis of cities, but of our new age of highly urbanized knowledge-based capitalism'[365]. It is here that we find the 'central contradiction of contemporary capitalism. The clustering force [of the creative classes] is at once the main engine of economic growth and the biggest driver of inequality'[366].

His critics could not have put it better.

As more people are drawn to the city, house prices and business rents increase and become unaffordable for anyone but the moneyed elites. Cultural hubs are forced to move deep into the suburbs, searching not only for manageable rents but the young people who make these hubs viable. In turn, the expansion of the creative classes spreads gentrification to places where it was once unthinkable. The team behind Pop Brixton has opened an equivalent, Peckham Levels! in a previous empty multi-level car park[367]. Box Parks like that in Shoreditch have opened in Wembley and in Croydon.

And thus, where deindustrialisation was felt most sharply in the centre of cities, today's cities are pushing the poor to the fringes and beyond. This doughnutting dynamic is what American urbanist Alan Ehrenhalt has called the 'Great Inversion'[368]. London's poor were once jammed in the East End. Now they are increasingly found on the inner edges of the M25 in places like Enfield, Romford and Dartford[369]. Or worse, Essex[370].

This exodus is not just the much-fretted exodus of the white working class, although the 600,000 'white' people who left London between the 2001 and 2011 censuses should not be ignored[371]. It is a banishment of the working classes, who are increasingly people of colour. It was once the familied middle classes of London's workforce who endured extended commutes. Now it is cleaners and security guards taking multiple buses to get to work. Nonetheless, although service workers might have been pushed out of central London, their work remains in the city. Baristas and cleaners may not be able to afford to live in Zone 1. Or even Zones 1-3. But they still need to come in and work there. As a result, London's average daily commute time is now 81 minutes. Tellingly, Black, Asian or other minority ethnicity (BAME) Londoners have longer journeys and are twice as likely as white Londoners to travel by bus. Especially the night bus[372], where routes like the N21 take exhausted cleaners from Peckham into the City before dawn[373].

Florida largely attributes this inequality to land ownership and property prices. He has good reason to. London has the highest property prices in the country and the highest proportion of renters. In 2018, the average London house price was over £600,000, doubling since 2009[374], and it would take the typical London couple with one child 20 years to save for a deposit for their first home. In Brixton, house prices increased by 76 per cent from 2006-2016[375].

Here London, Florida argues, is not only experiencing gentrification but 'plutocratisation' whereby a global elite of property developers buy up London real estate as both an investment and a way to store money, almost a 'global reserve currency'. Increasingly, new housing developments are being sold sight unseen to overseas investors who have little intention of living in them: almost all the flats in the £8 billion Battersea Power Station development were sold off-plan, with major sales pushes in Asia in particular.

Only 60 residents in St George Wharf Tower, the UK's tallest residential building, are registered to vote. These buyers have made London home to a new global elite that dominates areas like Mayfair and the UK's richest street, Kensington Palace Gardens. Despite former Mayor Boris Johnson's appeals to the contrary, developers' 'safety deposit boxes in the sky' are of little relief to those Londoners who can only dream of saving for a house deposit or for those in the mandated 'affordable' units who are forced to use the 'poor doors' around the side of these buildings.

Florida fears that out of control property values will price out his patented creative classes and quotes fellow urbanist Jane Jacobs as stating that 'when a place gets boring even the rich people leave'. What the creative classes brought, they have inadvertently encouraged the elites to take away. And all in the innocent search of a dream life, one created, and hijacked, by capitalism.

But this is just one scene in the crisis of cool capitalism that grips the city and plagues the London dream.

Back on the corner of Windrush Square, we see the rest of

the plot. Here the Ritzy Picturehouse Cinema, once described as a 'hipster oasis' with 'hip, nerdy staff'[376] (despite being owned by Cineworld, the world's second largest cinema chain), is attracting plenty of punters paying £14.10 to watch *The Favourite.* They seem oblivious, or unsympathetic, to the long running dispute between the Ritzy and its workers, who are backed by the BECTU union.

In 2016, the union had been promised moves towards the London Living Wage[377]. Ritzy Picturehouse has refused to back this promise even as the owner, Cineworld, made profits of £120 million in 2017[378]. Campaigners claim that Cineworld CEO Moshe 'Mooky' Greidinger earns over £2,500,000 a year[379]. Meanwhile, Ritzy staff in Brixton are still battling with regular strikes, for living wages and basics like sick pay and parental leave for all staff. These are the workers Florida deems the 'service class': those doing the routine tasks that service the consumptive experiences of the creative classes they aspire to be.

The struggles of these service workers reveal the class structure that punctures and propels the London dream; that for some to accumulate and consume, others must serve and suffer. They all dream of a better life. The tension between the hopes of London dreamers and the exploitative conditions they endure will be the stuff of the remainder of *The London Dream.*

And still, they come, chasing their London dreams. Many of those who aspire to creativity are kept in the reserves of the service classes. And it is these service classes that are the new urban working classes, enduring precarity not unlike that faced by the dockers that came before them. All of them compounded the street-level struggles that defined Victorian London[380].

They come to a city divided by class, as it always has been. And even if these classes are cooler than they once were, they still feel very Victorian.

Section 3

Marginal Creativity

Chapter 10

All Class

Class is the underlying grammar of British-ness. No one really knows what it is.

That class is important to the British is hardly an original insight. If you overlook all the imperial adventures and British dominance of the slave trade, an erasure which seems to happen fairly efficiently, the establishment, exploitation and reproduction of a class system is the country's original sin.

These sins are also openly, if silently, celebrated; all around Britain stand monuments to and of the aristocracy. Henry VIII's rampant wife killing, let alone his flagrant later-life disregard for hygiene, would not make him a popular contemporary figure, although Tudor house intrigue would have made for great click-bait. Nonetheless, Greenwich and Hampton Court palaces remain heavily promoted tourist attractions.

Celebrations of Queen Victoria and Prince Albert overlook the hungry 1840s and the complete political marginalisation of women and the poor. Stately homes are a matter of national pride, rather than a place of remembrance for those who toiled on their soil. *Downton Abbey, Victoria* and *The Crown* sell a particular sense of British-ness around the world. The monarchy remains popular and has established itself as part of the charm of Cool Britannia. Aristocratic patterns of land ownership continue to dominate the country: a third of all land in the UK and around half of all rural land is in aristocratic hands[381]. In London, the Crown, the Church and five aristocratic estates own over 1,000 acres of prime central London real estate[382].

To be sure, the British are immensely cynical about the upper classes and there is regular disquiet about the reproduction of establishment rule[383]. Nevertheless, it feels impossible to separate aristocratic rule and class divisions from British-ness, and certainly English-ness. It is not for nothing that migrants paying for British citizenship are forced to learn their kings and queens as part of the 'Long and Illustrious History' section in the Life in the UK test necessary to stay in the country[384]. Speaking of 'proper' manners remains commonplace, even among the commoners.

And yet, despite the ubiquitousness of class, like all good sins, it is not so easy to approach directly. Sure, we can laugh about it and obsess about it but to diagnose the cause of class is far too confronting. Instead, class is just *there*. For sociologists, this is a recipe for classification and conjecture. For Londoners, class is about struggle and survival, accumulation and consumption. And the tide of gentrification.

Enculturing Class

The meaning of class, like so many things, appears clearer in the mirror of historical narratives. The great British class system has pre-capitalist roots in feudal land ownership that, without a revolutionary dispossession of the nobility, continues to strongly influence both British attitudes and its economy. As this landowning elite increased its wealth through investments in the expansion of the empire, including in the slave trade[385], and the Georgian era enclosure of agricultural land forced the landless to move to cities in search of work, properly capitalist class divides emerged. These divides produced a mass of labouring humanity, an increasingly visible middle class and an aristocracy reluctantly transitioning its privilege from land ownership to trade and commerce.

City life made societal class divides more readily apparent. In Victorian London, class positions could be easily distinguished and upper-, middle- and working-class labels became more common, even if Marx was using different terms. These labels were often derived from positions at work – Do you own, manage or labour? – but also the cultures that corresponded with that socio-economic status. But identifying class positions was not as easy as it might have been in the countryside, where one's position in the household made social standing very clear. On city streets, the casual observer had less of an opportunity to size up the work and wealth of those they encountered.

Neither did shopkeepers and lenders. For those scraping by on Victorian London's low-wage economy, credit was a daily necessity. Lenders had no possibility of conducting credit checks and most of the poor had no property to act as security. Lenders, often landlords or local shops, were forced to make their decision to offer credit based on what was in front of them: appearance and expression. In English, class.

Thus, looking like you had wealth was a form of capital in itself. In a wonderfully British convolution, this meant that seeming to have a middle-class disposition was as important as having middle-class money. A strange economy of appearance emerged where appearing to have wealth required spending money, which in itself required access to credit[386].

Jerry White argues that 'this fragile credit nexus involved, at some time in their lives, almost the whole population of London in the threat of ruin and a substantial minority in ruin itself' [387]. Such pressure created unique sub-cultures in mid-nineteenth century London. Debtors could not be arrested on Sundays or within their house, unless bailiffs were invited or came through an open door or window. Committed debtors could then hole themselves up 6 days a week, if they could afford to, and leave the house 1 day a week as 'Sunday-men'[388].

It is perhaps this obsession with 'keeping up appearances' that led social anthropologist Kate Fox to claim that 'class in England has nothing to do with money, and very little to do with occupation' [389]. Instead, she suggests that linguistic class codes, as part of larger cultural representations, are the primary signifier of class status in England. Saying 'sorry' rather than 'pardon' is a class act, as is choosing between grey track pants or red trousers.

In London, however, a city thrown together by those escaping traditional binds and attempting to recalibrate them in a different context, cultural class customs are difficult to police. Indeed, just as Brits have spread across the Commonwealth in search of new lives, escaping class bounds is all part of the London dream.

And yet, the city's elegance and inequities have been built on class divides and traditions. Indeed, the city is literally divided by class. From the seventeenth century, power and privilege began to accumulate in the West around Westminster, particularly after the Great Fire of 1666. With royalty, both great and glutinous, came the estates that lie under today's West End. In turn, these estates attracted prestige and wealth on their green fringes. London's wealth spread out from Westminster and the old City, creating enclaves of wealth and fine Georgian squares in Marylebone and Bloomsbury[390].

On the other side of the city, the natural Easterly position of the docks led to precarious seafaring communities forming in Eastern locations such as Bermondsey, Limehouse, Rotherhithe and Wapping[391]. Factories developed and, with London's winds typically coming from the West, wealthier Westerners were able to avoid the worst of the odours of the industrial revolution.

Newcomers – from Huguenots to the Irish – were forced to cram themselves into existing communities outside of the Eastern boundaries of the City. The working-class East Enders that are part of the legend of the city emerged. While these class divides have been disrupted and increasingly replaced by an inner-outer divide, even a casual visitor to London can notice distinct differences between the glamour of the West and the grit of the East.

These traditions are built into the story London sells to the world, so that tourists often seek to play out posh fantasies when staying at places like the Savoy and taking afternoon tea at

Harrods. While these establishments might outwardly embrace the class snobbery their customers are paying to experience, on the production side class structures are established through the lop-sided struggle between the hotels' global elite owners and their marginalised migrant workers.

As a result of these sedimented economic divides, a purely cultural interpretation of class is an inadequate lens for understanding the divisions in British society, let alone in London. And so, in 2011 British researchers began to ask new questions of the relationship between culture and economics. In order to reimagine class for contemporary Britain, a team of sociologists led by Fiona Devine and Mike Savage gathered responses from 161,400 people for the BBC. A more detailed nationally representative survey was also conducted[392].

When *The Great British Class Survey*[393] was released in 2013, the researchers claimed that it produced a 'sophisticated, nuanced picture of what class is like now'. Gone are the upper, middle and working classes. No need for the bourgeoisie or the proletariat. The language of U and non-U is consigned to the past, amusing as it is to distinguish someone's status by whether they invite you round for supper, dinner or tea.

Inspired by French sociologist Pierre Bourdieu, Devine and Savage's team asked questions about the size and status of your social network (social capital), the sophistication of your cultural tastes (cultural capital) and your household income, savings and whether you own or rent your house (economic capital). Notably, there are no questions about occupation, which is the measure used by the Office for National Statistics to construct socio-economic classifications. Instead, using complex calculations of cultural, economic and social capital, the researchers identified seven class classifications:

1. Elite
2. Established middle class

3. Technical middle class
4. New affluent workers
5. Traditional working class
6. Emergent service workers
7. Precariat.

Whether or not you agree with these categories, their announcement certainly revealed the continued salience of class consciousness in the UK. At least of the strictly non-revolutionary kind. When the BBC Class Calculator became public and 'visiting the theatre' was reported as a sign of cultural capital, there was an otherwise unexplained 191 per cent increase in demand for theatre tickets in London[394]. Calculating class may be complex, but knowing that it is at the core of British-ness is not.

The calculator places me in the quarter of Britons in the established middle class, although I suspect the arrival of my twins – due as I write – may change that. For most of my London life, though, I would have been classified as an emergent service worker. This class has high social and cultural capital, but poor economic capital: the average income of £21,000 is far below London's median wage and just above the London Living Wage.

Unsurprisingly, the emergent service worker class is young and concentrated in urban areas, especially in university towns and in London, with particularly strong concentrations in Hackney and Tower Hamlets in the East End. They are young and ethnically diverse with a distinct over-representation of arts and humanities graduates[395].

This is the class that flocks to London for university and after graduation. They dream of meaningful creative work and cool experiences, while being prepared to put up with precarious employment and the indignities of house shares, overdrafts and reheated pasta. It's basically like being at uni again, except you have to get up in the morning.

Working for Class

Marx would have seen all of this social and cultural stuff as bourgeoise rubbish and a mere symptom of economic position. A business owner with more popular cultural tastes and no friends is still in a position to exploit his employees. Equally, a migrant day-labourer who throws on red trousers before trudging to the job site is given no special treatment from his employer, although his English colleagues might have other thoughts. Class is about more than identity, lifestyle and wealth. To understand class in London, and anywhere else, we must focus on work. Or, more specifically, the economic conditions that determine who works and how.

On this point, Richard Florida and Marx form an unlikely alliance: class is determined by your place in the productive process. What binds Florida's creative class, for example, is:

not just its value and attitudes but the place it occupies in the economic structure. Class membership follows from people's economic functions. Their social identities as well as cultural preferences, values, lifestyles and consumption and buying habits all flow from this[396].

Of course, Florida's creative strategy has little else in common with Marxist theory. For Florida what you are getting paid for matters far more than what you are getting paid. Nor does it matter whether you employ or are employed. Or, increasingly, are self-employed. Class may be about work, but Florida seems uninterested in the exploitation of those who labour, especially if they do so creatively.

Nonetheless, he identifies London as 'the archetypal example of a class-divided city'[397]. This divide, however, is not between the bourgeoisie and the proletariat, or the elites and the masses. Instead, London is divided between the creative classes who are 'paid to use their minds' and the service classes who 'perform routine work directly for, or on behalf of, clients'[398]. While the former dominate the contemporary mythology of London as the place to be, it is the service class who make up a higher proportion of working Londoners[399].

Florida's third category is the working class, those who are paid to 'manoeuvre heavy machinery and perform skilled trades' [400]. He reports that London's working class are almost entirely extinct, which is 'staggering in a city where Karl Marx spent the last decades of his life writing *Das Kapital*' [401]. This is a fundamental misunderstanding of both what Londoners were doing in the nineteenth century and what Marx meant by the working classes.

Marx's working classes, or the proletariat, were those with no choice but to sell their labour. In Marx's time in London during the Victorian era, some would have been engaged with heavy machinery or trades, particularly on the docks and in the processing factories and workshops across the city. But they also provided services, from domestic work to costermongering and waste disposal.

These working-class Londoners lived in places like Bethnal Green, where class struggle meant solidarity and strikes. Today, Bethnal Green is on the frontline of a different kind of class struggle, one between Florida's creative and service classes, all of them living out some version of the London dream (or just dreaming of escaping the city). Marx would have been more interested in those troops waiting in reserve.

Struggle in the Suburbs

Bethnal Green has changed about as much as the British sense of class, which is to say completely and not at all. Part of the Tower Hamlets Borough, Bethnal Green lies directly to the East of Shoreditch and Silicon Roundabout. Unsurprisingly, it is one of the Eastern edges of that class struggle given the name of gentrification.

Once a Cockney stronghold, Bethnal Green is now a very East London combination of migrant communities and young people seeking cheap rent and the gritty sense of cool engendered by diverse locales. Is there any place where London dreams are stronger?

A third of residents in the Bethnal Green Ward are of Bangladeshi origin and only 26 per cent own their home, compared to 64 per cent in England[402]. Across England, the proportion of multiple adult occupancy homes was around 4 per cent in the 2011 Census. In parts of Bethnal Green, it reaches 40 per cent[403]. For some, these house shares are a replication of university life and a smart and social way of splitting bills and living costs. For others in Bethnal Green, this is a way of accommodating multiple family members when income is limited. They are two forms of the same struggle.

In January 2017, the *End Child Poverty* group reported that the Bethnal Green and Bow parliamentary constituency has the highest rate of child poverty in the UK at 54 per cent[404]. In April 2017, the *Evening Standard* property section led with the headline *Hotspot in waiting: Bethnal Green set to rival Shoreditch with trendy bars and new homes in the Victorian chest hospital*[405]. The article's lede does not pull its punches:

It might be one of the last surviving pockets of authentic East End London, resisting the gentrification that has embraced much of Tower Hamlets, but Bethnal Green's resistance is weakening, wooed by a series of major new developments and fashionable small conversions that are warming it up for a place in the league table of hotspots.

This is a battle fought street-to-street, almost building-to-building. Maybe even flat-to-flat as hip newcomers replace poorer ones, often from ethnic minorities who have in turn replaced the old Cockneys. The streets are packed with class remnants and artefacts. Working-class boozers are still hanging on, although many have become among the 50 pubs that close in London every year[406]. Chicken shops abound with their migrant proprietors and their three main constituencies: school children, the hungry poor and slumming drunks.

Cool cafes are popping up everywhere, hovered over by a generational array of council houses. This week the Bethnal Green Working Men's Club, a fixture of the area since 1887 and now an 'anything goes music and performance venue', features a charity production of *The Vagina Monologues* and Ura Matsuri, an evening of alternative Japan Matsuri.

In Florida's calculations, Bethnal Green sits on the crossroads of the creative class and the service class. Where Shoreditch is almost all creative class, Florida's Martin Prosperity Institute calculates Whitechapel to the South and Mile End to the East are dominated by the service class[407]. In the vegan café where I've come to meet film-maker Paul, the service class make up half the population and only 31 per cent have at least an undergraduate qualification. Just across the road, it is the creative class that is dominant and 55 per cent have a university qualification[408]. I've made my way through some hot spots of gentrification in writing this book, but nowhere compares to Bethnal Green for the richness and complexity of its class structure.

Florida may argue that London's working classes have moved on, or have been moved out, and what is left are the emergent creative classes and an ethnically diverse service class that is just hanging on. And yet, whatever the rates of change, Bethnal Green is still a form of working class. It is just that everyone is now paying higher rent and some are drinking better coffee.

Paul does both. Although perhaps more tea than coffee.

Film Classes

When I arrive to meet Paul, he is already sitting in the patio area out of the front of the Gallery Cafe, seemingly unbothered by my absence. He is at home here. A vegan place with a performance space, the cafe donates all profits back to the community organisation within which it sits. It is no wonder that it has been voted the best café in Bethnal Green 3 years running. A gentle hint of grey hair and a smoothie of unknown origins make for the perfect establishing shot, as does his friendly handshake. This is a scene of simmering class complexity that could only really be found in the East End of London.

Upon meeting him, most English people would instantly identify Paul as middle class, albeit with a sophisticated countenance. With a BA in Film Studies and an MA from the London Film School, this aspiring film-maker's income, cultural tastes and sophisticated social network would probably place him in Devine and Savage's emerging service worker class. Florida would place Paul in the creative classes remaking London. Marx might have just called him one of the proletariat. None of these classifications captures Paul's gentle charisma. These are the classed complexities of the new Bethnal Green.

Having lived in the area for 7 years, Paul has witnessed the enormity of Bethnal Green's circular class transformation. Second-hand bookshops have closed. Trendy coffee shops have come and gone. In a change that all Londoners would recognise the symbolism of, Paul remembers that 'the chicken shop closed down, and turned into an art gallery, which then did chicken shop-themed art'. He points out the railway arches down the street, where working-class labour of the heavy machinery kind still happens, and worries that the glass and car service places will soon be replaced by trendy restaurants and clubs.

Still, for the moment Bethnal Green has what a boy from a small village in the Shires wants out of London, at least while it is still 'recognisably Bethnal Green'. It is from Bethnal Green that Paul has established his place in the matrix of London film making networks. He had been in California and in France before that and had spent some time doing temp work in Brighton during the 2008 financial crisis. Paul tells me that, tempting as the spectre of Brexit makes it to move out of London, perhaps to places like Berlin, 'once you start building a network, it's very hard to move', especially because if he 'went to a new city, no one would have a clue who I was'.

Besides, there are few places that would offer such opportunities for work. The UK provided 21 per cent of the global box office[409], with London at its core. A total of 65 per cent of the film and video production workforce are in London and the South-East (thus including the major film studies on the Western edge of the city) [410] and ONS data shows that London generates 77 per cent of the film industry's £13,442,598 turnover[411].

Cinema has long been part of the London scene, especially from the 1920s to 1950s where American glamour provided a dazzling escape from the grime of London life. White notes that a 1947 survey reported that, when asked what they had done the previous evening, 21 per cent said they had gone to the cinema. In 1949, 41 per cent of London's youth said that they went to the cinema every weekend, cramming into glamorous halls all across the city, including the 5,000-seater Trocadero in Elephant and Castle[412].

The cinema was a significant part of the London scene reported by *Time* in the 1960s and while it declined sharply during London's dark period in the 1970s and 1980s, British cinema, along with Brit Pop and the YBAs, drove the Cool Britannia revival of post-industrial London in the 1990s.

The production and consumption of cool in London can never escape class and film is no exception. *Panic!* An Arts and Humanities Council report on inequality in the British creative and cultural industry reported that 12.4 per cent of those working in film, TV and radio are from working-class origins, defined in the report by the ONS occupational classifications[413]. Moreover, just 13 per cent of directors and 16 per cent of screenwriters are women[414] and only 4.2 per cent are from Black, Asian or other minority ethnicities (BAME) backgrounds.

Working in film, Paul patiently explains, when projects finally take shape, 'you need to put a crew together very quickly and you don't really have time to interview lots of people, which is why there's so much nepotism in the film industry...'. Jobs are not really advertised. Instead, crews are created by selective word of mouth; Paul would not even put a call out on Facebook. The process is a recipe for insecurity as, 'when you're crewing up for things, you only really hear about things if someone thinks to call you'.

As Paul recognises, this organic system makes social capital essential. You can have the best ideas but someone has to fund them. You can be the most proficient at your part of the production process but that is not much use if you do not know who is hiring. This is all part of life in the creative classes; the success of an industry and success within an industry is about creating clusters of like-minded professionals.

Moreover, being able to enter these clusters is as much about knowing the right people as having the cultural capital and the skills to make the most of them. Creatives do not just want to work with people they know but people they get along with and share similar interests. Whether cultural capital is part of class can be debated but it is certainly a form of privilege. Developing and sharing cultural capital is also part of the London dream of a place of cool, civilised and cultural consumption.

Moreover, as Paul tells me, not only is it a very culturally white and middle-class industry, but the big decisions about funding are always likely to come from the most privileged backgrounds. Likewise, to be able to survive on low rates while you are waiting for your shot requires a lot of financial privilege.

But, as we have seen, the social and cultural elements of class do not tell the whole story, even if they are a vital cog in the reproduction of creative privilege. Most of all, the film industry is fractured by class because of the working conditions it enforces.

And still, they come.

Holding Classes

London's dominance of the film industry means that those wanting work have little choice but to move to the city. London not only attracts graduates wanting to work in the film industry but students moving to study at London's prestigious (and not so prestigious) film schools. As Paul has told me, though, the industry does not have a regular labour market. The British Film Institute (BFI) reports that about half of those engaged in the British film industry are freelance. Of those formally employed, 97 per cent are in firms with fewer than ten employees[415].

Moreover, many in the film industry regularly work in non-film jobs. Equally, even when working exclusively in film they are often not working in film without being technically unemployed – they are just between contracts. As such, it is difficult to say whether there is an oversupply of film workers. But there is definitely a fluid and ready supply of workers compelled by the awareness of competition to take the work in front of them while battling for something more.

Faced with these conditions, struggling creatives, no matter how talented they are – and Paul is definitely talented – are forced to hustle for any work that comes their way, like Victorian dock workers in Marx's time in London. Film industry freelancers, often working in networked crews, are competing for daily or weekly rates.

BECTU, the union for media and entertainment workers, suggests that an Assistant Producer on a feature film with a budget of more than £30 million should receive £12 per hour[416]. As Paul offers, though, these rates are not always paid because the union is not always strong enough to enforce them and aspiring workers are often desperate (or privileged) enough to ignore them. He knowingly tells me:

if you're early career, you know, say you're fresh out of film school,
you're a competent editor, but you haven't got any big successes

under your belt, you'll come and cut something for £100 a day, if
you're lucky, but you'll also be editing stuff for mates for nothing.

The alternative is to try and find a regular gig in London's service classes. At his least productive point, Paul was working as a mail boy for an insolvency service, with a 'Hitler of a boss' who was a former policeman. If he was 2 minutes late a meeting would be called and he would be threatened with the sack. After all, he was just on a temporary contract and there are lots of people they could get for the job. He was 29 and the only job he could get paid him the same wage he got aged 16. With less respect and less responsibility. Then there were the bar and café roles, which did not turn out much better.

Paul pauses this recounting of his service history and reflects. With wry English joy, he tells me, 'I've never had much luck with service jobs, to be honest.' He is a perfectly personable fellow, it's just that his creative mind is always searching for better ways to do things, which is not always what bosses are looking for from their temporary service employees.

Now, though, rather than having to 'say yes to absolutely everything' and taking shitty service jobs and working on poor quality film projects, Paul is doing a couple of days a week working in Dalston in a role generously dubbed 'Development Producer', working on developing ideas for documentaries or films. Fortunately, his wife earns a good wage and they have been able to keep their East London foothold during down times.

This security has taken Paul out of the service industry jobs he had previously relied on to supplement his income. But, even if he enjoys the work, it is not what he wants to do. What it does do is allow Paul to continue to work on his own stuff. Unpaid, of course. It is a personal investment in his future in search of his dream to get a shot at directing feature films.

While he battles gamely for this investment to pay off, Paul is circulating in London's creative reserve. In the film industry, as with most creative industries, this surplus is constantly on the boil, looking for new openings. For Paul, this involved relentless re-training and searching for funding opportunities. He had had two shots at the 'Microwave' scheme run by Film London. This scheme seeks to help people make their first feature film through training, mentoring and funding. This is all a wonderful opportunity, but the 16-17 weeks of the application and training period is all unpaid, save for some minor allowances.

All the writing, casting, auditioning, storyboarding meant that Paul had to turn down work although, the second time around, 'luckily the bulk of it took place in January through February...when things are dead anyway, so I wasn't losing out on work, because there was no work'. And so, he waits. After we have met I hear that Paul has started on a PhD programme and is still battling away on his projects and on those of others.

Unsurprisingly, this reserve army did not feature in Savage's culturally orientated definition of class. Nor do workers like Paul, who straddle routine service labour and precarious creative work, fit easily within Florida's distinction between the creative and service classes; research shows that in most countries creatively trained people are more likely to work outside of the creative industry than within it[417]. So often in London, the toil of service work is the price paid by those chasing a creative dream.

For Marx, however, the existence of this surplus is the foundational moment in the existence of working classes. For there to be exploitable workers, there needs to be a sense that they could be replaced. In London, this surplus is not always unemployed. Like Paul, they are often just not employed in the work they want and are fighting to make their way out of post-industrial purgatory. These struggling cultural workers also know that if they drop out, there is always someone else to take their place.

Creative workers across London feel this precariousness. Even with a union presence, few in London's floating film networks can be bargaining over rates. Especially when they are working for free.

As an academic, Emily knows this disciplinary effect well, and not just because she is a committed Marxist.

Chapter 11

Dreaming of Classes

'I'm quite nervous about the term "academic",' Emily says with a curiosity that is both academic and angst-ridden.

Academia seems too conservative, too cliquey. And yet Emily likes the idea of being able to communicate history. Working as a part-time faculty member at a range of universities in London, however, she is 'not totally enchanted by everything that [she] sees', which is a very academic euphemism.

Emily is sure that she is a Londoner, though. This has nothing to do with being born in Shepherd's Bush. She had been raised in the tranquillity of the home counties but only applied to universities in London; Emily was 'desperate to live here' as London was 'the most exciting place'. She ended up at a university in East London which, as an aspiring historian, was exactly where she wanted to be. It was where suffragette Sylvia Pankhurst used to live and it was where London's history resonated the most.

She loved the scale of the city. The intimacy of it. The vastness of it.

I loved living in Hackney, I loved the diversity of Hackney, I loved being surrounded by people that wore all different kinds of clothes, that you could get any kind of food, that you could hear all of these different languages. It just felt so exciting.

At first, Emily wanted it too much, though. She had come to live in Hackney during a gap year and 'wanted to be [a Londoner] so much that I guess I wasn't a Londoner to begin with'. Such outward enthusiasm is an automatic sign of an outsider, at least in a city as cynical as London. Now, as a historian with a doctorate, she sees all of London.

Here Emily not only fits into the long tradition of provincial dreamers but the slightly more modern tradition of London as a place of knowledge and of civility. A city of light where one is able to transcend the narrow existence available outside of the city bounds.

Emily comes from one of the two oldest centres of higher education in the United Kingdom and indeed the world; the University of Cambridge was founded in 1209 and teaching was occurring at the University of Oxford as early as 1096. Still, with 372,000 students in the capital across 39 institutions[418], London is very much the UK's dominant university city[419].

London is also very much an international student city, arguably the most popular student city in the world with 107,200 international students from over 200 countries[420]. For students all over the world, London is the place to be. For intellectuals, as Samuel Johnston and James Boswell would have attested, it has long been the place to be for those seeking civility and enlightenment.

The reputation of London as an enlightened city, in addition to one of wealth, pleasure and grime, was forged during the eighteenth century. The predominant narrative of London in this time, Jerry White suggests, was of an 'Age of Politeness', one of 'artistic and scientific genius, of reason, civility, elegance and manners'[421].

Nonetheless, universities were slow to develop in London. Despite its reputation as a cosmopolitan centre of civility, opposition from Cambridge and from Oxford restricted higher education to London's medical schools, which were not officially recognised as universities. It was only in the nineteenth century, with its ideology of enlightening refinement, that the University of London (called London University in 1826) officially came into being with a Royal Charter on the cusp of the Victorian era in 1836.

This new university was a secular alternative to its Cambridge and Oxford counterparts, the 'People's University', as Charles Dickens called it in 1858[422]. By the early twentieth century, the University of London had absorbed most of the existing colleges in London, including UCL, King's College and the London School of Economics. Others were soon to follow: Goldsmiths in 1904, Imperial College in 1907 and Queen Mary in 1915. Now, according to Richard Florida's City Lab, London (along with Los Angeles) has the highest concentration of top-ranked universities in the world[423].

London as a centre of knowledge does not stop with the University of London's 18 constituent colleges and over 200,000 students. Today, the city has over 1,000 museums and galleries[424]. There are also 380 individual libraries, including the British Library with its 150 million books, and 800 bookshops[425]. Even during World War II London 'nurtured a largely state-supported intellectual class – writers, artists, film-makers, actors, entertainers, spies, boffins, bureaucrats' [426] – that, along with American soldiers, produced 'a unique excitement' [427] at odds with the black-out conditions and risk of invasion.

This is civilised London, academic London, enlightened London. It was as much a part of the making of modern London as the industrial revolution.

We should not gloss over these advances. In particular, nineteenth-century scientific developments did much to improve the lives of Londoners. London should, and does, take great pride in being an intellectual centre of the world. And yet, as the history of London so strongly demonstrates, exploitation and enlightenment are a cosy couplet.

This co-existence is evident in the emergence of coffeehouses in early-modern London. When Pasqua Roseé, an eccentric Greek-Italian-Turkish migrant, opened London's first coffeehouse on the site of Jamaica Wine House in 1652, ideas and information were hard to come by. And yet, this information was fundamental to the fledging suppliers and speculators of capital. The coffeehouse provided a solution; a place for entertaining, for meetings, for auctions, for books and for enlightened discourse, as well as for company offices. Most influentially, coffeehouses openly posted the latest stock prices[428].

While Pasqua Roseé's coffeehouse was likely nothing more than a semi-mobile shack, the Jamaica Coffee House that replaced it was a far more permanent feature of City life. By the start of the eighteenth century, London boasted of having over 3,000 coffee houses in the City[429]. In time, as markets tend to facilitate, these coffee houses came to specialise. One might visit a specifically Whig coffee house or pop into the Jerusalem Coffee House to catch up on East Indian issues.

Unsurprisingly, the Jamaica Coffee House specialised in West Indian interests. Those with such interests could make a social call at what locals now call the 'Jam Pot' for news and financial information, as well as communication with the islands. William Beckford, for example, kept up with his sugar interests in Jamaica through letters sent by his agent, James Knight, to him at the Jamaica Coffee House[430].

The existence of establishments such as the Jamaica Coffee House tells a story of a London well and truly emerging from the dark ages. A place of 'penny universities' with unlimited refills. A place where information and ideas about a rapidly expanding world could be exchanged outside of formal networks and away from the vulgarity of gin palaces. A place for civil discourse over a bitter black concoction made palatable only by the sugar flowing in from the West. As the recently arrived Huguenot Maximilien Misson mused upon encountering the London coffeehouse scene:

You have all Manner of News there: You have a good Fire, which you may sit by as long as you please: You have a Dish of Coffee; you meet your Friends for the Transaction of Business, and all for a Penny, if you don't care to spend more[431].

Philosophical discussions in the coffee houses of early-modern London were fuelled by the proceeds of slavery. Indeed, as historian Chris Harman argues:

Philosophers might talk about equal rights in the coffee houses of Europe. But the sweetened coffee they drank was produced by people who had been herded at gunpoint onto ships in West Africa, taken across the Atlantic in appalling conditions (more than one in ten died on the way), sold at auctions and then whipped into working 15, 16 or even 18 hours a day until they died[432].

This pairing of civility and savagery was certainly not limited to the vulgar discussions of traders and stock jobbers. It was the very basis of a British Empire that was expanding throughout the world and funnelling the proceeds of its accumulation and exploitation through London. It might have been an age of politeness but eighteenth-century London was also, in Daniel Defoe's words, a 'great and monstrous Thing'[433].

This pairing of politeness and monstrosity is not a historical aberration, even if today this couplet is much cleaner and much cooler. We have seen this contradiction at play in museums and in the film industry. They are equally evident in the conditions on the expanding margins of academia in London. These reserves are the fulcrum of London's university system, a system based on class exploitation and civilised dreams.

Challenging Mentalities

There is perhaps an image of university employment as a cushy gig; 'academic' was the third most popular potential job in a recent YouGov survey[434], although that possibly says more about the kind of people who are procrastinating on the internet by completing surveys. Universities, after all, are supposed to have the common good in mind. Queen Mary, University of London, for example, gives its purpose with no little idealism:

Queen Mary University of London is dedicated to the public good, pursuing the creation and dissemination of knowledge to the highest international standards, thereby transforming wider society and the lives of our students and staff. [435]

Moreover, academic staff do not hold the same level of public sympathy as professions like nursing and teaching. There are no politicians to decry the effect of Brexit on 'hard-working academics'. No one says that we need to spend less on nuclear submarines and more on semiotic scholars, as sensible as that would be.

Perhaps we do not help ourselves. Lecturers have a reputation for turning up when they like it, not responding to emails and having summers off, all in the name of 'academic freedom'[436]. More than that, we often bask in our refusal to conform to workplace norms. Lecturers in a suit, working just a little too efficiently, are rightly viewed with suspicion by their colleagues. Fancy new haircut? Shouldn't your mind be on something more important? The whiff of genius can excuse any manner of workplace sins. Many academics might even be accused of cultivating this image to be excused of their practical responsibilities[437].

When I used to tell my friends that I got up when I wanted[438], the eye-rolling was audible. These friends are not all that sympathetic now that I have to get up early to look after my newly arrived twins. And still, if I turned up for work at 8:30am, I would quickly lose my social capital around the office. For all this, I am not complaining. And yet, mental health issues among academic staff are higher than almost any other profession. A recent survey[439] reported that 43 per cent of academic staff in the UK described some form of mental disorder[440]. A total of 30 per cent of PhD students, perhaps those with the most ambitious dreams and the most precarious conditions, develop a psychiatric condition[441]. By contrast, 22 per cent of those working in the defence and emergency sectors report similar issues[442].

For Emily, the reasons for this mental degradation are clear on both a professional and a personal level. It is the casualisation of work, itself caused by the marketisation of the sector as part of a larger neo-liberal economy, that is to blame. Emily believes that it is this insecurity, combined with the crushing dreams of an academic life, that is leading to a 'huge mental health crisis that's about to explode in academia'.

As has so often been the case in London's history, every shift towards a more civilised city is one towards suffering, for some.

Growing Pains

It is no coincidence that the growth of the UK university system mirrored that of the spurts of cool in post-industrial London. As the Swinging Sixties were developing, there was a systematic expansion of institutions and students in the UK university system in the 1960s[443], which was matched by a doubling of academic staff[444].

The second wave of expansion in the 1990s, which led to a mass participation system marked by Tony Blair's goal of 50 per cent participation in higher education by 2010 as part of the ambition of the 'learning society'[445], was not followed by an increase in public funding[446]. Moreover, the expansion of the sector came with a marked change in rhetoric from the 1963 Robbins Report[447] to the 1997 Dearing Report[448]. Here higher education shifted from a societal good to one that both benefited the individual and provided the labour required by employers in a post-industrial society. Specifically, the Dearing Report called for higher education to 'serve the needs of an adaptable, sustainable, knowledge-based economy'. If the 1960s had a firm anti-establishment message, by the time Cool Britannia and the 1990s came around it was a matter of making a mint out of this maxim.

The problem with the knowledge economy inspired expansion of the university system was that everyone was getting the message. In a system where only around 15 per cent of the population attended university, a degree gave a student a real boast. Today, it is only degrees from elite universities, or post-graduate degrees, that provide such an advantage[449]. Students are no longer competing with non-students for a job but competing with each other and seeking to find every advantage.

This consumer insecurity was only exacerbated by the tripling of fees by the Conservative-Liberal Democrat coalition in 2010. Students, now forced to pay £9,000 per year as an 'investment' in their future, were corralled into the role of demanding consumers. Those who did not were either not paying attention or were privileged enough to get a leg up on the competition from their social status.

Now, instead of speaking truth to power and acting as the critic and conscience of society, universities were setting up innovation units and asking for investments. Students had become consumers, with universities appealing to their future employment prospects as much as anything else. Queen Mary, for example, describes a series of 'Graduate Attributes' as part of their 'commitment to students'. These attributes have the emancipatory elements we expect of higher education, such as 'evaluating information critically', having a 'global perspective' and 'learning continuously in a changing world'. The kicker comes at the end: 'We believe this approach will add value to our graduates and enable them to compete in an unpredictable marketplace'[450].

This is the new university, one in which knowledge is consumed as much as it is learnt. A place where learning to challenge the world is less of a political act than an individual economic investment. A place where research without a measurable impact that is capable of generating funding is barely research at all. These are the universities of Thatcher and of Blair. These are Florida's universities, ones that produce and attract the creative classes. For Emily, it was a betrayal of everything the university stood for.

The Causes of Casual Lives

On the surface, the mass expansion of higher education in the UK should have been a boon for those who work in the sector. It has not been, except for those with corner offices and non-existent office hours. With the mass growth of universities not corresponding with an expansion of public funding, pressure on teaching staff was inevitable. More recently, the emphasis on funding universities through research outputs and impacts has produced a pronounced focus on obtaining research funding that 'releases' the researcher from teaching obligations. Their courses become the battlefield for an indeterminate supply of those precarious academics desperate for cash and for teaching experience.

This casualisation was something that Emily found on her return to her former London institution. Having come back from Essex to London after a stint in Paris, Emily was completing a PhD when she began working as a teaching assistant. Originally interested in drama and theatre, Emily had appeared in a few plays and teaching allowed her to perform the subject that she loved.

The conditions under which she was compelled to perform were far from loveable. Where the seminars she had once attended were taught by the course convener, she was now teaching these seminars as a PhD student. There was no real training, no real collaboration and no real office space. There was also no real job security. She found herself, 'sat in a smelly room, where everybody feels a bit undervalued'. The truly desperate thing is that just getting access to one of these offices is taken as a sign of progress.

These conditions are commonplace at universities across London. At Queen Mary, the institution just quoted as being 'dedicated to the public good', three-quarters of teaching staff are on precarious contracts[451]. Across the sector, half of all academic teaching staff are on insecure contracts[452]. If studying at university is all part of becoming part of the creative class and the promised world of the cool economy, those who teach have an increasingly different experience.

More specifically, existing on the margins of academia is an experience defined by insecurity that goes beyond the self-doubt of the academic imposter syndrome. You never quite know whether there is going to be any work for you next semester, despite your best efforts. Even if you are lucky enough to be in a position where work is readily available, you never know if you will be able to emotionally and practically cope with taking on the amount of teaching required to make a living. Sure, an extra course might allow you to save for the dry summer months, but can you possibly mark that many papers, speak for that many hours and learn that many different virtual learning systems?

Refusal is not really an option; causal teaching staff become very territorial and the person in possession is likely to continue to be employed. Turn down a course? Say goodbye to ever teaching it again, unless your replacement is foolish enough to give it up. Here creativity at work is as much about working out how you will get by as it is about creating and disrupting knowledge. It is finding out which researchers are going on leave and how to get from institution to institution in time for the next class.

Most of all, in Emily's words, insecurity exists because, 'the pay [for casual teaching contracts] was abysmal, so I couldn't live on it'. Most cultural and service workers have known the feeling; will you be given enough shifts/courses this week/semester in order to pay the rent? She 'quite literally could not afford to be ill', coming in to perform for students when she was really unwell.

To get by she was doing temping work for Office Angels, which was as demeaning as it sounds. Here in this new form of post-industrial reserve army, she was depressed, out of money and struggling with 'the thing that [she] had always wanted to do' that she now felt unable to continue with. It did not help that, as a young female academic, she was implicitly charged with more pastoral work, a gender divide firmly embedded across academia where women take on far more unpaid 'academic citizenship' than men[453].

The Academic Drug Gang

The insecurity that Emily and so many other academics experience in London is not a blip in the system; precarious work is the very basis upon which academic employment is based. This is a system that Alexandre Afonso, an Assistant Professor at Leiden University in The Netherlands, compares to that of the drug gangs[454] studied by economists Steven Levitt (of *Freakonomics* fame) and Sudhir Venkatesh. Levitt and Venkatesh found that drug dealers were willing to take on the low financial rewards and imminent danger because of the possibility of making it to the top[455]. Get Rich or Die Trying, as the saying goes. They might also have suggested that most of those who took up this labour felt like they had no other options but to die trying, as male unemployment in the neighbourhood they studied was three times the national average and median income less than half.

This structure where income is extremely skewed at the top and street-level dealers were earning less than the minimum wage is an example of dualisation. Dualisation occurs when a labour market is split between insiders in secure employment and an expanding range of precarious outsiders[456].

As Afonso states:

Academic systems more or less everywhere rely at least to some extent on the existence of a supply of 'outsiders' ready to forgo wages and employment security in exchange for the prospect of uncertain security, prestige, freedom and reasonably high salaries that tenured positions entail.

Academics everywhere might problematise the intentionality of choice in this statement but the logic of the academic job market is readily clear. Anyone seeking to make it in the industry is competing with a wave of similarly talented and ambitious outsiders. This is an economic dynamic that Marx would have easily recognised; a relative surplus of doctoral students and early career academics has created a reserve army of labour that disciplines existing lecturers. This is post-industrial class struggle. This is how people are exploited in the cool capital, no matter their sophistication.

Put simply again, lecturers who refuse insecure contracts are easily replaced. As with all flexible contracts, the risk is transferred from the employer to (sometime) employees. Teaching at a university level is generally held in higher esteem than retail work. And yet, it should come as no surprise to the reader that the level of precarity among academic staff led Sally Hunt, then general secretary of the University and College Union, to accuse universities of 'importing the Sports Direct model' of minimum wages and maximum insecurity[457].

The surplus supply of potential academics that enables this system exists because of the mass expansion of PhD graduates not only in the UK but in the OECD, all competing in a global job market. The share of PhDs in the OECD population doubled from 2000 to 2009[458].

London's reputation as a place of cosmopolitan civility means that academic work is harder to come by here than anywhere else. It may not be the coolest version of the London dream but, as Samuel Johnston knew well, being an intellectual in London is a powerful rendition of the London dream.

Afonso claims that the ready supply of outsiders allows the privileged insiders (those with research funding) to outsource the more troublesome (teaching) parts of their job onto outsiders. These outsiders may appear desperate for any work that comes their way but that is only because of their lack of an alternative. Sure, I'll teach this course for you, especially if the alternative is retail work. And, we both know that if I do not, someone else will.

If you have not cracked into the privileged elite of permanent employment, it is a matter of taking up what is offered or moving on from a colossal economic and emotional investment in the academic world. Hearing that a permanently employed colleague had received a research grant that would 'buy out' their teaching was always wonderful news for those snapping at the margins of an academic department. The unfortunate irony, one of post-industrial capitalism more than just academia, is that it is those taking on casual contracts that prevent the need to hire faculty on permanent contracts. Why hire a full-time lecturer and pay for their possible research outputs (and summer existence) when you can keep rolling out module-by-module contracts?

I was acutely aware of this logic and once (meekly) tried to call my employer's bluff: when convening five courses within a single department, I argued that if I refused they would have to hire someone else, and I could then apply for the full-time job that administrators had deemed unnecessary. It did not work out well for me. Or at least nothing changed.

So it is for much of the post-industrial world[459] and especially the creative industries, where the surplus supply of potential employees struggling for their dream job keeps the ambitions of the employed in check.

Hope, Dreams, Class Struggle
Economically, as *The Economist* points out with all its usual self-

awareness in the 2010 article *The Disposable Academic,* a PhD is often a waste of time, offering only slim marginal benefits over a Master's degree[460]. This misses the point. Most PhD students are not striving for financial benefit. Anyone clever enough to obtain a doctorate is *probably* clever enough and sufficiently self-aware to realise that there are easier ways of making money.

Instead, many have already invested in an academic identity that is difficult to shift. This identity is 'passionate, enthusiastic, and full of expectation'. It is one that, as David Knights and Caroline Clarke show in their study of business academics *It's a Bittersweet Symphony, this Life: Fragile Academic Selves and Insecure Identities at Work*[461], is almost an over-commitment that compels the invested to preserve against all rationality. We might say the same about life in London.

This idealised notion of academic life and academic identity drives the supply of PhD students. It also contributes to the mental health problems that occur when Sunday night dreams become less about changing the (academic) world and more about producing PowerPoint slides[462].

To work as a historian, in London, was Emily's dream. And it is this dream that weighs so heavily on so many in the creative classes in London. There is pressure, Emily says to:

> ...*collude in saying that it's all wonderful...but things are getting, actually, a lot worse, a lot more insecure.*

These stories, whether of doctoral students or casual teaching staff, are too commonplace in academia to do justice to here[463]. They are also a routine finding in research on precarious cultural work, where it is common for participants to comment something like , 'It's great to have a job that you love, but it shouldn't make you ill.' [464] We could not be farther from Florida's vision for the revitalised creative city. But it is the very image of the cool, creative and enlightened city that drives dreamers to London, only to compete with those that have come before.

And still, they come; new Emily's are arriving in London every day.

That Emily was able to continue is a testimony to her determination and dedication to her craft. But life as a Doctor has not changed much. Teaching contracts continue to be offered on a casual basis. Often times she does not know whether a course will even run until the last minute and whether the money you were relying on will come in. Unpaid work continues to be a functional requirement; the only way into more permanent and more secure work is through research publications. Casual staff certainly do not get paid for that.

But Emily, like many others in her position, is fighting back. Casualisation is being challenged across the university sector[465]. As she says, 'if you are only going to be somewhere for a term, why not go on the picket line?' It is a question being pondered by an increasing number of London's precarious workers.

Likewise, Emily is still excited about London: she is not going anywhere. Neither are London's students, their lecturers and London's creative classes, from advertisers and graphic designers to scientists and data analysts. London, like academia, Emily says with some determination, 'is worth fighting for'.

It is this hope that propels the London dream and continues to supply London's workforce. Dreamers may be well aware of the difficulties they face when entering London but, for most, the idea of London is worth the fight. London's class divisions are reproduced through this hope. So is the city's service sector.

Chapter 12

Acting Up

It took a while for Mandla to find his place in London. Literally. When his taxi pulled up on his street in Holloway late on his first September night in 2003, he could not see the Number 92 he was searching for.

He was not expecting to find the door number written in marker pen. This does not happen in quiet, organised Sweden where he was raised. I'm not sure I've seen it happen too often in London either.

For Mandla, it was a bracing reminder of what he was expecting after he finished high school in Stockholm and moved to London to study drama. Mandla thought about New York. He had heard that it was more aggressive, though. Besides, London was nearer and 'in my head'. So it was for the 20,000 Swedes in London[466]; Mandla tells me that Swedes joke that London is the fourth largest city in Sweden. I've heard this a few times before, although it speaks more to the Swedish idea of London than population data.

Most Londoners' idea of the Swedish would probably include blonde, blue-eyed and some version of reserved or reticent. While I had been warned that Mandla was too handsome to talk to, he fits none of these Swedish stereotypes. What Mandla does do is stand out from the crowd. Although we have never met, I have no trouble recognising his determined presence among the throngs outside Shoreditch High Street Station, even as the evening darkness descends at its inhumane November pace.

Mandla has come straight from rehearsal. The show, a physical theatre performance exploring issues of identity and discrimination, is opening in a couple of days at a fringe theatre in Marylebone. Reviewers would later describe his performance as 'energetic'. The show itself received distinctly mixed reviews. I wonder if this is often the case. His muscular, if compact, figure certainly commands attention. We've ended up in a buzzing Redchurch Street pub, the kind that instantly makes me feel old, and deaf. Over a ginger beer in the garden outside, Mandla has no trouble communicating his journey to London:

> I got quite interested in acting, so I did some courses after school. And then I heard about a drama school and they were holding auditions in Stockholm for this course in London. So I auditioned, and I got accepted, and once I graduated high school, I just moved to London, and enrolled.

Adjusting to London was not as simple. Growing up, Sweden had felt boring and he could not wait to get out. London made him appreciate 'the comfortableness, the cleanliness' of Stockholm. His new home was dirty. It was difficult. It was exciting in a way that Sweden was not.

Compared to Stockholm, London was 'like a country, like a world'. He was meeting people from places he had never encountered before. Even if the standard of living had dropped, the world was opening up for him. There was no time to dwell on the potential difficulties ahead of him. Instead, Mandla thought, 'kind of like, right. So this is what it's like living in London.'

Still, drama school was confounding. He was surrounded by much older, much more experienced students. Many were public school educated. A lot told stories involving their 'gap yah', Mandla says, nailing the (received) pronunciation. Welcome to the great British class system. Or at least the creative, London version.

It was this world that Mandla wanted to enter into in 2003. Nothing had changed when he graduated. He definitely did not want to go back to Stockholm, where nepotism was rife and opportunities limited. Of course, class-based social capital is important in London. As Paul told me, gig-based cultural fields operate through insular, often privileged networks. It is just that London's creative networks are a lot more diverse; gatekeepers are as important in London as Stockholm, but there are a lot more gates here.

If many of the barriers to creative employment are class-based, race adds another dimension. In the arts, the desire to demonstrate a commitment to diversity opens some doors; it also restricts the rooms one can enter.

It is a battle Mandla has no choice but to wade through. It is one 40 per cent of Londoners know well. Many would say that diversity is no opportunity.

BAME!

Mandla's web profile lists the following details:

Height: 5′ 9″ (1m 75cm)
Weight: 10st. 10lb. (68kg)
Build: Muscular
Age Range: 21-28
Ethnicity: Black-African

It was this last detail that likely got him his first job: a stabbing victim on Crimewatch. He was grateful for this opportunity to enter an exciting new world, even if he was barely on his feet. Something was amiss though. Auditions were coming in, they were just for the same kind of roles. It got boring very quickly. This was not what Mandla imagined when he left drama school and 'people kept saying, "oh my god, there's going to be loads of work for you, you're young, you're black, and black guys are *in* right now. Black guys are *in*".'

This was not quite the case. London has the highest proportion of actors from BAME in the country. And yet, only 19 per cent of theatre actors in London are from BAME background[467]. Worse,

Mandla found that those in positions of power did not want black actors. They wanted mixed race guys to pass off as black. They wanted to cast Hispanic-looking guys or people who look Filipino, whatever was the passing trend. Mandla does not hide his disgust: 'we're not a fad'.

The demand to 'sound more black' gets equally short shift. Well-spoken, although proud of his now instinctively London accent, Mandla found himself being asked by 'some white, middle-class director' to 'sound more street', even when it had nothing to do with the character. He stays away from these characters now, unless there is a degree of nuance beyond the stereotypes being reproduced by, and for, privileged outsiders.

Londoners across the city battle these stereotypes and not all have the same energy, talent or opportunity as Mandla. Despite the celebration of the outward celebration of diversity in London, ethnic inequalities are rife. Half of BAME Londoners report experiencing racial discrimination and more think that some jobs are effectively closed to ethnic minorities[468]. They are right; BAME public sector employees in London are paid up to 37 per cent less than their white colleagues[469].

Migrants, especially those from a BAME background, are at the front stage of London's story. Officially, London is open to them. When it comes to employment, BAME Londoners find opportunities to be far less accessible. Even more so when it comes to employment in the arts. For Mandla, finding work – the right kind of work – means searching for ways to keep afloat when opportunities are running dry.

The Survival Job
Unemployment is not a problem Mandla faces. He is rarely permanently employed. Nor is he not employed for long periods either. He has plenty of avenues to make some cash. Mandla acts, on stage and in film, specialising in physical performances. He dances, although he would not class himself as a dancer. He

has lucrative modelling options, which he fell into by accident.

In between these gigs, he makes his money by bouncing around what he calls 'survival jobs'. Of course he does. When I asked Mandla if he takes on non-creative work, he pauses for a moment and shoots me a look. It is the look you give when asked a question that is way too obvious.

Yeah, no, I always have to take a lot of stuff. I do, jobs for actors. Catering, working as a waiter. I did that for 5 years. I worked as a bartender. I also do promo, promotional work, where you work with brands, you promote brands and stuff.

In the previous chapters we saw that although film-maker Paul and academic Emily were existing precariously on the fringes of their dream professions, they only occasionally dropped into the ranks of the service class that acts as the safety net and holding bay for creative workers. Mandla spends much of his time here, though, only jumping out when creative work is available.

He is not alone in this struggle; two-thirds of theatre actors take on non-entertainment industry jobs to get by[470]. This is not a new idea; the trope of the actor/waiter, writer/barista is well-established. We tend to frame this 'starving-artist' narrative in terms of individual choices; that these conditions are the price paid for following one's dream. Sure, it is great that they are pursuing their big break, but maybe they should start looking for a real job. Even if your second job actually pays more than the first[471]. But few would consider investing in their survival job to be a viable option, at least until they are forced to; the fantasy of the dream job in the dream profession is remarkably strong.

It is perhaps because of this embrace of the dream narrative that those who desire secure work in the creative sector are held responsible for their fate. The answer to the precariousness of creative work is often to advise students on how to navigate their brand and their expectations[472]. If you turn down the possibility of a secure profession, say as an accountant or a lawyer, it is up to you to make it work. Indeed, despite all evidence, research by the BFI on social exclusion in the creative industries demonstrated an overwhelming belief in the meritocracy of the industry[473]. If you want to make it, and you have the talent, London will give you the opportunity. Or so the story goes.

And so, performers float between roles, hustling for places in more prosperous and more advantageous gigs while dreaming of a different life. These performers become micro-entrepreneurs. Not only are they forced to build up their 'brand', they must also negotiate an economy where gigs are short-term and fluid. These roles are opportunistically obtained through established networks and are disposed of at a moment's notice by performer and employer alike.

It is easy to lump these roles together: hospitality work, promo work, perhaps some kind of side hustle of questionable legality[474]. All these can be classified by the likes of Richard Florida as menial service industry roles, albeit with a hint of grinding glamour. For those competing for these gigs, though, there are defined micro-hierarchies of better roles and better shifts.

I certainly get this sense from Mandla. Not only is he making his way as an actor, but he is also making his way up through the associated side industries. Waiting and bar work is for beginners. So is handing out Red Bull on the street. He is doing far more prestigious stuff, serving London's creative classes at corporate events run by the likes of Google, Coke and Adidas. Then there is the modelling, which pays far more than acting ever has.

Performers like Mandla engage in this work out of resigned necessity, floating back and forth between the creative and service worlds. A 2014 *London Theatre Report* from the editor of *The Stage*[475], Alistair Smith, revealed that only one-fifth of fringe performers were being paid more than the national minimum wage. A third of actors were paid nothing at all. Further research by Casting Pro Call[476] reported that 75 per cent of actors across mediums in London earned less than £5,000 from acting in the previous year. A total of 46 per cent made less than £1,000 with one in five not getting any acting work.

In response to these reports, Malcolm Sinclair, the then president of Equity, the union for creative auctioneers, stated:

We are taking this issue extremely seriously; there is a huge issue over 'low pay, no pay'. We don't want to damage the fringe, but on the flipside, people out of drama school are desperate to get work, and they are being exploited.

He is clear on the cause of this exploitation:

Compared to when I started there are so many more drama schools, and university courses there are far more young actors coming out and it feels like there is less work around. There are too many actors and too few jobs.

This is Steven Levitt and Sudhir Venkatesh's drug gang logic all over again[477]; a surplus of entrants chasing a dream possible only for the elite (or the fortunate). There is about as much sympathy for aspiring actors working service jobs as there is for the danger endured by street-corner drug dealers. No one forced them to take on this risk, we think. Creative dreamers are welcome to spend their youth chasing their passion while we slog it out in offices and shops, but they have no right to cry about their choices.

As we have seen, though, it is not just creative performers facing these conditions. London's economy is reliant on talented young people chasing their dreams. By way of their desires for the new and the cool, these fresh faces make London the place to be. Because so many believe that London is the place to be, however, those who do not rise to the top of their field often end up servicing the cool economy.

The working conditions they are forced to endure also subsidise this economy. The likes of the fringe theatre could not exist if performers were paid decent wages. As the director of Lauderdale House, an arts and education centre in Highgate, Katherine Ives, states:

> ...if you had to pay everybody minimum wage I think the amount of fringe theatre would probably halve. It's not morally right, but we're in a climate where subsidies for creative venues are very minimal. Even if you sell out a show on the fringe, the venues are very small and the ticket prices are not high, there's not much money there to be made[478].

That we worry about ticket prices being too high rather than wages being too low tells us much about cool London and its theatre industry, where the gloom of production is put in its place by the shine of consumption.

Consuming Performance

Theatre is a central character in the story of a civilised, happening London, whether it is Elizabethan Shakespearean plays, Victorian music halls, generic West End musicals or subversive fringe productions. Tourists from all of the world specifically come to London to 'take in a show'. Watching theatre, whether a mass musical or a participative fringe production, is very much a local affair.

It is one that is specifically local to where Mandla and I are sitting; the first permanent public theatre in London (aptly called 'The Theatre') was opened just across the road from us on Curtain Road in 1576. After overcoming the reassertion of Royal control, if not government censorship, theatre in London boomed as the Georgian era became the Victorian one. The abolition of the restrictive 1737 Licensing Act in 1968 led to new freedoms.

By the time The Globe was reconstructed in 1966, post-industrial London had a claim to being the theatre capital of the world, something it is not shy about. Descriptions of London's theatre scene are often breathless. Witness:

London's West End is known the world over as the home of theatre. Millions of theatregoers descend on England's capital each year, and plays in London are often top of the agenda. Visitors come to enjoy spectacular performances in a spectacular city. As one of the major attractions for residents and visitors, such productions are always high in demand.
The rich diversity of the city's theatre scene means there is always something to enjoy. Whether you're looking for a hot piece of new writing or a revival of a classic, London has something for you.
The theatre buildings themselves are also awe-inspiring, with some having hosted plays for centuries[479].

The figures are staggering too, enough to support a claim that London has the largest theatre scene in the world. It has 241 professional theatres, from the West End auditoriums to tiny venues above pubs. In 2012/13, 22 million attended the theatre in London, bringing in £618.5 million, which is more than the cinema industry[480].

The industry employs 3,000 performers and 6,500 FT non-performers. There are an additional 10,000 part-time and freelance staff. In the words of the aforementioned *London Theatre Report*, 'London theatre is widely held to be booming, both artistically and at the box office[481].'

It is, as long as you look at consumption of theatre rather than its production, particularly on the margins. Like Paul and Emily, performers like Mandla are forced to walk an unstable line between the need to take on the multiple shifts required to exist in London and the unpaid work necessary to continue pursuing their passions

They can find themselves working every day for 3 weeks, just to make sure that the rent is sorted. And here lies the problem, Mandla cautions.

You do have your dry seasons, right? So, sometimes you almost start clinging on to the promotional job, the survival job…just booking up on loads of shifts.
Sometimes, at some point, you forget about the acting stuff, and the auditions. Because it's gone dry…I had a moment like that, where sometimes I would actually be focused, like on that more than the acting. And it actually got to a point where I was like, 'No. You know what? No. No I can't.'

It was here that working in a community of actors (90 per cent on most promo jobs, he estimates) pays off. As a result, quasi-colleagues are understanding (if a little jealous) when you had to take a day off for a 'big job'. His friends also egg each other on to make more of an effort, to get out of their comfort zone.

As much as London and the logic of capitalism holds him down, Mandla is always looking for ways to get up. And he is. His list of roles is growing rapidly and agents are searching him out on Instagram, even if Mandla refuses to work on his online brand. He has modelled for some household (or maybe just East London house share) names. Still, life is lived gig to gig. We laugh about the implausibility of getting a mortgage in London. Being able to travel for work seems a far more reasonable aspiration, even if Hollywood holds little appeal.

So, what does the future hold for Mandla? He loves to travel, and his unexpected modelling work has taken him to Italy and to the Netherlands. Recently, it took him to New York, a place he had turned down 15 years ago. What did he make of it?

D'you know what? It's really funny, I really liked it and I'd love to go back, and I'd love to work there but I grew to appreciate London even more. I really did. I was like, 'You know what? No. You know what? London is actually, I actually really like London. I'm actually glad I live here.

Despite the challenges, London is still the place to be for Mandla. It continues to be for so many other performers. They would likely agree with Mandla's renewed appreciation for the city; with a sudden smile, he tells me that London is 'awesome though. I mean, it is my home. It's just, like, soul-wise, creatively, it's very stimulating.'

As we part, I ask if he is anxious about his rapidly approaching show.

'I'm always a bit nervous. You have to be. But I'll be okay on the night.' With that, he bounces off into the buzz of the city's November darkness.

There is a lot more of London left for Mandla.

Chapter 13

Serving Flat Whites

I was recently asked by my parents to show some long-standing family friends around London. The No.1 concern of this middle-aged Antipodean couple? Finding good coffee.

Rumours of London's coffee poverty are rife among potential travellers from the Southern colonies. Australian and New Zealand travel guides to London often include rather patronising sections on WHERE TO FIND GOOD COFFEE. An illustration:

In recent years, Londoners have enjoyed a huge surge in artisan coffee shops. The café culture isn't yet on par with that of Melbourne or Sydney, but it's getting pretty close. If you know where to go, Antipodean-style flat whites, glasses of cold brew and high-quality beans can be found throughout the city[482].

The Antipodes are an unlikely source for such snobbery, given that the European settler cultures of these two nations were largely derived from attempts to escape the rigours of British class structures and the morality of cultural refinement. Unlikelier still, the flat white, now a hipster style icon, comes out of an attempt to maintain masculine appearances.

For Australians, the flat white was a product of post-war Italian migrants' efforts to assimilate into Melbourne. Unable to comprehend the Australian binary of white coffee and short/long black coffee, the flat white was an Anglicised version of something between a cortado, doppio or a macchiato.

Across the Tasman Sea, Kiwis were not entirely taken by European interpretations of black and white. The cappuccino was for children and the latte was 'considered a weak drink for intellectuals, political liberals and new mothers' [483]. Even now a 'latte-sipping liberal' is a serviceable insult. The flat white emerged as a stronger beverage with none of the foamy feminine indulgences of a cappuccino or latte. Either that or it came out of an attempt to make the best out of a cappuccino where the low-fat milk failed to rise: a flat, white, coffee[484].

For blokes who pride themselves on rugged resilience, Antipodean cultural masculinity is a remarkably fragile thing. In a wonderfully chaotic turn, this fragility has reinvented London's coffee culture. As has happened so often in London, the flat white was thrust into the city's marketplace by migrants desperate to reproduce a sense of home, and to make a bit of money from this cultural difference.

And so, New Zealanders James Gurnsey and Cameron McClure, along with Australian Peter Hall, opened *Flat White* in Soho because they found it 'nigh impossible to get a flat white; the strong, delicious creamy coffee of our namesake'[485]. They define the flat white as 'An antipodean style coffee which is served as a strong shot of espresso served in a small cup with textured milk; a damn good strong coffee'[486]. Just to make sure that you know it is okay to have something as feminine as *textured milk*, they add a second definition:

flattie noun. colloq. flat white;
I'm gonna smash back a couple of flatties bro / NZ / mate / Austral.

When *Flat White* chalked their first blackboard in 2005, it was one of a kind. Now, these artisan cafes are everywhere. Even the big players now promote their craft shops. Starbucks started to sell flat whites in 2010. I took advantage of their desire to enter the market when I was new to London, unemployed and broke but with literary desires that involved writing from cafes. When I went to Starbucks and had an awful flat white, I had an idea. I wrote an email complaint (being careful not to identify any staff member) and received a £10 voucher. That brought me four more coffees and four more hours out of the house while writing my first book. It is now reportedly Starbucks' most popular product[487], although I'm not sure how much my fraud had to do about that[488].

The surge in the flat white's popularity tells us much about London. Coffee has become a four-billion pound mainstream mega industry – Allegra Strategies report a 1,328 per cent increase since they started researching the UK coffee industry in 1999[489] – challenging tea as Londoners' beverage of choice. But coffee is more than a drink.

As we have seen in previous chapters, the rise of the coffeehouse was at the vanguard of the emergence of civilised London. Today, artisan coffee is again a cultural event, a status symbol and a cool experience; especially as a flat white's texture is perfect for Instagrammable foam art from hip baristas. It is no wonder that the café is taking the place of the pub as Londoners' preferred meeting place, especially as the distinction between work and play dissolves for millennial workers.

What goes unspoken in these glowing accounts of London's café culture are those doing the serving. In the hippest of cafes, skilled baristas might have a cache of cool rivalling that of cocktail 'mixologist'. Few would reach the London Living Wage. Others, especially in the chain brands, are scraping by at the bottom end of the legal minimum wage: £8.21 for those over 25, £7.70 for 21-24s, £6.15 if you are aged 18-20 and £4.35 for those under 18.

These café, bar, restaurant and shop workers are the front line of the service industry, often the meeting point of cool consumption and miserable production. They may be tied behind the counter but their dreams are just as strong as the creatives typing away on the tables in front of them. Aidan's certainly are, and they are very specifically Australian.

Exploiting Antipodeans

We have known each other a long time, Aidan and I, a friendship forged by family connections and separated by the Tasman. It's been a while since we have seen each other but he is typically friendly when I get in touch through Facebook Messenger.

Aidan is happy to meet me anywhere, he says, even if we are in the midst of the mythical 'Beast from the East' that blanketed London with snow in March 2018. Being between jobs does give you a bit of flexibility, he later tells me with his characteristic grin.

We have found ourselves in a pub just North of Silicon Roundabout, one full of enough down-at-the-mouth day drinkers to call itself an East London boozer, although there is a definite hint of geeky creativity. Maybe even the odd suit. It's the East End of London on display, or at least the palest version of it.

Aidan is at home here, although he had come to London almost accidentally. He had applied for a visa while in a relationship but they had never got around to organising their trip. When that relationship ended, he thought, 'Well, I've already got this visa, I might as well go use it.' Aidan knew one person in London and wanted to do some travelling, so why not come over and 'see what happens'?

He was certainly not the first Australian to make the trip; the 2011 census reported 107,918 Australians in London, although numbers are dropping[490]. Add in some 57,094 New Zealanders[491] and this makes for a pretty sizeable Antipodean population partaking in what us Kiwis colloquially (and thus always) call the great OE (Overseas Experience). Australians are concentrated in the South West of the city in areas like Wandsworth and Clapham, as well as strongholds in Shepherds Bush and Hammersmith, having been priced out of Earl's Court. But the community is also moving East to places like Finsbury, where Aidan has spent his 3 years in London.

Like many Australians, Aidan arrived in his twenties as part of a Youth Mobility Visa scheme allowing those under 30 to live and work in the UK for 2 years. It is the relative ease of obtaining these visas, the presence of an existing community, and the prospect of being connected to the rest of the world for the first time in a city where there is 'always something going on' that drives many to the home of their natural enemy, sporting wise at least. Most of all, London can be used as a base to travel from while hanging around with other Australians, complaining about the weather and pissing pounds up against the wall.

This Australian rendition of the London dream is perhaps the most hedonistic of all. In the adventure section of news.com. au, for example, Ash London provided *Ten Reasons You Need to Spend a Year Living in London in Your 20s*, the last of which was BECAUSE YOU CAN:

> *Let's face it. One day you might get married, might have kids, might have a mortgage or a career that requires you stay put in Oz. But now? Now you can be selfish. Now you can hop on a plane to the other side of the world and have an incredible adventure. You can spend all your money on weekend trips to Greece and concert tickets, and come home after a year or two flat broke with a full heart.*
> *At the end of your life, you'll never wish you travelled less — but you might wish you saw more of the world while you were young enough to do so*[492].

Aidan agrees whole heartedly and tells me with his infectious laugh that Australians have 'this expectation of being wildly drunk humans on a Wednesday and a Thursday and then having to work all weekend'.

And yet, in the Australian mythology of London, these dreams are both strong and always already crushed. Alex Stanhope, writing in *Vice*, articulates this sentiment when arguing that *London is the Worst City on Earth*:

For Australians, London was invented in the early-2000s, when we scored some new UK visa arrangements and started migrating en masse. I remember hearing about London squat parties, how the drugs were cheaper than beers and how Orlando Bloom was really down to earth. I remember thinking maybe I could go there and get an internship for a production company. By 2010, I was finishing uni and I had a dream. A Big Dream to become a screenwriter for a soap opera. Yeah, I don't know why either. But that was the dream and London was soap opera ground zero, so I made the move in 2011. ...I found London ugly. I grew tired of working constantly but never having money. I resented the sky and its sad, broken sun. I grew tired of being ignored by everyone except Polish waiters and the cleaners from Bangladesh who, like me, had come dreaming of something greater than Sainsbury's gin hangovers and mildew. We were all so disappointed[493].

Aidan was not disappointed; he knew London was going to be 'Grey and shitty'. Even still, arriving in 'bollocks cold' January London during a hot summer in Melbourne is enough to shock even the most jaded Londoner's system. But, still, there was 'a strange, kind of excitement and fear' on his arrival. An expectation, perhaps, that London was a way out of his Melbourne rut.

London was fun and it provided a 'kind of a launching pad'. After spending all his money travelling and enjoying himself, though, it was time for Aidan to get serious. He has a degree in marketing and 5 years' experience as a marketing and communications manager in Melbourne. Despite this, Aidan had expected to put to use his 11 years in hospitality. Even still, the initial rejections from marketing jobs were a shock: sorry, you don't have any London experience. Maybe not even sorry.

But, while no one cared for his marketing experience, Australian coffee makers are a hot commodity. As Aidan came to learn:

back in Aus, it's like, 'Yeah, I mean, the English just love
Australians.' Which they do, in their bars and their cafés...but in a
workplace, they're very much still along the lines of, like, 'Oh, I don't
know what your degree is?' So, there's that, kind of, almost, in the
right environment, we love Australians. In the wrong environment,
or in an untested environment, then we don't know...

Many migrants face the same barriers. While London provides an opportunity to move up in the world, often it begins by taking a step back. And so, Aidan had to turn to what he knew and what people gave him credit for: making flat whites on the service end of the creative economy.

He walked into three cafes and did three trial shifts, a practice endured by hospitality workers across the city. For cafes, bars and restaurants, of course, this practice is entirely sensible to an individual's suitability for the role [494]. When potential workers are abundant, it feels logical to push risk from employer to employee.

All three shifts were unpaid. One, after extending his morning trial to the whole day and promising food and pay, delivered only on the food. They still offered Aidan a job, though, as did the other two cafes. He decided on taking the one closest to where he lived. With a wry smile and a chuckle, Aidan takes a sip of his beer and tells me that, 'they didn't really talk about, kind of, the financial reimbursement side of things, it was just, like, "cool, this is what we pay people"'.

He was offered £6.74 an hour and, without any point of reference, took it.

You cannot survive in London on £6.74 an hour. Aidan did what he had to do: he worked 90 hours a week:

I'd have one day off probably every 2 weeks, normally like a Monday
or something. But that was just, kind of, it. Like, I would do a
morning and a night, or a two nights in a row, or whatever...the café

that I was working for had opened a restaurant at night, so I went from the café in the morning to the bar at night, restaurant at night, and had an hour, an hour and a half, an hour and 45 minutes, to go home, get changed, have a shower, change clothes into the night gear, and then back to the place to be at the restaurant. And it was just hectic, it was exhausting.

Aidan's situation was not unique; 62 per cent of the 163,000 Londoners working in the Accommodation and Food Services industry were paid less than the London Living Wage in 2017, by far the highest of any industry[495]. Overall, 20 per cent of employees in London are paid less than the living wage, with over half of them working in either the hospitality or retail sectors[496].

At this point in his London journey, Aidan was supposed to be completing a Masters online. He could not afford to work less to complete the degree, though, so he 'binned that off'. Applying for professional jobs proved equally difficult, as Aidan would have to take half a day off for interviews. Instead, the café/bar became his social life. It became a place to make friends that were not Australians and to share his boundless enthusiasm for life.

Still, this was tough work. It was exhausting. It was not what he came to London for. Aidan thought about going home if things did not improve. They did. He was able to drag himself out of the service sector to take on a role on the margins of the flat white economy. The job was a basic email marketing role for a tech company, paying £20,000 a year. He was now an 'emerging service worker', but it was a break that would provide marketing experience and, most importantly for Aidan, 'it meant that I didn't have to work 90 hours a week'.

After a year or so he was made redundant when the company was sold, which was perhaps a blessing. He had spent too long in a dead-end job and, he says with a chortle, 'most of that's a drunken blur, to be fair...' At least he was living some part of the Australia edition of the London dream.

Aidan went back to Australia, briefly, to convert his Youth Mobility Visa into a 5-year Ancestry Visa and recommitted to London, thinking 'Well, if this is all I've done in London it would probably be a disappointment.' He came back and started a marketing executive role for a tech company. This was a job he wanted to do. Cool company, interesting spot, doing fun work. He had the sense that, 'finally I'm kind of getting somewhere where I want...I'm finally getting paid, and it was all worth it'.

He was fired. Or at least he did not pass the probation period. With a cheeky smile he tells me that, 'At the end of the probation at 6 months, they were like "Yeah, look, we thought you would have probably progressed a bit further," and I was like, "Yes, I thought I would have a bit more training."'

He remains positive though:

I still had this really buoyant feeling, because one, I was, although I wasn't getting paid any longer, I was like, Yes, I'm away from this environment, and that made me far happier, and I went to Christmas, and did all those type of things, and the start of the year has been really positive for getting interviews and, like opportunities...I'm feeling like my time in England is almost starting, or almost, perhaps, starting again, because things have opened up far more drastically than they were when it was just like, Okay, the only job that you can do is being in a bar, or being in a café.

Later that month he started a new marketing job at an international education agency. Aidan's London dream lives on. Australian as his version might be, many Londoners have been living the same lives. They drag themselves into shifts at cafes, bars and restaurants knowing that this is not what they came to London for. But, just like Aidan, it provides them with a foothold in the city and an opportunity to apply for other, more creative and meaningful work. And, if times are tough, they know they can always fall back on the skills that keep the city running. This struggle, this class struggle, cannot be separated from the London dream.

Serving London

As Richard Florida remarked in his (non) mea-culpa, *The New Urban Crisis*, the most creative cities are also the most unequal[497]. Those that feel the pain of this inequality most are the service classes who have been pushed out to the periphery. 'Yes', he says to Oliver Wainwright in *The Guardian*, 'there are many artists and musicians who struggle, but the creative workers have colonised the best spaces in cities, pushing the service workers out to the periphery.' The real issue, Florida offers, is the 'immiseration of the service class'[498]. He went on to explain that the rise of populism had:

> *forced me to confront this divisiveness, I realised that we need to develop a new narrative, which isn't just about creative and innovative growth and clusters, but about **inclusion** being a part of prosperity. It was the service class – the class I had forgotten – that was taking it on the chin*[499]

Here Florida has it wrong and in more than just his uncritical promotion of the creative economy. Firstly, as we have seen, the divisions between the creative classes are often fluid. Aspiring creative workers like Mandla and Aidan regularly take 'survival jobs' in the service industry. Moreover, the problem is not so much that the service classes are excluded from London's creative economy. Instead, Florida's service class are necessary for the reproduction of London's cool and creative economy. This goes beyond the obvious requirement for baristas to serve coffee and drivers to deliver food and packages. More than this, the service class exist as the holding bay for the creative classes.

Paul, Emily and Mandla did not think of themselves as service workers, even when doing the most menial work. But servicing London was a way of avoiding unemployment while waiting for greater opportunities.

If Florida was made famous by publicising a new logic of creative capitalism, the woes he is now concerned with are as old as capitalism and its class structure. We are now ready to outline a theory of the class struggle hidden within the London dream. To do so, we need Marx, journalist Francesca and the ongoing struggles of London's literary dreamers.

Chapter 14

Grub Street Dreams

Francesca was born into journalism, even if she avoided it at first as, in her words, 'my father was a journalist'. Born in Italy, she moved to London aged two and was educated in Barnet. Having completed a BA in French and Italian at the University of Sussex she started off teaching English as a foreign language.

It was not enough, though, and she needed to break out. What better place to get away from it all than Australia and a communications diploma in Sydney? Such a journey is a very British dream.

From there Francesca got a start in community radio, which led to an opportunity with Radio Netherlands, covering news and current affairs. Having come into journalism almost by accident it became 'somewhat of an obsession'. At Radio Netherlands she '...loved all the shifts and the excitement'.

When she came back to the UK with small children, though, the shifts necessary for radio journalism were not really an option. Instead, it was freelancing and print that appealed and London was the place for it, if out of necessity more than anything. And not just for family reasons. If you want to be a journalist, Francesca states matter-of-factly, 'it has to be here'. Almost two-thirds of journalists work in London, compared to 29 per cent of all jobs[500].

London and written journalism was a different world from radio and the Australian lifestyle. Francesca found that London is not an easy place to be and it's 'not an easy place to be a journalist', but she loves:

all the museums, I love the variety, I love the theatre, I love all the galleries, and adore the Tate Modern, and the British Museum, all

of that and I think that there's so much, its endless and pockets
of it are so interesting. And I like the cultural mix, I mean it's so
cosmopolitan, and I think I'd miss that, elsewhere.

She loved working in travel writing too. In retrospect, though, Francesca informs me:

It probably wasn't a very good choice...I wasn't aware, 6-7 years
ago when I started to get back into it quite how journalism was in
a state of flux. With the onslaught of digital media, and apps, and
everything, and it just moved too fast...so I felt like I'm sort of
climbing, climbing up and down.

Francesca has entered journalism at a time when its very meaning is changing. Click-bait listicles can be aggregated from other listicles more cheaply than investigative research. Travel websites are often unwilling to actually pay people to go to the places they are writing about. I remember a student of mine doing an internship for a travel website who, when a writer quit, was asked to write a feature article about their experience of travelling through Morocco. That my student had never been was not a problem and a bit of Googling, and her brilliance, produced an excellent piece. She received neither a by-line nor a pay cheque, though she did have a valuable learning experience.

The line between editorial and advertorial is also disappearing, particularly in travel writing. Now, 'instead of sending your completed article to the editor, who would edit it, you're sending it, or people who do advertorial send it to the client, who will tweak it according to these needs'. Otherwise, press releases are just lifted straight from PR departments[501]. It is no wonder that so many journalists are turning to PR, especially because, as Francesca advises me, 'that's where the money is'.

The cause of this state of flux is clear to journalists, and to readers, everywhere: the rise of a digital age that has made consumers of information potential producers and disrupted established income streams. Before the fall, journalism was an insular industry of established outlets, steady producers and reliable consumers. Today, digital disruption has meant more outlets, more producers, more distracted customers and falling revenues.

In some ways, the opening up of the production and publication of ideas and knowledge (or just 'content') has produced meritocratic advantages. Journalism has long been an 'old boys club'. Over half of British journalists attended Oxbridge and a similar percentage came from independent schools[502]. Black Britons are 'underrepresented by a factor of more than ten'[503]. Digital journalism has nudged open these social and cultural entry barriers. For example, British-Eritrean journalist Hannah Pool has claimed that:

> One of the best things about modern technology is how it is breaking down the old boys' club, brick by brick, Tweet by Tweet. It used to be that you had to have a mum or dad in the business to get your first by-line, now you can just set up a blog[504]

Unfortunately, digital consumption and production has also established new economic barriers. The digital democratisation of journalism has allowed an almost unlimited supply of writers competing for an ever-dwindling trickle of advertising pounds. Moreover, newspapers are closing and their staff are going freelance, further fuelling the growing pool of precarious journalists. Interestingly, despite warnings of writerly doom, the number of journalists in the UK rose by 12 per cent from 2012-2018. Whether the growing number working in PR are actually journalists is a matter of debate[505].

These conditions have had a dire effect on pay; the National Union of Journalists reported that a fifth of journalists earn less than £20,000 per year[506]. And yet many, especially those established in London, are doing well[507]. Once again, we have a dualistic economy, with a declining number of established insiders doing well and a range of outsiders struggling. Being able to get your work online and being able to get paid for it are very different things. Boris Johnson and I have an equal opportunity to get our work on a website. *The Daily Telegraph* gives him £275,000 a year for his musings and I'm lucky to get a few quid, despite our work being equally incoherent.

Equal access is a problematic opportunity for freelance journalists, who are the fastest growing branch in the business. Freelance journalists are compelled to become multi-skilled micro-entrepreneurs, with all the freedom and precarity that comes with it. It is no surprise that the 30,000 journalists reported to be working exclusively online in the UK earn significantly less than those who appear in print[508], even if many are in steady jobs at established outlets.

With all this competition from professionals and amateurs alike, and with revenue collapsing, journalists like Francesca are regularly being asked to work for free, which she refuses to do. That does not stop others, though, especially young journalists. Francesca's frustration is close to the surface. Journalists working for free are 'making it difficult for everyone, because they know that there'll always be someone who will write for free, in the hope that it will lead somewhere, which it rarely does'.

Beyond individuals giving away their labour, many publications – often online, but sometimes national print outlets – are reliant upon an army of unpaid interns. As an unpaid London internship costs around £1,100 a month, even if travel costs are covered, only the most privileged can take on this route for long[509]. Where you might once have worked your way up from the mail room, 87 per cent of new journalists have completed at least one internship, with 95 per cent of those being unpaid[510]. These gigs are highly sought after; coming to London for an internship has become a stepping stone in the London dream.

And yet, in spite of all of these struggles, writing remains a fantasy profession and London is the place to do it. 'Author' is regularly nominated by Britons as their dream job, with journalist not far behind, just ahead of academic[511]. And this is despite the average full-time author's annual earnings being a miserable £10,437[512]. Unsurprisingly, only 13 per cent of authors make a living solely from writing and the median earnings of all authors is a measly £3,000 (falling 49 per cent from 2005-2017)[513]. As a result, these authors forge 'portfolio' careers like so many on the margins of the creative classes.

Francesca is still in the business but, with magazines closing and the editors with whom she had forged relationships moving on:

> it's just been constant trying to find work. I do less and less of that now. If things come my way, and I want to do them, I will, but pitching cold into the void and trying to get an answer, I do less and less of because it is very demoralising and you don't get an answer a lot of the time.

Now, instead of battling with the supply of journalists always desperate enough to undercut each other, like 27 per cent of journalists[514] Francesca is taking on a range of jobs that might be closer to the service class. She is doing some translating, invigilating exams, tutoring students again and working on the fringes of education. It is not that Francesca was now a poor journalist, far from it. It is just that most journalists are poor, now.

It is all part of London's story and the class struggle that propels the London dream, where the aspirant fantasies of Londoners feed into an economic system they have no choice but to join. And, as much as London has changed, this dynamic has stayed the same. London is a city constantly being transformed.

New residents, new business, new events and new crises. Industrial economy, post-industrial economy. Warehouse of empire, cultural hub of the world. These changes, however, mask the city's consistency. London has always been the place to be and a place of struggle. Nothing exemplifies this consistent duality like the plight of the city's literary aspirants.

Grubby Dreams

London has long had a mythological status for those with literary pretensions. Rightfully so. 'As a centre of intellectual production,' Jerry White writes, 'London's position in the English-speaking world was scarcely less pivotal than its role as world finance capital.'[515] Slightly less profitable, however, which is a shame for us Londoners with dreams of making a living from pen and paper, fingertips and keyboards.

Like most industries in London, the manufacturing of words was tightly clustered. Book publishing centred around Paternoster Row just North of St Paul's, flourishing from the beginning of the eighteenth century. For journalists, Fleet Street was the place to be. No industry as precarious as journalism could last in central London, however. After *News International* moved out in the 1980s others slowly followed and the last reporters moved out in 2016. Still, Fleet Street remains a metonym for the British press and, as we have seen, London remains at the core of London's literary culture.

London's newspaper industry expanded rapidly in the nineteenth century, flaunting the city's reputation as the intellectual centre of the empire. London was the hub of communication technologies, from the ports, to the railroads and the telegraph, which ensured that news flowed out from London and, as a result, flowed into London first[516].

Publications from every angle and for every interest were produced, although duties often kept them out of the hands of London's working classes and thus restricted the development of working-class publications and working-class consciousness. These 'taxes on knowledge' kept prices artificially high until 1861[517].

London's role at the centre of British intellectual culture is perhaps stronger now than during the Victorian era. As we have seen in everything from the great migration of students, to the rise of London's creative economy and its dominance of cultural production, London drains the brains from around the country. As Richard Florida insists, this clustering of talent is the key to its contemporary success.

Beyond its intellectual status, there is another Victorian dynamic that is being reproduced in twenty-first century London, one that Francesca found herself inadvertently thrust into. It is the simultaneous fantasy of a literary London life and the precarity of this existence. Victorian London may have been the capital of literary production but that was no guarantee of individual success. Instead, as White writes, 'The difficulties of writing for a living in London were notorious[518].'

And, if Fleet Street was the home of literary glamour, Grub Street was the sanctuary of the 'hack writer' (driven as hard as the horse pulling a hackney carriage). Once the home of Samuel Johnston, this Moorgate street – renamed Milton Street and largely swallowed up by the Barbican – played host to the fringes of literary society. It was as bohemian as it was impoverished and ambitious.

Beyond the hacks on Grub Street, writing was a pursuit for those who survived on service jobs of the time, from tradesman to clerks, and those trapped by professions and traditions. For educated women like George Eliot, for instance, writing was a way out of the binds of the era. Writing offered the same salvation for those destined to a career in the civil service[519].

The supply of these dreamers and their resistance to economic rationality meant that competition was fierce. White's reading of Victorian conditions resonates today:

As for other London industries, poor reward had much to do with an overstocked labour market in a low-wage economy...attracted to it a middle-class reserve army of labour whose education and literacy seemed to offer the possibility of earning easy money – even fame – by writing. Yet despite the every-spreading shelves of print, there were always more writers than columns to fill.[520]

'But still', writes White, 'they came.'

This is the story of London, one as relevant in Victorian London as in today's creative economy. The best interpreter of the class struggle within the London dream is Marx.

A Theory of the Exploitation of the Creative Classes

Grub Street writers, along with Francesca and today's literary dreamers, do not suffer these indignities because of the quality of the work. Not necessarily at least. Instead, the supply of writers means that editors can reduce rates to a level where they will still continue to receive quality submissions. If people will write for free, that does not leave much room for manoeuvre. To be sure, top talent and identifiable names that draw clicks and scrolls will still get top rates. The rest of us compete for scraps[521]. For Marx, this is the elementary logic of capitalism, whether we are talking dockers, sweatshop workers or copywriters.

Marx argued that workers are only able to be exploited because of the uneven relationship between employers and employees, capital and labour. This relationship is predicated on the vast majority of the population who do not have the means to reproduce their lives without selling their labour power[522]. To put it in more practical terms, only a small percentage of Londoners are able to exist through rents, profits and investments. Fewer still live off their land. The rest have to work to make a living.

Here the origins of the word 'proletariat', or Marx's working class, provide welcome context. In ancient societies, proletarians were the lowest class of citizens who, unable to provide property for the state, contributed by providing progeny; the proletariat were those who literally had nothing to give but bodies for the state[523]. So it is for the worker, in both nineteenth and twenty-first century London, who is forced to sell their labour because they have no other means of reproducing themselves.

Moreover, people without the means to reproduce themselves independently are not only compelled to work. They are disciplined to accept conditions offered by employers because there are more potential workers than jobs. That is, for the capitalist wage system to operate efficiently, an excess of workers must exist such that the threat of losing one's job remains; workers must *want* to be exploited as the employee generally benefits more from employment than the employer.

In Victorian London – and today's developing world – an unemployed worker risked starvation, and ultimately death, while their employer can easily replace the worker[524]. In twenty-first century London the consequences of unemployment might not be so drastic, but the logic remains the same: only the most talented employees are irreplaceable.

As Jack London astutely observed when discussing competition for work and the consequent cutting of wages in 1902, 'sweating, starvation wages, armies of unemployed, and great numbers of the homeless and shelterless are inevitable when there are more to do work than there is work for men to do'[525]. As a consequence, there is a 'sifting-out process' in which 'the least efficient must descend to the very bottom, which is the shambles wherein they perish miserably'[526]. 'It must be understood', London is at pains to say, 'that efficiency is not determined by the workers themselves, but is determined by the demand for labour.'[527] And, he might have added, the supply. And that is where the London dream, and the dream for a better life embodied by migrants around the world, fits into this story.

This logic was most starkly displayed in the banner the *New York Times* found on the walls of a Foxconn factory making iPhones in China, 'Work hard on the job today or work hard to find a job tomorrow.'[528] And yet, stories emerged of long lines of keen job applicants outside of Foxconn plants[529]. This was cited as evidence that Western critics of Chinese manufacturing were misguided; the Chinese people *wanted* these jobs. It is better evidence that people will do whatever they can to better their lives, and profit-minded employers will do everything they can to exploit this vulnerability.

The desire to move away from rural communities in search of hard toil and mental degradation reveals the axis around which capitalism, and London's economy, turns; people want, or rather need, to be exploited. In a world of seemingly inexhaustible cheap labour, there is always someone willing to bear the conditions you cannot. As Emily found, there are always other precarious academics looking for teaching work. Mandla just had to look around at one of his survival jobs to find others looking for gigs. Francesca is being forced out by newcomers compelled to write for nothing.

Marx argued that these replacements form a:

> *disposable industrial reserve army, that belongs to capital quite as absolutely as if the latter had bred it at its own cost. Independently of the limits of the actual increase of population, it creates, for the changing needs of the self-expansion of capital, a mass of human material always ready for exploitation.*[530]

This industrial reserve army becomes, in Marx's terms, the 'lever of capitalistic accumulation, nay, a condition of existence of the capitalist mode of production'[531]. As a consequence, Marx argues, the reserve army of labour is the '...pivot upon which the law of demand and supply of labour works'[532].

Thus, those not being employed within a given field but still searching for work there have a vital economic function. By being excluded from the industry and yet standing as potential workers, they compel employees to accept and endure conditions they are presented with. That was Aidan's experience at his first café. Paul and Mandla rarely have the opportunity to consider their wages when looking for work, at least not at their creative jobs. For Francesca, increasingly, the options are working for free or working elsewhere.

Moreover, as these creative Londoners' experiences illustrate, today's reserve army of labour is not lining up at a Job Centre. This surplus population is working, desperate to be exploited in a more interesting and personally profitable way. These new workers are on zero-hours contracts in cafes, bars and hotels. They are delivering food to weary professionals and workplaces, sent by companies unburdened by the minimum wage. Like Hannah and Emily, they are being recruited for short-term administrative roles while actively searching for a cultural industry job. Even in this promised land, it is a lucky worker who starts on more than the London Living Wage.

And so, even though more Londoners are employed than ever[533], of the 872,000 jobs added to the London labour market from 2012 to 2014, 95 per cent paid less than the London Living Wage[534]. This is London's reserve army of labour, working at survival jobs and hoping for an opportunity to live their dreams.

And still, they come. The city they are coming to returning to its Victorian roots.

Section 4

Serving the City

Chapter 15

Servicing the City

London receives 19 million foreign tourists every year[535]. A quick glance at the popular pop-up maps of the city reveals that the London they seek is a product of Victorian imaginations.

Sure, we can find some of the old (Westminster Abbey, 1080, 1.2 million visits[536]) and the new (*Coca-Cola* London Eye, 2000, 3.5 million visits), but most of London's iconic sites were either constructed or repurposed during the Victorian era.

The Tower of London might have been built by William the Conqueror in 1066 to keep an eye on the City of London but it is the restored nineteenth-century version that draws 2.7 million tourists each year. The Palace of Westminster has its origins in the eleventh century but was rebuilt in the Gothic Revival style after the fire of 1834. Likewise, Buckingham Palace was substantially expanded and put into official use by Queen Victoria at the start of her reign in 1837. Trafalgar Square opened to the public in 1844 and construction started on Tower Bridge in 1886.

The centre of all pop-out maps, the Elizabeth Tower *qua* Big Ben, was completed in 1859. Even the British Museum, an eighteenth-century invention, expanded significantly with the growing British empire during the nineteenth century.

The heart of contemporary Victorian London is the area in South Kensington known as Albertopolis. Founded by the proceeds from the Great Exhibition[537], the cultural institutions of Albertopolis are the defining legacy of Victorian refinement. From the Natural History Museum (1873), the Royal Albert Hall (1871), Imperial College (1888) and the Royal College of Music (1882), Albertopolis showcases an era of ambition and of advancement.

These values are quite literally inscribed in the Victoria and

Albert Museum, where the figures of Inspiration and Knowledge are carved into the niches of the façade of what Londoners now call the V&A. Imagined as the Museum of Manufactures in 1852, the V&A came into existence when the first stone was laid at its current South Kensington site by Queen Victoria in 1899. Here, in her last public appearance, Victoria articulated the defining aspiration of her reign, 'I trust that it will remain for ages a Monument of discerning Liberality and a Source of Refinement and Progress.'[538]

Like many Londoners, the basic fabric of my London life is Victorian, although it is not very refined and does not always feel like it is progressing particularly fast. Like all Londoners, my life is increasingly captured by the urban dynamics provoked by the Victorians and the first iteration of metropolitan capitalism. From intensive infrastructure projects to great accumulations of wealth and misery, both Victorian and twenty-first century London have captured the imagination of those seeking a better life and hurled around those already eking out a London existence.

I live in the Borough of Ealing, the Victorian 'Queen of Suburbs'. Ealing owes its existence to the rise of the Great Western Railway, which reached its previously pastoral fringes in 1838. The rise of suburbs like Ealing allowed a new middle class to escape the anxiety of the city. This would not last long. Once London's population rose from one million in 1801 to nearly six million by the end of the century, London became a city characterised by the conglomeration of suburbs we know today. A conglomeration connected by an invention that captured the age: the railway.

Indeed, I moved to this suburban village because I was able to catch the Great Western Railway in the direction of Brunel University, named with unearned ambition after the great Victorian inventor Isambard Kingdom Brunel. When my life took a turn for the better and I obtained a job in Holborn, I was able to transport myself by squeezing onto the tube in Zone 3.

The tube, which was the world's first underground metro system when it opened in 1863, is very much a product of the Victorian imagination. Like many of these products, it sought to create order out of the chaos of this new form of human existence, connecting Londoners thrown together with an intensity and inequity never seen before. These compressed disparities were reproduced within suburban homes across Victorian London.

I live in the servant's area of a Victorian mansion, now deemed a 'Garden Flat' in equal parts aspiration and desperation[539]. The presence of servant specific areas is common to Georgian and Victorian-era housing, such was the ubiquity of servants in upper and middle-class homes and the desire to keep these servants in their place. I try not to be bitter about my desk being shifted to the servant's quarters in the attic of the Bloomsbury Georgian building that houses my university[540].

This fashion for domestic servants facilitated, and was facilitated by, the flow of young women into the city in search of improved prospects. Employing servants was a sign of social mobility and the evidence of middle-class mores[541], an overt display of privilege similar to that enjoyed by the rising middle class of the developing world[542]. This fashion facilitated, and was facilitated by, the flow of young women into the city in search of improved prospects; three-quarters of all young women in early-modern London were new migrants[543]. The 'Juvenile Transference Schemes' of the late 1920s, which encouraged boys and girls to move from depressed provincial areas to find employment, provided so many young women to be domestic servants that it was called the 'white slave trade'[544]. Today, many Filipino girls have similar experiences in London.

In 1796 there were reported to be 200,000 servants in London[545]. That one-fifth of Londoners worked in service tells us much about the early-modern city, the availability of labour, the pull of city life, and the push towards waged labour. Even the impoverished Marxes had a maid.

Like many of the dynamics of the Victorian era, however, domestic service has returned to the forefront of London life. Just as with the early-modern metropolis, this dynamic has been propelled by a migrant-fuelled population boom and an increased wage inequality. The potential domestic workers are still predominately young women and are still exceptionally vulnerable to exploitation.

This time, however, the supplying provinces of these young women are not limited to middle-England. Instead, the latent workforce is called up from Eastern Europe, Latin America (via South Europe) and South East Asia. Since the enlargement of the EU to include eight Eastern European (EU8) countries in 2004, employment in 'Personal Service Occupations' has more than doubled in London[546].

Many are accommodated in the servants' quarters of the Knightsbridge or Mayfair mansions of London's new elite, where there are more servants now than in 1790[547]. Some of these servants, often from the Philippines, India or Indonesia, struggle in a state of semi-slavery, attached to wealthy families who trap them in iceberg homes by confiscating their passports and ensuring they have no other means of subsistence[548].

Live-in cleaners are relatively rare, however, particularly given that the size of the average London household has fallen from 5.8 in 1842 to 1.9 in 2013[549]. Instead, different forms of exploitative service work have emerged. Organisations across London outsource their cleaning operations to private companies in order to avoid providing institutionally guaranteed benefits[550]. Many domestic workers have even less security, subsiding as self-employed contractors or agency workers at the sharp end of London's gig economy. They still work in middle-class suburban homes, as well as London's offices, but they are never accommodated for more than a few hours at a time. Instead, they scurry from job to job, trapped by language limitations and competition from other provincial girls that push earnings well below the London Living Wage. Or the national minimum wage[551].

These cleaners exist as a precarious labour force only because there are so many of them available. London's middle-classes may struggle to save for a house, but hiring a cleaner once a week (often informally) is common practice for young Londoners. Especially those in house shares[552]. Hoovering rented carpets is not part of the millennial fantasy of London life, nor is mediating multi-lingual arguments about who cleaned the toilet last. Menial labour is something to be done by someone else, at least at home. Or it is something to be confined to the past. It is a past rapidly coming to the fore.

Contemporary imaginations of Victorian London do not shy away from the misery of the era. Dickens and Jack the Ripper are as much a part of the story of Victorian London as the tube and London's museums. This story, however, is framed as evidence of progress. London was once a city of slums and child paupers, but that is only something that happens over *there* now.

It is easy to agree. The worst excesses of Victorian London, whether disease and blood sports or child labour and the workhouse, are no longer a feature of London life. And yet, the boom of twenty-first century London – both in population and wealth – has brought references to Victorian inequality to the surface[553].

Hiring a cleaner from an app was entirely unthinkable for the Victorians. That the middle classes believe that engaging a migrant cleaner is an affordable alternative to doing their own chores is a very Victorian dynamic.

These migrant service workers are part of the new working class. The demographics of this class may have changed but its role has not. The vulnerability of the working classes is necessary for a cool version of capitalism to function as much as vulgar industrial iteration. Once again, civility and misery are a couplet. They never really split.

This story is the story of the London dream. It is one personified by the indomitable Daniel.

'I Heard that London Was a Place of Opportunities'

Daniel didn't turn up for our first interview. I receive an apology email later that morning; he had been mugged by three men in Brixton the previous evening and had been unable to get in contact with me. He was at work now, though, did I still want to meet?

There is no keeping Daniel down.

Later that week we arrange to meet outside of Warren Street Station. As ever, my anxiety makes me early and I'm enveloped in the hubbub of London's morning commuters. A dishevelled homeless man, reeking of alcohol past and present, has forgotten that I gave him change five requests and 10 minutes ago when Daniel approaches me with the briskness of a man on the move. Collared shirt, immaculate appearance. This was not the office cleaner I had imagined.

Originally from Ecuador, Daniel's family had moved to Spain when he was five. He finished high school in 2009 at the height of the Great Financial Crisis, a time when Spain's youth unemployment was at 40 per cent and rising[554]. His hopes of finding work as an electrician were going nowhere.

London and a good friend with a couch offered a solution. His friend had been working in London's massive cleaning industry and had returned to Spain for Christmas. He was insistent: the only way to escape his situation was to move to London. One week later, Daniel was on his way. When he arrived in 2010, there were 25,000 Spaniards reported to be in London. By 2016 that number was 79,000[555]. Many are following Daniel's difficult path from exclusion and unemployment at home to marginalisation and exploitation in London. And from despair to draining hope.

Daniel's English was limited to 'the basic hello, goodbye and the numbers' and he was soon sleeping on another friend's sofa. Still, he had hope. He got a job working for a cleaning company through his South American connections because, in his words, 'cleaning [in London] is about South Americans'. He is right, to a degree[556]. London's cleaning industry tends to be divided into Africans, East Europeans and South Americans, often coming in through the EU. Each has their own cultural networks through which employment is exchanged, creating whole cleaning 'teams' of the same nationality[557]. It might be of a different kind but social capital is as important in the service classes as their creative counterparts. Indeed, when you are working on the margins of formal employment, connnections are everything.

His cultural connections gave Daniel a start, but it was only 2 hours on Friday, Saturdays and Sunday night and he only got the job because no one else wanted it. Most likely because his employer was able to get away with paying him only £3.50 per hour because Daniel was under 21 at the time.

Like so many migrants to London, he was at the bottom of the chain. This only spurred him on:

...it gave me some energy, to say well this is not going to be forever, I want to live here, this is the way to live here. So, I couldn't...well, I was not complaining at all, because you have to survive. I have to do any type of job.

He was quite literally on the move through this precarious industry, working two, three, even four jobs at once, each shift only a few hours at a time. To be one of the 91,000 cleaners in London[558], Daniel states matter-of-factly, 'is just to keep running'. As soon as he finished one job, 'I used to run another job...From one side to another building and then get ready to go home and sleep a little bit and wake up in the early morning.'

Each job was only temporary for employer and employee alike. Daniel was not only prepared to endure this fluidity but use it to

his advantage. With knowing determination he tells me that '…
in this city, industry, you are not permanent. If something better
comes, you get offered 5p, 10p more yes you leave…I have changed
several times. So, I always improve on where I used to be.'

This was the definition of precarious work; zero-hours
contracts dependent upon maintaining a productive relationship
with his manager. This was a life where there was always a sense
that you were one shift away from not having any more shifts.
A life where you are entirely disposable so that, 'even if you
don't feel well one day and you call them, saying that they'll say
there are other who doesn't feel well too and they still come into
work'.

This life was a battle.

With managers to make sure that your holidays are paid and
that every hour worked was accounted for.

With London to get around the city, to find a place to rest
between shifts and to find somewhere to call home. And with
other cleaners for more security. When I ask if cleaners are pitted
against each other, he leans in and informs me that:

> *For a full-time job, yeah, it is a competition always. You have to
> find the key person, but always there is someone who knows about
> jobs. So, in terms of full-time there is competition and there are bad
> feelings too, you know. There are some people who are jealous of you
> and they try to mess [what you are cleaning] up.*

But £3.50 became £5.90. Irregular shifts became a thing of the
past, although he was still one of 76 per cent of cleaners earning
less than the London Living Wage[559]. Daniel's employers were
pleased with his work ethic and he progressed to be a supervisor.
And then a manager. Soon enough he was managing 55 sites.

But it was all too much. London is sometimes. He sighs

> *I just did that one job for one year and then I did my resignation,*

because of pressure from the clients, from my bosses, pressure from my head office too and it was too much for me. I had to run from here to there and give up...and if the cleaner doesn't want to do the job, I had to go out and meeting with them and sort out their problems. If they don't do a good job, I have a phone call from my client and then another phone call from my operation manager. I tried to know what's the problem. They said the job was from Monday to Friday, but I used to work from Monday to Sunday, so it was really, really hard and people think because you are wearing a suit, you have a nice job, but no. I prefer to be honest, when I resigned, I asked my previous manager, give me any type of cleaning job, I don't have to have any responsibilities- I'd reached that point where I was so stressed I said no, enough is enough. I don't want to wear out.

Even still, the future remains bright. He is still a site-manager and still looking up, starting a course in management when the next semester rolls around. Sat here in this homogenised chain coffee shop, well-presented and anxious to get moving, he looks every bit the Londoner.

Does he feel like one?

Yeah, I feel like it. I haven't had this feeling in any other countries when I travel around the world. I have been to Africa, I have been to North America, South America, Europe, many countries and London is like, they open the door. It doesn't matter who you are or where you come from. So, I feel very welcome in this city. I came here only to work and I don't want to go back to Spain right now, maybe in the future.

Daniel's toil has been made tolerable by the dream of a different life; both that he was going places in London and that a precarious life in London was better than a life back home. It is this dream, a specifically London dream, that has motivated Londoners for centuries. The hope and struggle for a better life has also maintained a healthy supply of human material ripe for exploitation by the city's employers.

And it is this that I cannot escape from my meeting with Daniel. His admirable struggle through adversity is finally starting to work out for him, but it bore fruit for his employers a long time ago.

Daniel suffered such exploitation because of the presence of so many like him, willed and willing participants engaged in 'the riot, the struggle, and the scramble for a living' [560]. The addition of aspiring and perspiring bodies to the maelstrom of the city's labour force is the fuel that lights the fire of capital and the deadweight that dampens the dreams of its present population.

This is neither Daniel's fault nor his folly. It is not the responsibility of migrants like him arriving in wealthier economies in search of a better life – it *never* is. It is the very stuff of capitalism and the contradiction in London's economy that continues to propel it: as London grows wealthier and the opportunities for consumption grow more diverse and plentiful, the toil and misery of the Londoners who reproduce it persists. If part of the London dream is a city of unlimited possibilities for adventure, culture and pleasure, these possibilities are serviced by those in search of the same dream but living a London nightmare.

It is not only in the cleaning industry that we come across such stories of hope and exploitation. A Victorian logic of labour abounds in London's service industries. Daniel would no doubt have stories to share with Abeo about agency work, even if Abeo's life in security is far less mobile.

Security and War

Abeo stares through me, my question left hanging in our tense office air. His eyes return to mine and the forced smile that has occupied his face slides away.

It's war

Nigerian born but proudly South London raised, Abeo is a seasoned soldier.

For 35-hours-a-week, but only for a few hours at a time, he inhabits someone else's chair in this university building in Bloomsbury, his shaven head and stoic eyes offering a fleeting image of pride to a city that is indifferent to his plight and yet reliant on his presence.

Offices like this across London do not open without security guards like Abeo. They use his physical presence to inspire a sense of security during the day and to turn the lights off at night. Few of the workers and students progressing to the floors above return his cursory greetings.

This is the first time I have spoken to Abeo about anything other than football, which I know nothing about, and the office air-conditioning, of which I know even less. I wonder what happened to Imran, the Pakistani guard with whom I bonded over cricket.

Abeo's invisibility should not be surprising, nor should it be wholly attributed to the callousness of my colleagues, if only because we are not really his colleagues. Instead, Abeo is employed by a contractor that deploys his labour to organisations across London on a flexible basis, a flexibility it passes on to Abeo. Like 118,000 other Londoners[561], his 'zero-hours' contract means that the agency has no obligation to provide him with work or the kind of rights that those anonymous employees take for granted.

One off day, one bad decision and Abeo is gone.

One day off sick and Abeo doesn't get paid.

His eyes narrow at the thought, the grey tufts in his fledgeling goatee hinting at the strain.

It's an exploitation. It's an exploitation. It gives them the power to

*get rid of you. You can't claim for sick benefit, you can't claim for
holiday. It's just an exploitation of staff...All of them are exploiters.
The contract they have with the organisation is not what they give
you...some agencies charge £20 an hour for their staff, but they give
you £8.*

The door buzzes. Abeo holds my gaze and leans over to push the
button that grants entrance to the building. The manner of his
resignation is effortless.

*You are programmed like a robot...working, working, working.
Because London is an expensive city to live in.*

His employer is part of the UK's booming £9 billion security
industry[562], an industry forged in a climate of fear and a sea
of unskilled labour. It is the latter that has allowed the likes of
G4S, the UK's largest security provider, to turnover £7.59 billion
in 2016[563], seemingly unaffected by a series of high-profile
scandals[564]. The fruits of its incredible profitability are probably
less apparent to its army of workers on zero-hours contracts,
much as the benefits of the FTSE 100 reaching record highs in
2017[565] must seem alien to the 20 per cent of working Londoners
earning less than the living wage[566].

This is the war that Abeo faces. But this is not the side he
wants to be on.

His toil is made tolerable by the dream of a different life. It
is this dream, a specifically London dream, that has motivated
Londoners, old and new, for centuries. The hope and struggle
for a better life has also maintained a healthy supply of human
material for the city's employers.

Today, Abeo's desk is the home of a full-time receptionist.
Alongside her to-do lists and family photos lie his well-worn
textbooks. Abeo is studying full-time for a degree in Operations
Management. He tells me with some animation that:

A man with no educational background is nothing. If you want to go into business you need a certificate. I want to go into business...if you are working on your own you have the power to do what you like.

It is this power that is lacking in Abeo's life. Like so many before him, Abeo is at the mercy of the city, of its employers, of its landlords and of the indifference of those within the properties he nominally protects.

Would he live anywhere else?

Not really, nah can't. I can only live in the city...

By the time I have written up our conversation, another body fills the reception chair. Abeo's absence goes unremarked.

Daniel's and Abeo's war stories, like most war stories, are both personally unique and socially clichéd. All across London migrants toil in industries seldom seen by those on the cooler end of the economy. The stories of those servicing London are as much a part of the city as those in public relations or film. They dream of better lives but find themselves struggling to service and secure the lives of other Londoners chasing their dreams.

And still, they come. Being exploited in London is better than not being exploited and not being in London. Although some gig workers would be forgiven for questioning this wisdom.

Chapter 16

London's New Paupers

0013: Uber from Roundhouse in Camden to our place just East of London Fields, £17. Not bad. A few clicks of the app and a driver was there in 3 minutes. Four cabs were circling and he seemed glad for the work. Five stars all around. Does anyone under 40 take a black cab anymore? Maybe bankers and tourists.

1017: Amazon delivery from some guy in a white van. He left quick. It's a desperately needed phone charger. Thank god for Prime.

1330: Shuffle off to the jazz festival at Victoria Park. That's what I love about London; there is always something to do, even if you don't want to do it. It's heaving. There are white-shirted staff everywhere in the marque. The one who empties out the £6 wine into a plastic cup looks a long way away.

1542: ASOS delivery. Three tops. None fit. They will have to go back.

1905: Deliveroo. Massaman Curry and Pad Thai. The usual. £3.29 is a small price to pay for not having to leave the house. The 30 minutes wait is fine for a Sunday night too.

2129: Another delivery. What is it this time and who delivers at this time of night?

Living the dream. Monday, the tube to Oxford Circus and two buzzing monitors can wait.

* * *

0010: Another ride is available. At least they are going a decent distance this time. The last four were under £10 but I only find out where they are going when I'm at the pickup point. Anyway, they had to be accepted, otherwise there is a risk of losing potential fares. Even if Uber has got softer after they were banned by TfL.

It's an easy pickup and they don't look like they will be sick in the car. It took a long time for Uber to cover it last time. If only you could just call someone.

The black cab drivers look miffed as my Prius glides away. Why? They might have taken The Knowledge, but Waze has just as much information and I didn't have to spend years learning how to use it. Anyway, I have a degree in engineering but no one would hire someone with my name. All I needed to get going with Uber was to pass the most basic of tests to get my commercial licence and a car lease. I work my own hours. It's just that there are so many of us competing for the same jobs. Most days it's a battle to earn a living wage. I have to drive 7 days a week to survive sometimes. And Uber could always cut me off. I'd go somewhere else but no private hire company can compete with them.

If I can stay up for an hour when I get home, I might be able to make breakfast for the girls.

1016: Where is this house? Three knocks, sign here. Another 69p earned. Fifty packages to go.

1331: Who pays £6 for wine in a plastic cup? I'm getting £7.83 per hour. Exactly. At least this work is easy to get. I just signed up on the app, proved that I could work in this country and now I can select the gigs I want. I just have to get here early to make sure they don't send me away. Seven hours to go, as long as clean up doesn't take that long. Then two buses and I'm home.

If I can find work on 6 days next week I can save some money. Then I might be able to go home and start my life again. Unless they kick us out first.

1542: I'm sure I've been here before. They take a long time to answer the door. I was about to leave the parcel on the doorstep. Don't they know I've got work to do?

1845: The Thai place. Always popular on a Sunday night.

There are five of us here, all familiar faces and familiar helmets. The uniform of the rider, the dudes, the pirates of the streets. One of these idiots doesn't even have a proper thermal bag. He is going to get complaints.

They are taking ages tonight but there is nothing I can do but wait. I get about £4.50 per delivery and these are my peak earning hours. Waiting time gets me nothing. When the flimsy plastic bags arrive, I weave through the streets, only to get to the place and not be able to find the flat. Why don't London houses have clear numbers? It's impossible in the dark. They seem happy to see me, though. Their eyes go to the bags rather than my eyes. No tip. Back to the bike. Only a couple of hours until the orders stop coming in. Tomorrow it is back to the café for my 7-11 shift.

2130: Just made the delivery in time. After 12 hours, I'm done. I could really have done with the day off today because my wife is ill and the kids are a handful, but if I called in sick I would have lost my route, possibly forever. So much for being self-employed. There has to be a better way than this.

Just another Sunday of London dreams. They are Victorian dreams in the twenty-first-century capital.

The New Paupers

When then Labour Party MP Frank Field and his senior researcher Andrew Forsey published their report into Uber and the gig economy in 2016, they did not hold back. In *Sweated Labour: Uber and the Gig Economy*[567], the authors state that:

> there is a sizeable group of people who bear the largely unseen human scars of the 'gig economy'. They are the hidden army who, despite being classed as self-employed, work very long hours, often with one particular company, in return for chronically low rates of pay. Moreover, they do so without the right to paid leave, to the National Living Wage, and to challenge an unfair dismissal, for example,

which are among the protections granted to workers and employees.

These conditions, they argue, 'bear a close resemblance with what the Victorians would have called "sweated labour"', which an 1890 House of Lords Select Committee defined as:

when earnings were barely sufficient to sustain existence; hours of labour were such as to make the lives of the workers periods of almost ceaseless toil; and conditions were injurious to the health of the workers and dangerous to the public[568].

This description applies to twenty-first century Uber drivers and Deliveroo riders as much as Victorian dockers and garment manufacturers. It is the logic of the twenty-first century gig economy, where companies have been enabled to use people on a short-term, freelance and temporary basis. Unsurprisingly, businesses in London benefit more from this system than the contractors they engage, even if these contractors need the work more than the companies need them.

Field and Forsey reported that some Uber drivers in London are earning as little as £2 per hour and are finding it increasingly difficult to find fares, which forces them to work ever longer hours. One driver explained why this happens:

Drivers will carry on working at low rates due to desperation. Low fares and too many drivers mean drivers have to work longer hours which is not safe for the drivers and [the] customers. [Uber have] flooded [the] market with drivers. My [earnings have] halved over [the] last 2 years.

It is not that Uber is a bad employer. Uber drivers are not technically employed. Like many gig economy companies, they classify their workers as self-employed, thus avoiding having to pay the minimum wage and offer basic employment rights.

Once again, these are very Victorian conditions. The experience of the poor in Victorian London was not one of formal employment contracts and enforced rights. Indeed, the very idea of 'employment' only came into usage in the nineteenth century[569]. Instead of formal employment contracts, many labourers were engaged on a temporary basis for days or hours at a time with minimum rights and maximum insecurity.

Of the 22,000 dock labourers recorded in the 1901 census, for example, only 8,500 were permanent hands[570]. The others were casuals who would have been employed for half a year on average, working through a 'call on' system of causal work. Potential workers would arrive early in the morning and hang around till the 'Calling Foreman' would ring the call-on bell, which happened twice a day. Lining up behind a fence to be chosen for work, often in gangs, workers would only be selected at this 'call on'. If they worked, they could eat. If they did not, they would have to work harder to find a gig tomorrow or risk going down the dreaded workhouse. Looking at the surpluses trudging away behind the fences, those who were lucky could certainly not afford to slack or to struggle.

Today, such a system would be seen as barbaric. The call-on bell has been replaced by the chime of a phone notification and the clamouring masses have become regulated by apps and algorithms. Anyone organising an Uber journey and seeing a flotilla of available riders, or walking past a gang of Deliveroo drivers waiting in a central London motorcycle bay, can bear witness to the logic of the Victorian docks at work today.

But there is a major difference. Although twenty-first century sweated labour has become cleaner, no Victorian employer would try to sell the benefits of insecure work. London's gig economy companies have less shame, instead promoting the benefits of flexibility, freedom and control. Uber, for example, invites you to, 'Only drive when it works for you. There's no office and no boss. That means you'll always start and stop on your time—because with Uber, you're in charge.'[571]

Gig economy contractors mostly speak of stress and insecurity. And a little shame. One Uber driver told Field and Forsey that:

> *We are pushed to do more hours a week [because] we don't make enough money to support ourselves. When I take the cost of expenses I am hardly left with £150 in my pocket for 60 hours which is way below minimum wage. My livelihood is my job. I support my family through this work. Uber has created the circumstances in which one can't survive*[572].

'Confronted with such evidence,' Field and Forsey ask, 'why do the drivers not seek higher earnings by working with another company?' The answer is that the drivers have few other options, especially as Uber is wiping out its competitors by lowering fares.

This is what I found when my journey into the world of Uber began in April 2019. Before then I had scrupulously avoided Uber, save for a few late-night journeys home with friends. In April, however, came the birth of my twin boys and regular trips back and forth from the suburban West London hospital. There are no black cabs waiting outside the hospital at 3am. The tube is not an option that early on a Tuesday morning. The two buses necessary to get home are not a practical alternative for a sleep deprived new father ferrying a family's worth of clothing and kit.

Uber it was, night after night, morning after morning, while my wife and new family recovered. During these rides I received a personal tutorial in Uber's role in the London dream. Drivers told me of their families, of their hopes and of their frustrations with Uber. There was the 6am Sunday pickup who was trying to make £60 for the day before he re-joined his family. There was the 2am ride who hated Sadiq Khan. There was the midday pickup who gave me his web design business card; he was taking a break while business was slow.

These drivers rallied against black cabs and any attempt to regulate their work. They were frustrated by the new congestion charge, from which those 'actively licensed with London Taxi and Private Hire'[573] are exempt. One driver told me that he would refuse fares when he found out they were going through central London, even if he was penalised by Uber. Overwhelmingly, though, these drivers wanted to tell me of their future plans and how they were using Uber to make their way in London. These drivers were living their version of the London dream. But their willingness to endure the conditions imposed by Uber should not be seen as a validation of the company. Instead, it shows the lack of options for those making their way in the city.

Of course, the drivers could search for other work. But the reason so many turn to Uber in the first place is the barriers they face in the formal labour market. Only 6 per cent of Uber drivers identify as White British[574] (compared to two-thirds of black cab drivers) and are often new migrants who face considerable difficulties gaining formal employment. Many of the most vulnerable Londoners have caring responsibilities that restrict the hours they can work. For them, Uber offers the opportunity to control their destiny and chase their London dream.

Driving has long been the work of choice for those Londoners with no other option. London, this vast and unplanned city, has always needed a skilled transportation industry to distribute goods from ports and people across the metropolis. In 1901, there were 120,000 road transport workers, with 68,000 of them carmen and carters[575]. Their lives were not easy. As Jerry White states, 'Hours were long – ninety-six a week not uncommon – and pay was low.'[576] In his 1890 *Life and Labour of the People in London*, Charles Booth reports that there 'is perhaps no man's employment which yields so small a return per hour' and 'Of men of this class there is always a surplus in London.'[577] And so it is today, where surpluses of potential workers enable the precarious self-employment that rules London's transportation industries, whether by Uber (and Uber Eats), Deliveroo, Hermes or the overabundance of smaller companies that avoid the scrutiny of the big players.

London's reliance on this surplus of labour was clear in reactions to TfL's 2017 refusal to grant Uber a licence to operate in the city. The Mayor supported the decision and black cab drivers celebrated. Consumers were annoyed. Responses to the ban included tweets bemoaning that 'London life just got even more expensive', 'Great, back to the rip off black cab monopoly, ill miss you uber if no one else will' and 'Banning @Uber because a few black cabs are stuck in the past is stupid. Black cabs cost way too much.'[578]

As I heard during my bleary-eyed rides through West London, it was the drivers who were most despairing, despite the conditions they endure. James Farrar, chair of the Independent Workers' Union of Great Britain's United Private Hire Drivers branch, stated that, 'This is a devastating blow for 30,000 Londoners who now face losing their job and being saddled with unmanageable vehicle-related debt.'[579] One London driver, on learning of the ban from a customer, 'finished the job and just pulled over to the side of the road to cry'. The driver, Zahra Bakkali who fled to London from Morocco in 1997, told the *Evening Standard*, 'I feel so proud of myself, driving a car; wearing exactly what I like to wear; making enough time and money to feed my children[580].'

But Uber refuses to die, overturning the TfL ban in the Court of Appeal in 2018[581]. Moreover, despite courts twice declaring that Uber must start formally employing its drivers, the company continues to appeal[582]. The gig economy will not go down quietly. It is certainly not only Uber who are at fault. London's courier and food delivery people also feel the pain of self-employment, and they are no less central to the propagation of the London dream.

Delivering the Goods

One of the core drivers of London's flat white economy is online shopping. Here technology and creativity combine to convince us to buy things online and to streamline the process. The army of foot soldiers required to deliver these products to the buyer – at least until Amazon's drones are perfected – are not quite as glamorous.

London might be the place to be, a place where there is always something to do, but that something is often staying at home while the world comes to us. But part of the consumer experience is getting what you want, now. It is no good having to wait for weeks, or even days, for items to be delivered. Our packages have to be delivered *now* and for as little as possible. And while we are at home too, please.

This is employment by consumer demand, but how these parcels arrive is not our business. It is not really the business of the company you bought the product from either. Instead, the foot soldiers are employed by sub-contractors such as Hermes, the subject of another Field and Forsey report, *Wild West Workplace*[583].

Field and Forsey took testimony from 78 of Hermes' 10,500 drivers and recorded stories of precarious lives, foodbank usage and suicidal thoughts. Some drivers reported being worse off after a day's work, despite Hermes' claim that drivers should be able to earn the equivalent of £9.80 per hour. Field and Forsey highlight one statement as exemplifying the concerns of the drivers:

A good many couriers are mothers who want work to fit in with childcare needs. Some are elderly people trying to supplement their meagre pensions, to keep the wolves from the door. Many of the couriers are vulnerable and desperate people who want to work and stay away from the need to rely on public funds to support them. But some couriers are so poorly paid and treated that they often have to visit food banks, just to feed their families. I'm living below the poverty line because of my crap wages. I'm given two hour bands to meet. What freedom have I got? I feel like I'm in a deep, dark corner.

These drivers are told they can work when they want. Just do not take too much time off. As one driver said:

I was told yesterday that I'd better not have too much time off when I said I was having a week off soon because 'they now have a load of Poles lined up that want work'.

Hermes' turnover increased from £261 million in 2011-12 to £442 million in 2014-15.

Life is not much easier for food delivery drivers, even if their working lives are a little more adventurous. Riders for companies like Deliveroo consider themselves to be the 'Pirates of the road', rebellious 'dudes', slipping their way through London's streets to make those extra deliveries[584]. Rider forums are full of screenshots of big days and big tips[585], and complaints about 'Frank', Deliveroo's 'super smart algorithm' that decides which rider to offer which order'[586].

Deliveroo was launched in London in February 2013, because founder Will Shu found it difficult to get restaurant quality food and 'made it his personal mission to bring great restaurants closer to their customers'. 'Customers', Deliveroo claims, 'are at the heart of everything we do.'[587] Those who do the deliveries certainly are not, despite claims of 'flexible work and competitive fees'.

In August 2016, riders conducted a one-day strike against a new pay plan, with some drivers carrying flags with 'Slaveroo'. At the same time, the government told Deliveroo that it must pay the minimum wage – unless it can prove that its riders are self-employed. It did, legally at least[588].

Now, 90 per cent of riders are paid per delivery. Only 15 per cent work solely for Deliveroo[589], both because work is confined to the meal-time rush and because fees are not high enough to compensate[590]. Although Deliveroo is starting to restrict the number of riders in certain areas, it is a regular London sight to see riders idling waiting in gangs. It is no wonder that there are regular rumours that food delivery drivers are delivering drugs as well as takeaways. London's poorest have always been its most entrepreneurial. On the streets of Victorian London, for example, as White reports, '...the great game of London life was played out, where brute strength was subservient to wit, quick-thinking, fast hands, a ready tongue and a sharp eye'[591].

These riders are also subject to some of the most vicious and Victorian crimes from moped gangs. In 2017, Deliveroo drivers refused to work in areas of London after acid attacks seemingly targeted at them. The attackers, often moped gangs, have become the Victorian pick-pockets of our time, stealing phones from unsuspecting Londoners. Marx would not have been surprised by this misery, although he did not foresee the shape it has taken.

London Stones

Marx had argued that capitalism forces a growing proportion to move from being self-employed and employers to selling their wage labour. Today, the new working classes are becoming immiserated not through employment but because they are again becoming micro-entrepreneurs, technically in control of their labour time. The self-employment of those who might have been unemployed also explains the paradox of the 2010s in London and in much of the developed world: if unemployment is falling, why is poverty so entrenched? From 2010 to 2016, Field and Forsey report, a third of those who have found new jobs are now self-employed[592].

These non-workers are a standard feature of capitalist economies. As Jack London states during his journey in the East End in 1902, with far more sympathy than the raw text implies:

*They are the stones the builder rejected. There is no place for them in
the social fabric, while all the forces of society drive them downward
till they perish. At the bottom of the Abyss they are feeble, besotted
and imbecile[593].*

In more recent years, with the emergence of immense urban
poverty in the developing world, sociologist Zygmunt Bauman
deemed such unfortunate souls to be the 'wasted lives' of global
capitalism[594]. More analytically, cultural historian Michael
Denning used the term 'Wageless Life' to describe those making
an improvised living outside of formal employment structures[595],
often those involved in the kind of street-selling and refuse
handling just described.

Today they are described as 'micro-entrepreneurs' by those
of today's sympathetic development theorists[596]. Just as tourists
visiting European cities are often confronted by migrants selling
trinkets, counterfeit luxury brands and umbrellas[597], Victorian
London had its costermongers, hawkers and pedlars along with
an infinite variety of other 'penny capitalists' lying outside of
wage labour[598]. Londoners searching through sites like jobtoday.
com would easily recognise these stresses.

It is, of course, much cleaner this time around. But
clean, cool and creative exploitation dreamt up on Silicon
Roundabout is still exploitation and it is no less precarious.
In London, consumption of cosmopolitan cool 'at one pole is,
therefore, at the same time accumulation of misery, agony of
toil, slavery, ignorance, brutality, mental degradation, at the
opposite pole'[599].

This is the London dream.

The Contradiction of Cool Capitalism, or the London Dream

The showpiece of the London dream is the mythology of a city
where there is always something to do. Gigs, games, exhibitions,

shows, root-top pop-ups and other vices: if you want to do it, London has it all. These are the cool experiences that propel the fantasy of urban life. But someone has to produce them.

And so, the dreams of London's creative classes are served by those labouring in menial service jobs, preparing, waiting, cleaning and guarding the city. These dreams are also delivered by those hustling for gigs on apps that send them across the streets of London, delivering meals, packages and passengers for a few pounds at a time. Uber, Deliveroo and the flocks of delivery drivers hurtling across London are wonderful, for consumers.

This is the contradiction of cool London: for you to be able to catch affordable taxis and get restaurant quality food brought to your door whenever you want it, someone has to be prepared to do it at a profitable price you can afford. And, for someone to be prepared to do it in spite of the precarious misery catalogued above, there must be others willing to replace them. For every Uber driver who says they just cannot continue, there are more joining every day. Workers in the gig economy may come and go at a remarkable rate but they are not in short enough supply that companies are compelled to improve their conditions to attract more applicants.

But the dreams of those who serve and deliver are as strong as London's flaunted and flaunting creatives. For the former, as for all of us Londoners, the city is the place to be. The place to be who you want to be and to chase excitement, opportunity and the possibility of prosperity.

And so, the consumer and the service provider, the coolest and the most miserable of Londoners have much in common. But not just their dreams. We are all at the mercy of London's employers who are able to take advantage of our willingness to endure the city for the idea of a different life. If you cannot keep up with the pace, there is always someone willing to replace you. Advertising designers and PeoplePerHour freelancers, academics and adjunct lecturers, film-makers and café workers are facing the same struggle as delivery drivers and those fruitlessly handing out *TimeOut* on street corners.

And so it should be no surprise that there are Londoners who have had enough. Some are leaving the city to establish little Londons in Brighton, Bristol or even Berlin. Many are heading back to the provinces because the city is no place for the littlest of Londoners. Others are going back to the continent because they do not feel welcome here. Some of the most precarious are standing and fighting, with a little Latin spirit.

Resistant Conclusions

Drums beat, flags are waved and Spanish flows out from megaphones. Horns fill the darkness and a mini carnival meets the streets outside of the Senate House gates. Protests outside London universities do not normally look like this. Sure, there is solidarity, humour and regular outbreaks of rhyming chants led by the least self-effacing, but even the most academic among us would not risk calling them a party.

Protests by the International Workers Union of Great Britain (IWGB) have a different flavour. Of course they do. The IWGB represents some of London's most precarious workers, most of them migrants and often from Latin America (via Southern Europe) or Africa. Formed in August 2012, it now consists of an eclectic set of semi-autonomous branches, including those representing couriers and delivery drivers, private hire drivers, foster carers, cleaners, security guards, game workers, electricians, and those working at the University of London (UoL).

The IWGB are representing London's new paupers, those most precarious in London's working classes. They are the Londoners you see camped out at the back of the bus, or asleep against the glass on the tube. They are the ones lurking upstairs at McDonald's between shifts. In *Capital*, Marx called them 'the lowest sediment of the relative surplus population'. Pauperism, Marx wrote:

is the hospital of the active labour-army and the dead weight of the industrial reserve army. Its production is included in that of the relative surplus population, its necessity in theirs; along with the surplus population, pauperism forms a condition of capitalist production, and of the capitalist development of wealth[600.]

While they might be a disposable surplus within London's capitalist economy, being taken into employment or self-employment when necessary and turfed out when times are tough, this is no comment on the value of these workers or the power of their dreams. It is because of the strength of their hopes for better lives, as well as the destitution forced upon them by what are apparently well-meaning organisations, that they fight so passionately for their rights. If this book has catalogued the link between the exploitation of service workers and the reproduction of cool London, the members who drive the IWGB are fighting back by bringing this contradiction onto London's streets.

The IWGB emerged out of one of the basic causes of exclusion and exploitation in modern London; few of London's cleaners speak English. Indeed, cleaning and behind the scenes roles in hospitality are one of the few (legal) jobs available to those without rudimentary English. Jason Moyer-Lee, a Spanish speaking American, had got in touch with cleaners and porters while completing his PhD at SOAS. After initially volunteering to translate for the mostly Latin American workers, as well as teaching English, Moyer-Lee became involved with Senate House's Unison branch[601]. He is now the general secretary of perhaps the most dynamic union in London.

Having started with a handful of members, IWGB's member-led approach, visibility and results have meant that membership has grown rapidly. For many Londoners, the union provided their first chance to have their voice heard. The IWGB now represents over 2,500 of the most vulnerable Londoners. They fight fiercely for better pay and conditions. Sometimes it is just to ensure that their members are paid at all. Most of all, they bring together in solidarity those most vulnerable Londoners who may not have felt they had any rights at all. It is no wonder that IWGB protests are so vibrant and passionate.

And Henry Chango Lopez, the President of the IWGB, is

usually leading the charge.

The Coarsest Demand

We are only a few hundred yards from the gates of Senate House, where recent IWGB protests have been held, but the atmosphere could not be more different. Henry and I have met outside of Senate House, where he works as a porter, and have made our way to the stark confounds of the Institute of Education Student Union cafeteria. The seating is state-school basic and Henry declines my offer of a coffee. He also rejects the option of anonymity as 'he is too well known now'.

This is not what Henry expected when he arrived in London from Ecuador 19 years ago. He knew nothing of trade unions then, or employment law, and did not have any documents until 2009. He was getting by in catering jobs and had workplace experiences typical of undocumented migrants: he had been sacked, been discriminated against and had money taken from him. At that time, he tells me, 'I could never do anything. I didn't know how the system worked.'

When Henry returned from a long break back home, he decided to look for a new job and a better life. He fought to get his documents sorted and found a job working as a porter at Senate House (part of the UoL). His father worked there and told him that work was available. It was part-time, 4 hours a day, but it was something. As Daniel, our aspiring cleaner, found, getting on the bottom ladder of London's service sector is a matter of finding cultural connections, especially if your lack of English prevents you from applying in the usual way. The difficulty comes when you have to protect your rights. It was learning to protect those rights that set Henry on his journey to IWGB President.

When he started at Senate House, Henry tells me, there was no union presence, with the exception of an older guy who was trying to convince the migrant cleaners, porters and security guards to join the union. 'Nobody would listen to him,' says Henry, as if it was common sense. Soon Henry started to have problems; his managers were trying to take money from his overtime.

So, one day the day of pay would come and there would be missing money and I would have to fight with the manager for the money. I knew that this woman was corrupt, because she used to do it to other workers.

It was time to do something. He had started to learn English, which only a minority of IWGB members speak, but Henry says, 'I think it was more...I don't like injustice and it makes me angry when someone is treating people unfairly and this woman was treating me and other workers very unfairly.' The problem was, who should they take action against?

While they worked within the UoL, their labour was outsourced to a company called OCS and then to Balfour Beatty. When the latter took over they, 'completely messed up the wages of the workers. So workers weren't paid all month, some of them 2 months.' London's cleaners, security staff and porters cannot possibly go that long without pay. They decided that 'enough is enough'.

This presented another dilemma: who would help them? At that time, many had joined Unison and were trying to organise by talking with union officials. But Henry and his colleagues weren't interested in the vagaries of union politics and particulars. And so, one day they just walked off the job not even knowing if they would be sacked for doing so.

With help from SOAS students and like-minded activists, they got some drums and started walking around the Senate House carpark. Their passion attracted others. and then 'workers came from the other halls of residence because they were also having problems with the company. We all got together and it was the first time all of the workers came out in anger.' The spirit of the IWGB was alive, even if they were still with Unison. They recovered £6,000 in unpaid wages that day, Henry tells me with understandable and understated pride.

Because he spoke English, Henry's friends put him forward to represent them with the union. Soon after, he was reading the *Evening Standard* on the bus home and saw an article about workers at UCL campaigning for the living wage. Those at UCL were getting £8. Henry and his friends were on £6, let alone the living wage. It's the same university, Henry thought, why aren't they getting the same? After all, those at SOAS already had the living wage.

He took the newspaper to his older union colleague, the one who had been trying to get them to join the union. Henry was not met with much enthusiasm. Once his friends caught wind, though, they also started to wonder why they were not campaigning. They started to organise to campaign for the London Living Wage, specifically targeting the UoL. After all, are not their wages ultimately coming from the university? Universities are also easier to shame than outsourcing specialists like Balfour Beatty. As a result, their leaflets and social media materials focused on the prestige of the institution and its pride in teaching about inequality and injustice.

Their social media heavy campaign, vibrant and unmissable demos, and student support made for a compellingly visible campaign. After 9 months of campaigning, victory! They were going to be paid the living wage.

It was not enough though and nor should it be. Those in Senate House employed by Balfour Beatty were not on the same conditions as their university-employed colleagues. They wanted sick pay and holidays and pensions. Another campaign was launched and Unison was asked to lead it. The union agreed with their proposals and started to talk to the university. But, Henry felt, these mostly British union officials did not really understand their needs. And so, 'there was a point when we decided, "okay, we're not going to wait, let's launch the campaign – even if they don't want to support us". They're not doing anything, so let's launch our campaign.'

It was called the 3Cosas. In English, 'sick pay, holiday and pensions'. Unison were not happy, Henry tells me, and put up posters saying they were not supporting the protest. Henry and his friends were angry. They decided to put a motion to the branch and flood the next union meeting. It was certainly packed because, Henry says, 'the officials brought in more people to ensure that they would not give us what we want and give us the support'.

They lost that battle but decided to continue with the campaign. The next step was to try and take over the branch of Senate House Unison so that it reflected the members, mostly cleaners, security staff and caterers. They hit another barrier. Unison had decided to hold the elections by ballot, rather than the usual show of hands. Many of the workers had changed address – a common problem when you are living month by month – but the union would not let the addresses be changed in the system.

They were a union fighting a union, the new migrant working class against the old British guard. Plus, Henry suspects, '[Unison] were kind of in bed with the University of London' and were trying to keep relations cordial. The outsourced workers had no motivation to do that. They just wanted basic rights. Then, Henry says, came the telling blow:

Unison delayed releasing the results and ultimately cancelled the election. After that, we just didn't know what to do. It was just so insulting what they did. We took our drums to Unison Headquarters, we said we're workers, why won't you support us at the Unison Headquarters with the drums and the placards. We said you were meant to support us as our union, you want our money but not our

votes.
Yeah, they called the police on us, they removed us from the area.

They were fighting on all sides and getting nowhere. But there was a small, independent union that were regularly supporting their protests: the IWGB. It too had come out of another mega-union, Unite, and was organising cleaners across London. After nothing came of Henry and his colleagues giving Unison one last chance at the next branch meeting, they left *todos juntos* to form a branch of the IWGB.

Henry became the Chair of IWGB University of London and the 3Cosas campaign intensified. But Unison were fighting them. The UoL refused to recognise them, and still do not, even though the IWGB has the vast majority of non-academic union members at UoL. They could not even negotiate on behalf of their members, only campaign. They were new to it all, Henry laments, and 'we didn't know much about these things, like how to represent the workers, I didn't know what it meant to be a rep'. But they were dedicated and, with help from others, built respect by advocating for those who felt they had no voice.

Still, the members of IWGB needed to do more than win small battles. They decided to hold a strike, which would be the first strike across all the UoL institutions. Through social media and video campaigns, IWGB had developed a fund and were able to support workers who might not have survived an extended strike. It was a 'big, big win'. They secured '6 months full pay sick pay' and 5 weeks holiday. Progress was being made.

Where managers would once openly shout at them or sack workers without process, they were now being treated with respect. The IWGB have a big and empowered membership and are starting to take on, and campaign for, workers from other UoL sites. Other unrepresented and precarious workers, like foster carers and delivery drivers, started approaching them for help and started their own branches of IWGB. Henry says the

Union message is simple:

> *the way we work is that anytime someone wants to campaign, we tell the workers we can help you with the skills, knowledge, but you have to do more. If you're not involved, we don't do anything. We rather don't start anything.*

But the battle is far from over. Even though they work within the University of London, they are still not employed by the University of London. They are certainly not giving up.

Civility and Servitude

'For almost 200 years,' the University of London's *About Us* section boasts, 'we have improved the lives of millions of people around the world through our unique approach to education, prompting Charles Dickens to term us the "People's University"'[602].

In December 2018, the IWGB launched a boycott of Senate House. They asked for people to pledge to:

> *not attend or organise any events at the University of London central administration (including Senate House, Stewart House, the Warburg Institute, the Institute of Historical Research, the Institute of Advanced Legal Studies/Charles Clore House and Student Central) until all outsourced workers (including cleaners, receptionists, security officers, catering staff, porters, audiovisual workers, gardeners and maintenance workers) are made direct employees of the UoL on equal terms and conditions with other directly employed staff*[603].

The IWGB claim that outsourced workers are paid less, have worse conditions, less opportunity for advancement and are regularly bullied[604]. Agency workers across London, along with the self-employed of Deliveroo, Hermes and Uber, would agree.

The UoL had initially committed to ending outsourcing, but is pushing back the date until a bidding process starts, during which 'in-house' bids will be considered.

Over 400 academics have signed up, causing 33 seminars and 170 events to be relocated as of April 2019. MPs like John McDonnell, Caroline Lucas and Frank Field have registered to support the cause, as has commentator Owen Jones. Not everyone gets it, though, especially the old guard. When the British historian Richard J Evans refused to cancel the UoL launch of his book on the Marxist Eric Hobsbawm, he claimed that Hobsbawm would not have approved of the boycott because, 'it was not an official picket line,' and, 'the fact that the IWGB union split away from Unison and Unite to operate independently would have struck [Hobsbawm] as undermining the trade union movement'[605]. I think Hobsbawm might have had a different opinion if he were to sit down with Henry and other IWGB members.

The university is not going lightly. In June 2018, it was reported that the university had already spent £415,134 on extra security during outsourcing protests[606]. Much of it on agency security guards. It created what Simon Childs called a 'Theatre of Security' within which visitors to Senate House were being forced to show ID badges before entering the building[607].

The University of London describe themselves as a 'conscientious employer' that 'takes its Public Sector Equality Duty very seriously' [608]. They claim to be 'dismayed by the inaccurate and misleading claims'. Moreover, the university insist that they are 'not involved in the contractual arrangements between its contracted out suppliers and their staff', which is kind of the point. They also stated that:

The University is aware that individuals working within its larger service contractors presently benefit from flexible working hours, which it understands for many, if not all, provides welcome

flexibility, including opportunities for work with other employers.
This level of flexibility would be difficult to replicate for directly
employed staff[609].

Gig economy companies often trot out this line. In response to another lost appeal on the employment status of their workers, an Uber spokesperson said, 'If drivers were classified as workers they would inevitably lose some of the freedom and flexibility that comes with being their own boss.'[610]

Similarly, Deliveroo, having won a case classifying their riders as self-employed, claimed that it was 'a victory for riders who have consistently told us the flexibility to choose when and where they work, which comes with self-employment, is their number one reason for riding with Deliveroo'[611].

In February 2019, the Boycott Senate House Twitter account posted a letter signed by 50 UoL cleaners[612]. They did not speak of the benefits of flexibility or the joys of being able to have multiple jobs. Thanking those who are 'supporting us and joining the fight,' they describe conditions where they 'have contracts which only guarantee 2 or 3 hours of work a day, when in reality we work many more hours'. As a result, the letter says, they have to chase overtime each week even when they have been working the same hours. Holiday pay is based only on their contractual hours. The cleaners also remind us that, 'Outsourcing engenders economic and social exclusion in which we, migrant workers, are exploited in ways that would never be possible with the mostly white academics and managers directly employed by the university.'

Tellingly, the cleaners insist that they are proud of working for a renowned university that 'prides itself in "treating individuals equitably", that recognises "equality of opportunities", "that supports diversity social inclusion" and that ensures that every member of staff is treated "with dignity at work"'. They go on to say, 'We are asking the University of London to live up to the principles it preaches and make them become a reality.' These are the lives of the unseen migrant workers who keep London moving.

Later, Henry kindly distributes some surveys to his members, taking pity on my monolingualism. Most were from Latin America via Spain or Portugal and have been here since the great recession hit Southern Europe, creating youth unemployment levels of 40 and 50 per cent[613]. It was no place and no time for migrants to be looking for work. So they had come to London because of its 'jobs and opportunities' and 'diversity and multicultural community' in 'one of the most famous cities in the world'. But life in London is tough, even if it now feels like home for many. They wrote that in London, 'you can only survive' because, several stated, wages are so low and housing costs are so high. They spoke of long shifts and inequality between workers. One wrote that:

If you want to live in London you have to do very hard work. I leave to work in the morning around 5am. I go to work by train it takes one hour…I am a security office receptionist working 12-hour shift. This means that I expending more than 14 hours a day.

This is London, where civility, servitude and hope can exist in the same building. This is the London dream. All of it.

As for Henry, he will continue the good fight. He has completed a degree in Social Sciences at Birkbeck and the IWGB is only growing. Since we spoke he has now become the full-time President of the IWGB. And he is definitely a Londoner, although his London is very different from others we have seen in this book. He tells me:

I really like London. Most of my life, I have lived in London, yeah it's a good place to live. I never have a problem. When you speak the languages, it's easy to socialise with these people. Now the fact that I have been involved in the trade union movement to know a lot of people and that's helped make my life even more like, easy to get by.

Waking Up?

The struggles of the IWGB and the workers they represent should be an inspiration for Londoners, especially the most vulnerable of us. They are willing to battle for their rights and for their London dream. Moreover, their campaign against the University of London has focused troublesome attention on the tension between the civilising mission of the university and the exploitative practices it seemingly relies upon.

But there is one thing that I cannot escape. Even when the IWGB succeeds, and battles often take years of sacrifice, they have only succeeded in winning back the most basic rights. Even the right to have rights. If the disavowed foundation of the London dream is class struggle, capital is winning.

Nonetheless, despite the conditions they are faced with at work and beyond, few of the migrant workers Henry represents are heading home. There is just something about London that inspires hope in even the most dire of circumstances. Even for those battling to survive, there is the possibility of community and the sense of opportunity.

This is the thing about London; if you want to make it, London remains the place to do it. And not everyone is miserable or living precarious lives. Recent research shows that two-thirds of the highest paid in the UK live in London and its commuter towns[614]. London's economy continues to grow, seemingly immune from the spectre of Brexit[615]. There are 76 buildings taller than 20 storeys due to be completed in London in 2019, with 541 currently under construction[616].

Those hoping to make it in the arts, in tech or in something in between are right to come to London to search for work, cultural connections and cool experiences. Less fortunate migrants hoping to survive in service industry jobs are not dupes either: quite simply, London provides the best chance of finding work, avoiding overt discrimination and making your way in the world. It always has, even if the consequences are often brutal.

While London's population is growing rapidly because of high birth rates and continued international migration, the city loses more than 50,000 people per year to other parts of the country[617] – even though over 200,000 arrive from parts of the UK each year[618]. Child poverty continues to rise[619] and the number sleeping rough in London grew by 20 per cent in 2018[620]. International surveys rank the quality of life in London lower than all UK cities with the exception of Glasgow[621]. Another report named London the best city in the world in 2019 on account of its universities, luxury shops and restaurants[622]. Tourist numbers continue to set records[623].

At the height of Victorian London, historian Peter Ackroyd suggests, the city 'was so large that practically any opinion could be held on it and still be true'[624]. What is true of Victorian London is true today. There are many stories that can be told about London.

'London is a place to make your fortune'

'London is a place to spend your fortune'

'London is a place where there is always something to do'

'London is a place to find work'

'London is a place where all are welcome'

'London is a place where the poorest are being forced out of the city'

'London is the place to be'

London is a city of hope, a city of misery. A city where there is always something to do and no shortage of precarious workers struggling to do it. It is all part of the London dream.

And still, they come. But for how much longer?

Endnotes

1 James Boswell, *The Life of Samuel Johnson* (London: Hutchinson and Co, 1791), 285.

2 Boswell, 286.

3 Boswell, 286.

4 Tony Parsons, 'London Is the Greatest City in the World,' GQ, 2016, http://www.gq-magazine.co.uk/article/tony-parsons-london-capital-world.

5 Sam Selvon, *The Lonely Londoners* (London: Penguin Books, 2006), 79.

6 I write these seemingly optimistic words while the world endures the chaos of Trump and of Brexit, wholly aware that the holder of this book may be reading in a time in which they are laughable.

7 Cynthia Cockburn, *Looking to London* (London: Pluto Press, 2017).

8 Karl Marx, *Das Kapital* (Oxford: Oxford University Press, 1995), 362.

9 Yvonne Kapp, *Eleanor Marx: Vol 1 Family Life* (London: Virago Press, 1972), 128; sourced from Lindsey German and John Rees, *A People's History of London* (London and New York: Verso, 2012), 126.

10 Karl Marx and Fredrich Engels, *Marx and Engels: 1844-51: Vol. 38* (London: Lawrence and Wishart, 1982), 377.

11 Francis Wheen, *Marx's Das Kapital* (London: Atlantic Books, 2006), 25.

12 Blanchard Jerrold, *London, a Pilgrimage* (London: Anthem Press, 2005); Peter Ackroyd, *London: The Concise Biography* (London: Vintage, 2001), 483.

13 Plato, *The Republic* (New York: Cosimos, 2008), 92.

14 All names are pseudonyms.

15 Cockburn, *Looking to London*.

16 Ben Judah, *This Is London* (London: Picador, 2016).

17 Alan White, 'Literally No One Has A Clue What Theresa May Means By 'The British Dream,'' Buzzfeed, 2017, https://www.

buzzfeed.com/alanwhite/everyone-wants-to-know-what-the-hell-theresa-may-means-by?utm_term=.bmQx0A4RQV#.ahJ21wEmvd.

18 Nesrine Malik, 'Theresa May Has a Dream. A Mawkish, Shabby 'British Dream," The Guardian, 2018, https://www.theguardian.com/commentisfree/2018/feb/01/theresa-may-british-dream.

19 Ade Sawyerr, 'Will There Ever Be a British Dream?,' Operation Black Vote, 2011, http://www.obv.org.uk/news-blogs/will-there-ever-be-british-dream.Z. Nia Reynolds, *When I Came to England: An Oral History of Life in 1950s and 1960s Britain* (London: Black Stock, 2001).

20 This is not to deny the presence and contributions of migrants to modern Britain, nor to reject the value of including a migration narrative into the story of Britain. As David Goodhart has implored in *The British Dream*, a migrant orientated British dream could help to develop cohesion where there is now division.

21 Ackroyd, *London: The Concise Biography*, 573.

22 German and Rees, *A People's History of London*, 13–14.

23 Cockburn, *Looking to London*, 10.

24 Original quote from Matthew Paris in 1255 but cited in Nick Merriman Sara Selwood, Bill Schwarz, *The Peopling of London: Fifteen Thousand Years of Settlement from Overseas : An Evaluation of the Exhibition* (London: Museum of London, 1996).

25 'EU Referendum: The Results in Maps and Charts,' BBC News, 2016, http://www.bbc.co.uk/news/uk-politics-36616028.

26 Corporate Research Unit, 'Spitalfields and Banglatown Ward Profile,' London Borough of Tower Hamlets (London, 2014), https://www.towerhamlets.gov.uk/Documents/Borough_statistics/Ward_profiles/Spitalfields-and-Banglatown-FINAL-10062014.pdf.

27 Ackroyd, *London: The Concise Biography*, 702.

28 'Immigration and Emigration: The Huguenots,' BBC, 2003, http://www.bbc.co.uk/legacies/immig_emig/england/london/article_1.shtml.

29 Jerry White, *London in the 18th Century* (London: The Bodley Head, 2012), 138.

30   White, 139.

31   'Changing Shadows,' *The Economist*, 2003, https://www.economist. com/christmas-specials/2003/12/18/changing-shadows.

32   White, *London in the 18th Century*, 218.

33   White, 137–39.

34   'The Origin of "Refugee,"' Merriam-Weber, accessed May 10, 2018, https://www.merriam-webster.com/words-at-play/origin-and-meaning-of-refugee.

35   Cockburn, *Looking to London*.

36   'National Statistics: Asylum,' Home Office, 2017, https://www. gov.uk/government/publications/immigration-statistics-october-to-december-2016/asylum.

37   Cockburn, *Looking to London*, 24.

38   German and Rees, *A People's History of London*, 26.

39   German and Rees, 27.

40   'Immigration and Emigration: East End Jews,' BBC, 2003, http:// www.bbc.co.uk/legacies/immig_emig/england/london/article_2. shtml.

41   'Changing Shadows.'

42   'Immigration and Emigration: East End Jews.'

43   David Goldberg, *This Is Not the Way: Jews, Judaism and the State of Israel* (London: Faber and Faber, 2012).

44   'Changing Shadows.'

45   Jerry White, *London in the 20th Century* (London: The Bodley Head, 2001), 131.

46   White, 133.

47   White, 130.

48   White, 130–31.

49   Office for National Statistics, 'Births by Parents' Country of Birth, England and Wales: 2017,' 2018, https://www.ons.gov.uk/ peoplepopulationandcommunity/birthsdeathsandmarriages/ livebirths/bulletins/parentscountryofbirthenglandandwales/2017.

50   White, *London in the 20th Century*, 131.

51   'Enoch Powell's 'Rivers of Blood' Speech,' The Telegraph, 2007,

https://www.telegraph.co.uk/comment/3643823/Enoch-Powells-Rivers-of-Blood-speech.html.

52   White, *London in the 20th Century*, 132.

53   Clair Wills, 'Passage to England,' Times Literary Supplement, 2017, https://www.the-tls.co.uk/articles/public/punjabi-immigrants-stories/.

54   Jack London, *The People of the Abyss* (London: Macmillan, 1903), 6.

55   Ibid.

56   London, *The People of the Abyss*, 65.

57   'Analysis of Real Earnings and Contributions to Nominal Earnings Growth, Great Britain: May 2018,' Office for National Statistics, 2018, https://www.ons.gov.uk/employmentandlabourmarket/peopleinwork/earningsandworkinghours/articles/supplementaryanalysisofaverageweeklyearnings/may2018.

58   'The Scale of Economic Inequality in the UK,' The Equality Trust, 2018, https://www.equalitytrust.org.uk/scale-economic-inequality-uk.

59   Moussa Haddad, 'The Perfect Storm: Economic Stagnation, the Rising Cost of Living, Public Spending Cuts and the Impact on UK Poverty,' Oxfam, 2012, https://policy-practice.oxfam.org.uk/publications/the-perfect-storm-economic-stagnation-the-rising-cost-of-living-public-spending-228591.

60   Jerry White, *London in the 19th Century* (London: The Bodley Head, 2007), 109.

61   White, 108.

62   White, 109.

63   White, 109.

64   'Hidden Homelessness in London,' London Assembly, 2017, https://www.london.gov.uk/sites/default/files/london_assembly_-_hidden_homelessness_report.pdf.

65   'Hidden Homelessness in London.'

66   Richard Brown and Brell Wilson, 'Running on Fumes: London's Council Services in Austerity,' Centre for London, 2015, https://www.centreforlondon.org/wp-content/uploads/2016/08/CFL3888_

Running-on-fumes_short_paper_12.11.15_WEB.pdf.

67 Joseph Addison, 'Thursday, June 12, 1712,' The Spectator, 1712, https://www.gutenberg.org/files/12030/12030-h/SV2/Spectator2. html#section403.

68 German and Rees, *A People's History of London*, 26–27.

69 Ackroyd, *London: The Concise Biography*, 703.

70 Ackroyd, 704.

71 Emma Tapsfield and James Glanfield, 'The Most Racist Programme I've Ever Watched': BBC Faces Twitter Backlash over Controversial Documentary The Last Whites of the East End – While Some Viewers Say 'It's Only Telling the Truth,'' Mail Online, 2016, http://www. dailymail.co.uk/news/article-3608136/The-racist-programme-honest-reflection-state-nation-Britain-divided-reaction-Whites-East-End.html.

72 '2011 Census: Key Statistics and Quick Statistics for Local Authorities in the United Kingdom,' Office for National Statistics, 2011, https://www.ons.gov.uk/peoplepopulationandcommunity/ populationandmigration/populationestimates/bulletins/key-statisticsandquickstatisticsforlocalauthoritiesintheunitedking-dom/2013-10-11.

73 Ackroyd, *London: The Concise Biography*, 706–8.

74 Nick Gutteridge, 'REVEALED: EU Migrants Pocket MORE Tax Credits Cash and Child Benefits than BRITISH Workers,' Express, 2016, https://www.express.co.uk/news/uk/655145/Brexit-EU-refer endum-European-migrants-benefits-tax-credits-British-workers.

75 Chris McMillan, '#MakeAmericaGreatAgain: Ideological Fantasy, American Exceptionalism and Donald Trump,' *Subjectivity* 10, no. 2 (2017): 1–19.

76 Susan Fox, *The New Cockney: New Ethnicities and Adolescent Speech in the Traditional East End of London* (Basingstoke: Palgrave Macmillan, 2015).

77 'A Guide to the Hostile Environment,' Liberty, 2018, https://www. libertyhumanrights.org.uk/sites/default/files/HE web.pdf.

78 Zac Goldsmith, 'On Thursday, Are We Really Going to Hand the

World's Greatest City to a Labour Party That Thinks Terrorists Is Its Friends? A Passionate Plea from ZAC GOLDSMITH Four Days before Mayoral Election,' Mail Online, 2016, http://www.dailymail.co.uk/debate/article-3567537/On-Thursday-really-going-hand-world-s-greatest-city-Labour-party-thinks-terrorists-friends-passionate-plea-ZAC-GOLDSMITH-four-days-Mayoral-election.html.

79 Ackroyd, *London: The Concise Biography*, 703.

80 'Our #LondonisOpen Campaign,' Mayor of London, 2017, https://www.london.gov.uk/about-us/mayor-london/londonisopen.

81 'Facing Facts: The Impact of Migrants on London, Its Workforce and Economy,' PWC, 2017, https://www.pwc.co.uk/services/legal-services/services/immigration/facing-facts--the-impact-of-migrants-on-london--its-workforce-an.html.

82 Fredrich Engels, *The Condition of the Working Class in England* (London: Penguin, 1845).

83 Henry Mayhew, 'Victorian London - Publications - Social Investigation/Journalism - The Criminal Prisons of London and Scenes of London Life,' The Great World of London, 1862, http://www.victorianlondon.org/publications5/prisons-01.htm.

84 Ackroyd, *London: The Concise Biography*, 486.

85 Henry Fielding, 'An Enquiry Into the Causes of the Late Increase of Robbers,' Internet Archive, 1751, https://archive.org/details/anenquiryintoca00fielgoog.

86 William Booth, *In Darkest England and the Way Out* (Cambridge: Cambridge University Press, 1890), 11–12.

87 Ackroyd, *London: The Concise Biography*, 490.

88 Henry Mayhew, *London Labour and the London Poor* (Ware: Wordsworth Editions, 2008), 6–8.

89 German and Rees, *A People's History of London*, 156.

90 Charles Dickens, *Oliver Twist* (London: Penguin, 2003), 63.

91 Graham Mooney, 'Shifting Sex Differentials in Mortality During Urban Epidemiological Transition: The Case of Victorian London,' *International Journal of Population Geography* 8 (2002): 26.

92   Ackroyd, *London: The Concise Biography*, 288.

93   Ackroyd, 291.

94   German and Rees, *A People's History of London*, 99.

95   White, *London in the 19th Century*, 30.

96   White, 30.

97   London, *The People of the Abyss*, 29.

98   Ackroyd, *London: The Concise Biography*, 500.

99   Mayor of London, 'London Datastore,' Historical Census Population, 2011, https://data.london.gov.uk/dataset/historic-census-population/resource/2c7867e5-3682-4fdd-8b9d-c63e289b92a6#.

100 Clive Emsley; Tim Hitchcock; Robert Shoemaker, 'A Population History of London,' Old Bailey Proceedings Online, 2017, https://www.oldbaileyonline.org/static/Population-history-of-london.jsp.

101 Mayor of London, 'London Datastore.'

102 White, *London in the 19th Century*, 30.

103 Dickens, *Oliver Twist*, 11.

104 London, *The People of the Abyss*, 34.

105 Robert Winnett, 'Get a Job, Iain Duncan Smith Tells Parents on the Dole,' The Telegraph, 2012, https://www.telegraph.co.uk/news/politics/9330574/Get-a-job-Iain-Duncan-Smith-tells-parents-on-the-dole.html.

106 White, *London in the 19th Century*, 29.

107 Documenting that activity goes beyond the scope of this book. See Lindsey German's and John Rees' *A People's History of London* for a powerful historical analysis of radical politics in London.

108 German and Rees, *A People's History of London*, 100–101.

109 German and Rees, 108.

110 German and Rees, 111.

111 Catherine J. Golden, *Posting It: The Victorian Revolution in Letter Writing* (Gainesville, Florida: University Press of Florida, 2009), 129.

112 Liza Picard, 'The Great Exhibition,' British Library, 2009, https://www.bl.uk/victorian-britain/articles/the-great-exhibition.

113 White, *London in the 19th Century*, 103.

114 Clement Shorter, *The Brontes Life and Letters Volume II* (London: Hodder and Stoughton, 1908), 215–16.

115 White, *London in the 19th Century*, 269.

116 Noted in White, 78.

117 White, 102.

118 H.A. Shannon, 'Migration and the Growth London, 1841-1891,' *Economic History Review* V, no. 2 (1935): 79–86; White, *London in the 19th Century*, 102.

119 White, *London in the 19th Century*, 103.

120 White, 116.

121 White, 102.

122 Ackroyd, *London: The Concise Biography*, 485.

123 Kimberly Conner, '20 Reasons London Is the Most Exciting City in the World,' Huffington Post, 2016, https://www.huffingtonpost.com/kimberly-conner/20-reasons-london-is-the-_b_9633332.html.

124 Katie Allen, 'Economic Output per Person in London More than Double Rest of UK,' The Guardian, 2016, https://www.theguardian.com/business/2016/dec/15/economic-output-of-london-more-than-double-rest-of-uk.

125 Richard Florida, 'The Economic Power of Cities Compared to Nations,' CityLab, 2017, https://www.citylab.com/life/2017/03/the-economic-power-of-global-cities-compared-to-nations/519294/.

126 Parsons, 'London Is the Greatest City in the World.'

127 White, *London in the 20th Century*, 188.

128 White, 206.

129 White, 208.

130 White, 76.

131 White, 338.

132 White, 325.

133 White, 326.

134 David Batty, *My Generation* (United Kingdom: Lionsgate, 2017).

135 Richard Florida, *The Rise of the Creative Class: And How It's Transforming Work, Leisure, Community and Everyday Life* (New

York: Basic Books, 2002).

136 Batty, *My Generation*.

137 Stryker McGuire and Michael Elliott, 'Hot Fashion, a Pulsating Club Scene and Lots of New Money Have Made This the Coolest City on the Planet,' *Newsweek*, November 1996.

138 David Kamp, 'London Swings! Again!,' Vanity Fair, 1997, https://www.vanityfair.com/magazine/1997/03/london199703.

139 Like so many new parents, Hirst moved out of London (to Devon) when his first child was born in 1995. I'm sure I will too, one day. Not today though, as I'm writing a book on London.

140 Rachel Lichtenstein, *On Brick Lane* (London: Hamish Hamilton, 2007), 276.

141 White, *London in the 20th Century*, 342.

142 Richard Florida, *The New Urban Crisis* (London: OneWorld, 2017), 58.

143 Nevin Martell, 'Brett Anderson and Mat Osman on Suede's Discography,' Filter, 2011, http://filtermagazine.com/index.php/exclusives/entry/brett_anderson_and_mat_osman_on_suedes_discography.

144 John Harris, 'Cool Britannia: Where Did It All Go Wrong?,' New Statesman, 2017, https://www.newstatesman.com/1997/2017/05/cool-britannia-where-did-it-all-go-wrong.

145 'You Can Walk Across It on Grass,' *Time*, April 1966.

146 Alan Ehrenhalt, *The Great Inversion and the Future of the American City* (New York: Vintage, 2013).

147 'Trust for London,' London's population over time, 2018, https://www.trustforlondon.org.uk/data/londons-population-over-time/.

148 'You Can Walk Across It on Grass.'

149 Joe Muggs, 'Is New Cross the New Camden?,' Evening Standard, accessed August 5, 2018, https://www.standard.co.uk/go/london/clubbing/is-new-cross-the-new-camden-6695175.html.

150 'New Cross,' UK Census Data, 2011, http://www.ukcensusdata.com/new-cross-e05000449#sthash.eAlmTa7g.dpbs.

151 'Ward Profiles and Atlas,' Greater London Authority, 2015, https://

data.london.gov.uk/dataset/ward-profiles-and-atlas.

152 'You Can Walk Across It on Grass.'

153 'London's Population by Age,' Trust for London, 2018, https://www.trustforlondon.org.uk/data/londons-population-age/.

154 White, *London in the 20th Century*, 171.

155 German and Rees, *A People's History of London*, 14.

156 Ackroyd, *London: The Concise Biography*, 455.

157 William Dalrymple, 'The East India Company: The Original Corporate Raiders,' The Guardian, 2015, https://www.theguardian.com/world/2015/mar/04/east-india-company-original-corporate-raiders.

158 The Economist, 'The Company That Ruled the Waves,' The Economist, 2011, http://www.economist.com/node/21541753.

159 'Britain and the Slave Trade,' The National Archives, accessed October 30, 2017, http://www.nationalarchives.gov.uk/slavery/pdf/britain-and-the-trade.pdf.

160 White, *London in the 20th Century*, 171.

161 White, *London in the 18th Century*, 168.

162 German and Rees, *A People's History of London*, 233.

163 German and Rees, 86.

164 German and Rees, 234.

165 Mayhew, *London Labour and the London Poor*.

166 Robert Douglas-Fairhurst, 'London Labour and the London Poor by Henry Mayhew,' The Guardian, 2010, https://www.theguardian.com/books/2010/oct/16/rereading-henry-mayhew-london-poor.

167 Mayhew, *London Labour and the London Poor*, 301.

168 Douglas McWilliams, *The Flat White Economy* (London: Douglas Overlook, 2015), 23.

169 Wandsworth Council, 'Battersea Power Station,' History of Battersea Power Station, 2018, http://www.wandsworth.gov.uk/info/200536/nine_elms/2101/battersea_power_station.

170 'The History,' Battersea Power Station, 2018, https://batterseapowerstation.co.uk/about/heritage-history.

171 'Coal-Fired Power Stations,' Hansard, 1984, http://hansard.

millbanksystems.com/written_answers/1984/jan/16/coal-fired-power-stations#S6CV0052P0_19840116_CWA_281.

172 'Battersea Power Station,' South Chelsea, accessed March 7, 2018, https://web.archive.org/web/20120310153152/http://www.southchelsea.freeserve.co.uk/page11.html.

173 Peter Watts, 'Mosque, Circus, Neverland UK ... the Best Failed Ideas for Battersea Power Station,' The Guardian, 2016, https://www.theguardian.com/cities/2016/may/31/battersea-power-station-london-mosque-circus-neverland.

174 Matt West, 'Almost All 866 Flats in Battersea Power Station Development Sold to Foreign Investors for £675m - and They Haven't Even Been Built Yet,' This is Money, 2013, http://www.thisismoney.co.uk/money/mortgageshome/article-2328459/Almost-866-flats-Battersea-Power-Station-development-sold-foreign-investors.html.

175 Julia Kollewe, 'Battersea Power Station Developer Slashes Number of Affordable Homes,' The Guardian, 2017, http://www.thisismoney.co.uk/money/mortgageshome/article-2328459/Almost-866-flats-Battersea-Power-Station-development-sold-foreign-investors.htm.

176 Ruth Bloomfield, 'It's Battersea Poor Station: First-Time Buyers Banished to Former Industrial Estate Half a Mile from Luxury Homes,' Evening Standard, 2015, https://www.homesandproperty.co.uk/property-news/its-battersea-poor-station-firsttime-buyers-banished-to-former-industrial-estate-half-a-mile-from-47706.html.

177 Sheila Hills, John, Brewer, Mike, Jenkins, Stephen P, Lister, Ruth, Lupton, Ruth, Machin, Stephen, Mills, Colin, Modood, Tariq, Rees, Teresa and Riddell, 'An Anatomy of Economic Inequality in the UK: Report of the National Equality Panel' (London, 2010).

178 Robert Watts, 'The Sunday Times Rich List 2017: Boom Time for Billionaires,' The Times, 2017, https://www.thetimes.co.uk/article/the-sunday-times-rich-list-2017-boom-time-for-billionaires-pzbkrfbv2.

179 Trust for London, 'Children,' London's Poverty Profile, 2016, http://www.londonspovertyprofile.org.uk/indicators/groups/children/.

180 Calvin Tomkins, 'The Modern Man,' The New Yorker, 2012, https://www.newyorker.com/magazine/2012/07/02/the-modern-man.

181 Jack Simpson, 'Battersea Power Station Deal Delayed Again,' Construction News, 2018, https://www.constructionnews.co.uk/markets/sectors/housing/battersea-power-station-deal-delayed-again/10033827.article.

182 BBC, 'Tate Modern Drew in Record Visitors in 2016,' BBC News, 2017, http://www.bbc.co.uk/news/entertainment-arts-39404206.

183 Tate, 'History of Tate,' Who We Are, 2017, http://www.tate.org.uk/about/who-we-are/history-of-tate#modern.

184 Cited in Tomkins, 'The Modern Man.'

185 ''Wobbly' Millennium Bridge Fixed,' BBC News, 2002, http://news.bbc.co.uk/1/hi/england/1829053.stm.

186 Tomkins, 'The Modern Man.'

187 Gabrielle Brace Stevenson, 'Ben Wilson's Chewing Gum Art On The Millennium Bridge,' Culture Trip, 2016, https://theculturetrip.com/europe/united-kingdom/england/london/articles/ben-wilsons-chewing-gum-art-on-the-millennium-bridge/.

188 www.uncsbrp.org, 'London's Finance Industry,' London's Economic Plan, 2017, http://www.uncsbrp.org/finance.htm.

189 Charles Booth, *Life and Labour of the People in London* (London and New York: Macmillan, 1890).

190 'Welcome to South Bank,' Home Page for South Bank, 2017, https://www.southbanklondon.com/index.

191 Daryl Rozario, 'London's Creative Industries – 2017 Update,' London Datastore, 2017, https://data.london.gov.uk/apps_and_analysis/londons-creative-industries-2017-update/.

192 Daniel Bell, *The Coming of Post-Industrial Society* (New York: Basic Books, 1976).

193 Slavoj Žižek, *First as Tragedy, Then as Farce* (London: Verso, 2009).

194 Fredric Jameson, *Postmodernism, or, the Cultural Logic of Late Capitalism* (Durham, NC: Duke University Press, 1991).

195 Thomas Frank, *The Conquest of Cool* (Chicago: The University of Chicago Press, 1997).

196 Jim McGuigan, *Cool Capitalism* (London: Pluto Press, 2009).

197 'About Us,' Goldsmiths University of London, 2018, https://www.gold.ac.uk/about/.

198 Coran Elliott, 'Landlords Spending Thousands on Flowers to Create "Instagram Friendly" Pubs to Boost Trade,' The Telegraph, 2018, https://www.telegraph.co.uk/news/2018/08/04/landlords-spending-thousands-flowers-create-instagram-friendly/.

199 'Zero-Hours Tate Staff Amazed as They're Asked to Stump up for Boss's New Boat,' Freedom News, 2017.

200 Geraldine Kendall Adams, 'Campaign Launched against Privatisation in Museums,' Museums Association, 2018, https://www.museumsassociation.org/museums-journal/news/21032018-campaign-launched-against-privatisation.

201 'Gallery Staff's Pay Should Reflect Success of Tate Modern 2,' Public and Commercial Services Union, 2016, https://www.pcs.org.uk/news/gallery-staffs-pay-should-reflect-success-of-tate-modern-2.

202 Hannah Ellis-Petersen, 'Anger as Tate Asks Staff to Contribute towards Boat for Nicholas Serota,' The Guardian, 2017, https://www.theguardian.com/artanddesign/2017/apr/27/tate-asks-staff-to-pitch-in-to-buy-boat-for-departing-chief-nicholas-serota.

203 Tomkins, 'The Modern Man.'

204 Susanna Rustin, 'Modern Master: How Nick Serota's Tate Skyrocketed to Success,' The Guardian, 2017, https://www.theguardian.com/artanddesign/2017/may/30/tate-modern-britain-liverpool-st-ives-nicholas-serota.

205 Charlotte Higgins, 'How Nicholas Serota's Tate Changed Britain,' The Guardian, 2017, https://www.theguardian.com/artanddesign/2017/jun/22/how-nicholas-serota-tate-changed-britain.

206 Ellis-Petersen, 'Anger as Tate Asks Staff to Contribute towards Boat for Nicholas Serota.'

207 Higgins, 'How Nicholas Serota's Tate Changed Britain.'

208 Higgins.

209 'Gallery Staff's Pay Should Reflect Success of Tate Modern 2.'

210 ONS, 'UK Labour Market: May 2017,' UK labour market: May 2017, 2017, https://www.ons.gov.uk/employmentandlabourmarket/ peopleinwork/employmentandemployeetypes/bulletins/ uklabourmarket/may2017.

211 LSE, 'Prosperity, Poverty and Inequality in London 2000/01 to 2010/11,' Social Policy in a Cold Climate, 2013, 51, http://sticerd. lse.ac.uk/dps/case/spcc/srr03.pdf.

212 Robert Booth and Caelainn Barr, 'Number of Londoners Abandoning Capital Hits 10-Year High,' The Guardian, 2017, https://www.theguardian.com/uk-news/2017/dec/29/londoners-leaving-capital-for-brighton-birmingham-and-bristol.

213 'House Price Calculator: Where Can I Afford to Rent or Buy?,' BBC News, 2018, https://www.bbc.co.uk/news/business-23234033.

214 Alex Sims, '14 Reasons to Go to New Cross Road, SE14,' Time Out, 2016, https://www.timeout.com/london/blog/14-reasons-to-go-to-new-cross-road-se14-102116.

215 Henry James, The Notebooks of Henry James (Chicago: The University of Chicago Press, 1947), 27.

216 Harry de Quetteville, 'The Silicon Joke?,' The Telegraph, 2018, https://www.telegraph.co.uk/technology/the-silicon-joke/.

217 Matt Biddulph, 'How London's Silicon Roundabout Really Got Started,' Gigaom, 2012, https://gigaom.com/2012/12/11/how-londons-silicon-roundabout-really-got-started/.

218 @mattb, '"Silicon Roundabout": The Ever-Growing Community of Fun Startups in London's Old Street Area [Tweet],' 2018, https:// twitter.com/mattb/status/866136681.

219 Tim Bradshaw, 'Silicon Roundabout: Is This the Heart of the UK's New Dotcom Boom?,' Financial Times, 2008, https://www.ft.com/ content/f815bdd4-4bfa-3e47-bfda-5948428001b7; Mike Butcher, 'Now We Have Silicon Roundabout Where Are London's Existing, Organic, Tech Hubs?,' Tech Crunch, 2008.

220 Prime Minster's Office, 'PM Announces East London "Tech City",' Gov.uk, 2010, https://www.gov.uk/government/news/pm-announces-east-london-tech-city.

221 It is now 'Tech Nation', a conglomeration of Tech City and Tech North.

222 Biddulph, 'How London's Silicon Roundabout Really Got Started.'

223 McWilliams, *The Flat White Economy*, 47.

224 McWilliams, 15.

225 McWilliams, *The Flat White Economy*.

226 McWilliams, 17.

227 Definitely not Australian.

228 Rozario, 'London's Creative Industries – 2017 Update.'

229 Milja Keijonen, 'London's Sectors: More Detailed Jobs Data,' GLA Economics, 2015, https://www.london.gov.uk/sites/default/files/ gla_migrate_files_destination/London%27s sectors - more detailed jobs data.pdf.

230 McWilliams, *The Flat White Economy*, 28.

231 Mayor of London, 'Culture for All Londoners' (London, 2018), https://www.london.gov.uk/sites/default/files/2017_draft_ strategies_culture_2.0.pdf.

232 Mayor of London, 'Sadiq Khan Places Culture at the Heart of the London Plan,' 2017, https://www.london.gov.uk/press-releases/ mayoral/mayor-places-culture-at-heart-of-london-plan.

233 Florida, *The Rise of the Creative Class: And How It's Transforming Work, Leisure, Community and Everyday Life*, xxi.

234 Florida, 8.

235 Florida, 8.

236 Simon Goodley and Jonathan Ashby, 'Revealed: How Sports Direct Effectively Pays below Minimum Wage,' The Guardian, 2015, https://www.theguardian.com/business/2015/dec/09/how-sports- direct-effectively-pays-below-minimum-wage-pay.Olivia Solon, 'Amazon Patents Wristband That Tracks Warehouse Workers' Movements,' The Guardian, 2018, https://www.theguardian.com/ technology/2018/jan/31/amazon-warehouse-wristband-tracking.

237 Alec MacGillis, 'The Ruse of the Creative Class,' The American Prospect, 2009, http://prospect.org/article/ruse-creative-class-0.

238 Florida, *The Rise of the Creative Class: And How It's Transforming*

Work, Leisure, Community and Everyday Life.

239 I also engage the academic artifice of black clothing as anti-fashion. It is mainly to hide any unfortunate food/coffee stains.

240 Oliver Wainwright, '"Everything Is Gentrification Now": But Richard Florida Isn't Sorry,' The Guardian, 2017, https://www. theguardian.com/cities/2017/oct/26/gentrification-richard-florida-interview-creative-class-new-urban-crisis.

241 Florida, *The New Urban Crisis*, xxiii.

242 Wainwright, '"Everything Is Gentrification Now": But Richard Florida Isn't Sorry.'

243 Florida, *The New Urban Crisis*, xxiv.

244 Danny Dorling, 'The New Urban Crisis by Richard Florida Review – "Flawed and Elitist Ideas,"' The Observer, 2017, https://www. theguardian.com/books/2017/sep/26/richard-florida-new-urban-crisis-review-flawed-elitist-ideas.

245 Richard Florida, *The Rise of the Creative Class, Revisited* (New York: Basic Books, 2014), vii.

246 Florida, 7.

247 Florida, vii.

248 Florida, xxiii.

249 Florida's emphasis

250 Not literally.

251 Frank Field and Andrew Forsey, 'Wild West Workplace: Self-Employment in Britain's "Gig Economy"' (London, 2016), http:// www.frankfield.co.uk/upload/docs/Wild West Workplace.pdf.

252 '20 Facts About London's Culture,' Mayor of London, 2018, https:// www.london.gov.uk/what-we-do/arts-and-culture/vision-and-strategy/20-facts-about-london's-culture#.

253 Florida, *The Rise of the Creative Class, Revisited*, 306.

254 Florida, *The New Urban Crisis*, xx.

255 'Johnson: How British Values Help to Make the World Richer and Safer,' CCHQ Press, 2016, http://press.conservatives.com/ post/151242631480/johnson-how-british-values-help-to-make-the-world.

256 Richard Florida, 'Class-Divided Cities: London Edition,' CityLab, 2013, https://www.citylab.com/life/2013/11/londons-class-divides /6056/.

257 Adam Woods, 'Who's Who on the Silicon Roundabout?,' The Campaign, 2011, https://www.campaignlive.co.uk/article/whos-silicon-roundabout/1053814.

258 McWilliams, *The Flat White Economy*, 51.

259 McWilliams, 63.

260 Sam Francis, 'Londoners Work "Three Weeks a Year More than Rest of UK,"' BBC News, 2017, https://www.bbc.co.uk/news/uk-england-london-39516134.

261 And, yes, a Starbucks.

262 To be fair to Robbie, the gluten-free beer is for me.

263 Christopher Rocks, *London's Creative Industries - 2017 Update*, 2017, https://www.london.gov.uk/sites/default/files/working_paper_89-creative-industries-2017.pdf.

264 'Mayfair,' Instant Offices, 2018, https://www.instantoffices.com/en/gb/a-guide-to-office-space-in-mayfair; 'Berkeley Square vs Canary Wharf – Which Is London's Premium Business Address?,' Morgan Pryce, 2011, https://www.morganpryce.co.uk/knowledge-centre/exclusive-news-articles/berkeley-square-vs-canary-wharf-which-is-london-s-premium-business-address.

265 White, *London in the 19th Century*, 172.

266 White, 173.

267 White, *London in the 20th Century*, 180.

268 'Statistics,' Creative Industries Federation, 2017, https://www.creativeindustriesfederation.com/statistics.

269 'Statistics.'

270 It was her transcription of my interview with Robbie that started our conversation.

271 Jamie Johnson, 'London Is Europe's Cocaine Capital – but Only during the Week,' The Telegraph, 2016, https://www.telegraph.co.uk/news/2016/12/13/london-overtaken-antwerp-europes-weekend-cocaine-capital/.

272 Patrick Greenfield, 'Middle-Class Cocaine Use Fuels London's Rising Violence, Says Sadiq Khan,' The Guardian, 2018, https://www.theguardian.com/society/2018/jul/27/middle-class-cocaine-use-fuels-londons-rising-violence-says-sadiq-khan-knife-crime.

273 'Personal Well-Being in the UK: 2015 to 2016,' Office for National Statistics, 2016, https://www.ons.gov.uk/peoplepopulationandcommunity/wellbeing/bulletins/measuringnationalwellbeing/2015to2016#people-in-london-reported-lower-worthwhile-ratings-than-uk-overall.

274 'Personal Well-Being Estimates,' Office for National Statistics, 2018, https://www.ons.gov.uk/peoplepopulationandcommunity/wellbeing/datasets/headlineestimatesofpersonalwellbeing.

275 Ackroyd, London: The Concise Biography, 493.

276 '"Half of Women" Sexually Harassed at Work, Says BBC Survey,' BBC News, 2017, https://www.bbc.co.uk/news/uk-41741615.

277 Tim Wallace, 'London Goes from Best to Worst for Gender Pay Gap,' The Telegraph, 2017, https://www.telegraph.co.uk/business/2017/11/27/london-goes-best-worst-gender-pay-gap/.

278 TUC, 'The Gig Is Up: Trade Unions Tackling Insecure Work' (London, 2017), https://www.tuc.org.uk/workplace-issues/employment-rights/gig-trade-unions-tackling-insecure-work.

279 'Women,' Trust for London, 2018, https://www.trustforlondon.org.uk/data/populations/women/.

280 Rebecca Wilson, 'Creative Sector Gender Pay Gap at 28%, Sphere Salary Survey Reveals,' Recruitment International, 2017, https://www.recruitment-international.co.uk/blog/2017/07/creative-sector-gender-pay-gap-at-28-percent-sphere-salary-survey-reveals.

281 Thomas Friedman, The World Is Flat: The Globalized World in the Twenty-First Century (London: Penguin Books, 2005).

282 Ben Paytner, 'Female Freelancers Are Paid Way Less Than Men For The Same Creative Jobs,' Fast Company, 2017, https://www.fastcompany.com/40482750/female-freelancers-are-paid-way-less-than-men-for-the-same-creative-jobs.

283 ONS, 'Population Dynamics of UK City Regions since Mid-2011,' Population dynamics of UK city regions since mid-2011, 2016, https://www.ons.gov.uk/peoplepopulationandcommunity/populationandmigration/populationestimates/articles/populationdynamicsofukcityregionssincemid2011/2016-10-11.

284 Social Mobility Commission, 'Social Mobility Index: 2017 Data,' Gov.uk, 2017, https://www.gov.uk/government/publications/social-mobility-index-2017-data.

285 BOP Consulting, 'Soho: The World's Creative Hub' (London, 2013), http://www.thecreativeindustries.co.uk/media/232461/soho-bop-report.pdf.

286 Paul Swinney and Maire Williams, 'The Great British Brain Drain' (London, 2016), http://www.centreforcities.org/wp-content/uploads/2016/11/16-11-18-The-Great-British-Brain-Drain.pdf.

287 The appeal of London for Oxbridge students has long been strong. When a train station was first built in Cambridge in 1845, it was built a sizeable walk from the colleges in order to discourage students from making the journey into London and enjoying themselves a little too much. Or so the story goes.

288 Swinney and Williams, 'The Great British Brain Drain.' It will not surprise anyone that these degrees and institutions are more likely to be achieved and attended by students who enter with a degree of cultural or economic privilege.

289 Sidney Pierucci, 'Why MICRO-INFLUENCER Marketing Is Still "The Game" in 2019.,' The StartUp, 2018, https://medium.com/swlh/why-micro-influencer-marketing-is-the-game-in-2018-fdeda0993c36.

290 Pierucci.

291 Susie Khamis, Lawrence Ang and Raymond Welling, 'Self-Branding, "Micro-Celebrity" and the Rise of Social Media Influencers,' Celebrity Studies, 2016, https://doi.org/10.1080/19392397.2016.1218292.

292 'Craft Content. Make Bank.,' TRIBE, 2019, https://www.tribegroup.co/influencers.

293 Taylor Lorenz, 'Rising Instagram Stars Are Posting Fake Sponsored Content,' The Atlantic, 2018, https://www.theatlantic.com/technology/archive/2018/12/influencers-are-faking-brand-deals/578401/.

294 White, London in the 18th Century, 187.

295 James Walvin, A Short History of Slavery (London: Penguin, 2007), 57.

296 White, London in the 19th Century, 187.

297 White, London in the 18th Century, 188.

298 White, 189.

299 White, 195.

300 Pat Hudson, 'The Workshop of the World,' BBC History, 2011, http://www.bbc.co.uk/history/british/victorians/workshop_of_the_world_01.shtml.

301 Flora Tristan, London Journal 1840 (London: George Prior Publishers, 1980), 2.

302 Ackroyd, London: The Concise Biography, 386.

303 White, London in the 20th Century, 311.

304 Ackroyd, London: The Concise Biography, 388.

305 Steven Kettell, 'Circuits of Capital and Overproduction: A Marxist Analysis of the Present World Economic Crisis,' Review of Radical Political Economics 2 38, no. 1 (2006): 24–44.

306 Zygmunt Bauman, Work, Consumerism and the New Poor (Berkshire: Open University Press, 2005) cited in; Colin Cremin, Capitalism's New Clothes (London: Pluto Press, 2011), 111.

307 I'm a middle-aged academic in no position to tell anyone what is cool. In the next section I will offer a sociological reading of cool. Nothing could be more un-cooler, other than this footnote.

308 Slavoj Žižek, 'You May!,' London Review of Books, 1999, https://www.lrb.co.uk/v21/n06/slavoj-zizek/you-may.

309 Pierre Bourdieu, Distinction (London: Routledge, 1984), 367.

310 You only live once and Fear of Missing Out, for the blissfully uninformed.

311 To be clear, this excitement to enjoy does not apply to all Londoners.

Many of the more religiously inclined still dwell in a disciplinary environment. Others who are just scraping by in service or manual work may have a disciplinary environment forced upon them. Moreover, I find my students increasingly anxious about the future and often more concerned about job security than freedom and vice. Or maybe finding job security that involves freedom to have vices.

312 Luke Scorziell, 'The Experience Economy with Case Lawrence,' The Edge of Ideas, 2018, https://theedgeofideas.com/2018/03/21/ep-33-experience-economy-case-lawrence/.

313 'Things to Do in London This Weekend,' Time Out, 2018, https://www.timeout.com/london/things-to-do-in-london-this-weekend.

314 Glyn Daly, 'Politics of the Political: Psychoanalytic Theory and the Left(S),' *Journal of Political Ideologies* 14 (2009): 290.

315 Robert Farris Thompson, *African Art in Motion* (Berkeley: University of California Press, 1974), 43 cited in ; McGuigan, *Cool Capitalism*, 3.

316 Dick Pountain and David Robins, *Cool Rules: An Anatomy of an Attitude* (London: Reaktion, 2000), 41.

317 Pountain and Robins, 26 cited in; McGuigan, *Cool Capitalism*, 4.

318 Frank, *The Conquest of Cool*, 26.

319 'The Politics of Cultural Studies,' *Cultural Politics* 2, no. 2 (2006): 137–58; 'The Coolness of Capitalism Today,' *TripleC* 10, no. 2 (2012): 425–38.

320 See Monica; Degen, Clare Melhuish and Gillian Rose, 'Producing Place Atmospheres Digitally: Architecture, Digital Visualisation Practices and the Experience Economy,' *Journal of Consumer Culture* 27 (2015): 1–22.

321 'Pop Up London,' Pop Up London Entertainment, 2016, http://thenudge.com/london-/pop-up-london.

322 *No Logo* (Picador: Knopf Canada, 1999).

323 Florida, *The Rise of the Creative Class: And How It's Transforming Work, Leisure, Community and Everyday Life*, 7.

324 Booth, *Life and Labour of the People in London*.

325 McWilliams, *The Flat White Economy*, 23–24.

326 McWilliams, 24.

327 Ollie O'Brien, 'Cool London?,' Mapping London, 2014, http://mappinglondon.co.uk/2014/cool-london/.

328 'Box Park Shoreditch: About,' Box Park Shoreditch, 2018, https://www.boxpark.co.uk/shoreditch/about/.

329 'Rent a Space - Ebor Street Wall,' Rent a Space, 2018, https://www.appearhere.co.uk/spaces/ebor-street-wall-shoreditch.

330 '#GOODBYESHOREDITCH,' Last Days of Shoreditch, 2018, http://lastdaysofshoreditch.co.uk/.

331 Mike Urban, 'The Death of Brixton's Pope's Road as Sports Direct Take Over,' Brixton Buzz, 2018, http://www.brixtonbuzz.com/2018/06/the-death-of-brixtons-popes-road-as-sports-direct-take-over/.

332 Rowan Moore, *Slow Burn City* (London: Picador, 2016), xix.

333 Sheila Patterson, *Dark Strangers: A Sociological Study of the Absorption of a Recent West Indian Migrant Group in Brixton, South London* (Bloomington: Indiana University Press, 1963), 54. cited in White, *London in the 20th Century*, 22.

334 They also came because, after the US effectively closed its borders to them through the 1952 McCarran-Walter Act, those seeking to escape unemployment and poverty at home had little other option but to head to the Mother Country.

335 Donald Hinds, *Journey to an Illusion: The West Indian in Britain* (London: Heinemann, 1966).

336 White, *London in the 20th Century*, 135.

337 White, 135.

338 Lloyd Bradley, 'Calypso and the Birth of British Black Music,' British Library, 2018, https://www.bl.uk/windrush/articles/calypso-and-the-birth-of-british-black-music.

339 Andy Wilson, '"Co-Existence through Calypsos and Cockney Cabaret": The Inter-Racial Movement and Dutiful Citizenship,' London Black Histories, 2017, http://www.blacklondonhistories.org.uk/tag/1960s/.

340 Martin Kettle and Lucy Hodges, *Uprising!: Police, the People and the*

Riots in Britain's Cities (London: Macmillan, 1982), 141.

341 Alex Wheatle, 'The Gentrification of Brixton: How Did the Area's Character Change so Utterly?,' The Independent, 2015, https://www.independent.co.uk/news/uk/home-news/the-gentrification-of-brixton-how-did-the-areas-character-change-so-utterly-a6749276.html.

342 Future Brixton, 'Have Your Say What Happens "Meanwhile at Pope's Road",' Love Lambeth, 2014, https://love.lambeth.gov.uk/have-your-say-what-happens-meanwhile-at-popes-road/.

343 The history of Pop Brixton comes from an excellent review by Jason Cobb, 'Exclusive: Grow Brixton to Pop Brixton – How a Green Oasis for the Community Turned into a 21st Century Business Park,' Brixton Buzz, 2016, http://www.brixtonbuzz.com/2016/06/exclusive-grow-brixton-to-pop-brixton-how-a-green-oasis-for-the-community-turned-into-a-21st-century-business-park/.

344 Lambeth Council, 'Future Brixton Masterplan' (London, 2009), https://moderngov.lambeth.gov.uk/documents/s57901/01 Future Brixton Masterplan 1.pdf.

345 Jason Cobb, 'Planning Permission Recommended for Grow:Brixton to Transform Site of Old Pope's Road Car Park,' Brixton Buzz, 2014, http://www.brixtonbuzz.com/2014/09/planning-permission-recommended-for-growbrixton-to-transform-site-of-old-popes-road-car-park/.

346 Taffus Maximus, 'Pop Brixton (Formerly Grow Brixton) Pope's Road Development,' Urban75.net, 2014, https://www.urban75.net/forums/threads/pop-brixton-formerly-grow-brixton-popes-road-development.322188/.

347 Cobb, 'Exclusive: Grow Brixton to Pop Brixton – How a Green Oasis for the Community Turned into a 21st Century Business Park.'

348 Jack Hopkins, 'Bridging the Gap between Bedroom and High Street: A Space for Start-Ups to POP up in Brixton,' jackhopkins, 2015, https://jackhopkins.wordpress.com/2015/04/14/bridging-the-gap-between-bedroom-and-high-street-a-space-for-start-ups-to-

pop-up-in-brixton/.

349 Lambeth Council, 'Pop Brixton - Lease Extension until November 2020,' 2017, https://moderngov.lambeth.gov.uk/documents/s929 26/Pop Brixton ODDR - SLA and Lease extension 003.docx.pdf.

350 Jason Cobb, 'Lambeth Council Extends Pop Brixton Lease for Two Years as Business Park Fails to Deliver Any Profit,' Brixton Buzz, 2018, http://www.brixtonbuzz.com/2018/01/lambeth-council-extends-pop-brixton-lease-for-two-years-as-business-park-fails-to-deliver-any-profit/.

351 Lambeth Council, 'State of the Borough 2016' (London, 2016), https://www.lambeth.gov.uk/sites/default/files/State of Borough 2016 - v3.pdf.

352 Lambeth Council, 'Officer Delegated Decision,' Brixton High Street Fund, Pop Brixton co-working space, 2014.

353 Taffus Maximus, 'Pop Brixton (Formerly Grow Brixton) Pope's Road Development,' Urban75.net, 2015, https://www.urban75.net/forums/threads/pop-brixton-formerly-grow-brixton-popes-road-development.322188/page-96.

354 'Working Lives,' Tube Creature, 2011, http://tubecreature.com/#/occupation/current/same/U/940GZZLUBXN/TFTFTF/13/-0.1029/51.4517/.

355 'Chasing Cool,' The Economist, 2014, https://www.economist.com/blighty/2014/04/08/chasing-cool.

356 I don't. I've just found out the cost of childcare in London and have brought my own sandwiches.

357 'Coldharbour,' City Population, 2011, https://www.citypopulation.de/php/uk-wards-london.php?adm2id=E05000420.

358 'Impact Hub,' Pop Brixton, 2019, https://www.popbrixton.org/members/impact-hub/.

359 'Get to Know Us,' Impact Hub Global Community, 2019, https://impacthub.net/get-to-know-us/#frequent.

360 Andy Wilson, 'Lambeth's Budget Challenge,' Love Lambeth, 2019, https://love.lambeth.gov.uk/lambeth-budget-challenge/.

361 Lambeth Council, 'Officer Delegated Decision.'

362 Rebecca Montacute, 'Internships - Unpaid, Unadvertised, Unfair,' Sutton Trust, 2018, https://www.suttontrust.com/wp-content/uploads/2018/01/Internships-2018-briefing.pdf; Orian Brook, David O'Brien and Mark Taylor, 'Panic! Social Class, Taste and Inequalities in the Creative Industries' (London, 2018).and Inequalities in the Creative Industries" (London, 2018

363 Florida, *The New Urban Crisis*, xi.

364 Florida, xxiv.

365 Florida, xiv.

366 Florida, 35.

367 'Peckham Levels,' Peckham Levels, 2019, https://www.peckhamlevels.org/.

368 Ehrenhalt, *The Great Inversion and the Future of the American City*.

369 Florida, 'Class-Divided Cities: London Edition.'

370 Graeme Archer, 'Let's Talk about the Exodus of 600,000 Whites from London,' Daily Telegraph, 2013, https://www.telegraph.co.uk/news/uknews/immigration/9888310/Lets-talk-about-the-exodus-of-600000-whites-from-London.html.

371 Office for National Statistics, 'Population Estimates for the UK, England and Wales, Scotland and Northern Ireland: Mid-2017,' Population Estimates, 2018, https://www.ons.gov.uk/peoplepopulationandcommunity/populationandmigration/populationestimates/bulletins/annualmidyearpopulationestimates/mid2017#growth-varies-less-across-the-uk-london-no-longer-growing-fastest.

372 'Annual Commuting Time Is up 18 Hours Compared to a Decade Ago, Finds TUC,' TUC, 2018, https://www.tuc.org.uk/news/annual-commuting-time-18-hours-compared-decade-ago-finds-tuc.

373 See Ben Judah, *This Is London* (London: Picador, 2016) pp. 203-213 for an evocative account of lives on the N21.

374 Hilary Osborne, 'Average Price of London Home Almost Doubles to £600,625 since 2009,' The Guardian, 2016, https://www.theguardian.com/money/2016/may/11/average-london-home-

doubles-price-house-property.

375 Sarah Marsh, 'How Has Brixton Really Changed? The Data behind the Story,' The Guardian, 2016, https://www.theguardian.com/cities/datablog/2016/jan/14/how-has-brixton-really-changed-the-data-behind-the-story.

376 Olivia O'Suvillan, 'Cine-Files: Ritzy, Brixton, London,' The Guardian, 2011, https://www.theguardian.com/film/2011/oct/05/cine-files-ritzy-cinema-brixton.

377 BECTU, 'Living Staff Living Wage,' Campaigns, 2018, https://www.bectu.org.uk/get-involved/campaigns/picturehouse.

378 Murad Ahmed, 'Strong 2017 Movie Slate Lifts Cineworld Sales, Profits,' Financial Times, 2018, https://www.ft.com/content/efdc62fc-2821-11e8-b27e-cc62a39d57a0.

379 Mike Urban, 'Boycott the Ritzy Campaigners Keep up the Pressure into 2018,' Brixton Buzz, 2018, http://www.brixtonbuzz.com/2018/01/boycott-the-ritzy-campaigners-keep-up-the-pressure-into-2018/.

380 Mayhew, London Labour and the London Poor.

381 'Aristocrats Own Third of Land in England and Wales,' The Independent, 2010, https://www.independent.co.uk/news/uk/home-news/aristocrats-own-third-of-land-in-england-and-wales-2130392.html.

382 'Who Owns Central London?,' Who Owns England?, 2017, https://whoownsengland.org/2017/10/28/who-owns-central-london/.

383 See for example Carole Cadwalladr, 'Whatever the Party, Our Political Elite Is an Oxbridge Club,' The Guardian, 2015, https://www.theguardian.com/commentisfree/2015/aug/24/our-political-elite-oxbridge-club; Owen Jones, The Establishment (London: Penguin, 2014); Philip Kirby, 'Leading People 2016: The Educational Backgrounds of the UK Professional Elite,' 2016, https://www.suttontrust.com/wp-content/uploads/2016/02/Leading-People_Feb16.pdf.

384 I'm not at all bitter about having to memorise a list of murderous kings and queens.

385 Catherine Hall et al., 'Introduction,' in *Legacies of British Slave Ownership* (Cambridge: Cambridge University Press, 2014).

386 White, *London in the 19th Century*, 216.

387 White, 216.

388 White, 218–19.

389 Kate Fox, *Watching the English* (London: Hodder and Stoughton, 2004), 81.

390 White, *London in the 18th Century*, 131–32.

391 German and Rees, *A People's History of London*, 46.

392 Mike Savage et al., 'A New Model of Social Class? Findings from the BBC's Great British Class Survey Experiment,' *Sociology* 47, no. 2 (2014).

393 'Huge Survey Reveals Seven Social Classes in UK,' BBC News, 2013, https://www.bbc.co.uk/news/uk-22007058.

394 Mike Savage, *Social Class in the 21st Century* (London: Pelican Books, 2015), 6–7.

395 Savage et al., 'A New Model of Social Class? Findings from the BBC's Great British Class Survey Experiment,' 242.

396 Florida, *The Rise of the Creative Class, Revisited*, 37.

397 Florida, 'Class-Divided Cities: London Edition.'

398 Florida, *The Rise of the Creative Class, Revisited*, 9.

399 Florida, 'Class-Divided Cities: London Edition.'

400 'Insight: Focus on the Southwest Ontario Region,' Martin Prosperity Insights, 2009, http://martinprosperity.org/tag/service-class/.

401 Florida, 'Class-Divided Cities: London Edition.'

402 Corporate Research Unit, 'Bethnal Green Ward Profile,' London Borough of Tower Hamlets, 2014, https://www.towerhamlets.gov.uk/Documents/Borough_statistics/Ward_profiles/Bethnal_Green.pdf.

403 'DataShine: Census,' DataShine, 2019, http://datashine.org.uk/#table=QS112EW&col=QS112EW0031&ramp=YlOrRd&layers=BTTT&zoom=14&lon=-0.0636&lat=51.5280.

404 'More than Half of Children Now Live in Poverty in Some Parts of the UK,' End Child Poverty, 2018, https://www.endchildpoverty.

org.uk/more-than-half-of-children-now-living-in-poverty-in-some-parts-of-the-uk/.

405 Ruth Bloomfield, 'Hotspot in Waiting: Bethnal Green Set to Rival Shoreditch with Trendy Bars and New Homes in the Victorian Chest Hospital,' The Evening Standard, 2018, https://www.homesandproperty.co.uk/property-news/buying/new-homes/bethnal-green-set-to-rival-shoreditch-with-trendy-bars-and-new-homes-in-the-victorian-chest-hospital-a119346.html.

406 'London Loses One Pub a Week, According to New Figures,' BBC News, 2018, https://www.bbc.co.uk/news/uk-england-london-4 4659180.

407 Martin Prosperity Insights, 'London, Brilliant!' 2013, http://martinprosperity.org/wp-content/uploads/2013/06/London-Insight_v01.pdf.

408 Florida, 'Class-Divided Cities: London Edition.'

409 BFI, 'UK Films and British Talent Worldwide' (London, 2018).

410 Heather Carey et al., 'A Skills Audit of the UK Film and Screen Industries' (London, 2017).

411 'Employment and Place of Employment in the Film Industry, 2017,' Office for National Statistics, 2017, https://www.ons.gov.uk/employmentandlabourmarket/peopleinwork/employmentandemployeetypes/adhocs/008458employmentand placeofemploymentinthefilmindustry2017?:uri=employmentan dlabourmarket/peopleinwork/employmentandemployeetypes/adhocs/008458employmentandplac.

412 White, London in the 20th Century, 336.

413 Brook, O'Brien, and Taylor, 'Panic! Social Class, Taste and Inequalities in the Creative Industries.'

414 'Employment in the Film Industry' (London, 2017).

415 'Employment in the Film Industry.'

416 BECTU, 'Production Branch Ratecard 2018,' Production branch ratecard 2018, 2017, https://www.bectu.org.uk/advice-resources/library/2449.

417 S Cunningham, 'Developments in Measuring the "Creative

Workforce",' *Cultural Trends* 20, no. 1 (2011): 37.

418 This count does not include foreign-based institutions, such as American 'study abroad' centres like mine.

419 'Student Numbers in London,' London Higher, 2017, https://www. londonhigher.ac.uk/ceo-blog/student-numbers-in-london/.

420 'Student Numbers in London.'

421 White, *London in the 18th Century*, xx–xxi.

422 'History of University of London,' University of London, 2018, https://london.ac.uk/about-us/history-university-london.

423 Richard Florida, 'Mapping the World's Knowledge Hubs,' CityLab, 2017, https://www.citylab.com/life/2017/01/mapping-the-worlds-knowledge-hubs/505748/.

424 'Top Ten Facts About Studying in London,' Study London, 2018, https://www.studylondon.ac.uk/why-study-in-london/top-10-facts.

425 '20 Facts About London's Culture.'

426 White, *London in the 20th Century*, 337.

427 White, 337.

428 White, *London in the 18th Century*, 175.

429 David Holmes, *Communication Theory: Media, Technology and Society* (London: SAGE, 2005), 77.

430 White, *London in the 18th Century*, 166.

431 Sidney W. Mintz, *Sweetness and Power: The Place of Sugar in Modern History* (New York: Penguin Books, 1985), 111.

432 Chris Harman, A People's History of the World, 2nd ed. (London: Verso, 2008), 249.

433 Daniel Defoe, *A Tour Thro' the Whole Island of Great Britain, Divided into Circuits or Journies* (London: JM Dent and Co, 1927).

434 Will Dahlgreen, 'Bookish Britain: Literary Jobs Are the Most Desirable,' YouGov, 2015, https://yougov.co.uk/topics/politics/articles-reports/2015/02/15/bookish-britain-academic-jobs-are-most-desired.

435 'The Values of Queen Mary University of London,' Queen Mary University of London, 2014, https://www.qmul.ac.uk/strategy/the-

strategy/values/index.html.

436 My awareness of these stereotypes may say more about my work ethic than my colleagues.

437 Apologies to all those wonderfully fashionable academics; there is nothing anti-intellectual about looking good or following pop culture. Moreover, there are some deep gender stereotypes in the mythology of the mad professor sketched out here.

438 Except on Wednesdays, when I'm rudely awakened by the dustman.

439 Paul F. Gorczynski, Denise Hill and Shanaya Rathod, 'Examining the Construct Validity of the Transtheoretical Model to Structure Workplace Physical Activity Interventions to Improve Mental Health in Academic Staff,' *EMS Community Medicine Journal* 1, no. 1 (2017).

440 I am one of them.

441 Katia Levecque et al., 'Work Organization and Mental Health Problems in PhD Students,' *Research Policy* 46, no. 4 (2017).

442 Anonymous Academic, 'Academia Is Built on Exploitation. We Must Break This Vicious Circle,' The Guardian, 2018, https://www.theguardian.com/higher-education-network/2018/may/18/academia-exploitation-university-mental-health-professors-plagiarism.

443 Ken Mayhew, Cecile Deer and Mehak Dua, 'The Move to Mass Higher Education in the UK: Many Questions and Some Answers,' *Oxford Review of Education* 30, no. 1 (2004): 66.

444 Ana Lopes and Indra Angeli Dewan, 'Precarious Pedagogies? The Impact of Casual and Zero-Hour Contracts in Higher Education,' *Journal of Feminist Scholarship* 7, no. 8 (2014): 28–42.

445 Tony Blair, 'Full Text of Tony Blair's Speech on Education,' The Guardian, 2001, https://www.theguardian.com/politics/2001/may/23/labour.tonyblair.

446 Mayhew, Deer, and Dua, 'The Move to Mass Higher Education in the UK: Many Questions and Some Answers,' 66.

447 Lord Robbins, 'The Robbins Report' (London, 1963).

448 National Committee of Inquiry into Higher Education, 'Higher Education in the Learning Society (The Dearing Report),' 1997, http://www.leeds.ac.uk/educol/ncihe/.

449 'With Greater Participation, Even "Greater Inequality,"' Times Higher Education, 2016, meshighereducation.com/news/expans ion-in-global-higher-education-has-increased-inequality.

450 Queen Mary University, 'The Queen Mary Statement of Graduate Attributes,' 2015, http://www.qmul.ac.uk/gacep/statement/.

451 'Strike - QMUL UCU,' Strike, 2018, https://qmucu.wordpress.com/ strike/.

452 'Precarious Work in Higher Education,' UCU, 2016, https://www. ucu.org.uk/media/7995/Precarious-work-in-higher-education-a-snapshot-of-insecure-contracts-and-institutional-attitudes-Apr-16/pdf/ucu_precariouscontract_hereport_apr16.pdf.

453 Jacqueline Z. Wilsona et al., 'Retaining a Foothold on the Slippery Paths of Academia: University Women, Indirect Discrimination, and the Academic Marketplace,' Gender and Education 22, no. 5 (2010): 535–545.

454 Alexandre Afonso, 'How Academia Resembles a Drug Gang,' LSE Impact Blog, 2013, http://blogs.lse.ac.uk/impact ofsocialsciences/2013/12/11/how-academia-resembles-a-drug-gang/.

455 Steven Levitt and Sudhir Venkatesh, 'An Economic Analysis of a Drug-Selling Gang's Finances,' Quarterly Journal of Economics 115, no. 3 (2000): 755–789.

456 Johan Davidsson and Marek Naczyk, 'The Ins and Outs of Dualisation: A Literature Review,' Working Papers on the Reconciliation of Work and Welfare in Europe 2 (2009).

457 Aditya Chakrabortty and Sally Weale, 'Universities Accused of "importing Sports Direct Model" for Lecturers' Pay,' The Guardian, 2016, https://www.theguardian.com/uk-news/2016/ nov/16/universities-accused-of-importing-sports-direct-model-for-lecturers-pay.

458 Afonso, 'How Academia Resembles a Drug Gang.'

459 Emmenegger, Partick; Häusermann, Silja; Palier, Bruno; Seeleib-Kaiser, Martin, ed., The Age of Dualization: The Changing Face of Inequality in Deindustrializing Societies (Oxford: Oxford University Press, 2012).

460 'The Disposable Academic,' The Economist 397, no. 8713 (2010).

461 David Knights and Caroline Clarke, 'It's a Bittersweet Symphony, This Life: Fragile Academic Selves and Insecure Identities at Work,' Organization Studies 35, no. 3 (2014): 335–57.

462 I knew I was working too hard when my dreams, unrelated to work, were organised in the format of PowerPoint slides. This realisation did not stop me having to work too hard.

463 See, for example, Anonymous Academic, 'Academia Is Built on Exploitation. We Must Break This Vicious Circle'; Anonymous Academic, 'I Just Got a Permanent Academic Job – but I'm Not Celebrating,' The Guardian, 2018, https://www.theguardian.com/higher-education-network/2018/jun/22/permanent-academic-job-university-system-unfair-exploitative; Alexander Gallas, 'The Proliferation Of Precarious Labour in Academia,' Progress in Political Economy, 2018, http://ppesydney.net/proliferation-precarious-labour-academia/.

464 R Gill, 'Academics, Cultural Workers and Critical Labour Studies,' Journal of Cultural Economy 7, no. 1 (2014): 12.

465 'Stamp out Casual Contracts,' UCU, 2018, https://www.ucu.org.uk/stampout.

466 'Population by Nationality,' Office for National Statistics, 2017, https://data.london.gov.uk/dataset/nationality.

467 BOP Consulting & Graham Devlin Associates, 'Arts Council England Analysis of Theatre in England' (London, 2016), https://www.artscouncil.org.uk/sites/default/files/download-file/Analysis of Theatre in England - Final Report.pdf.

468 Joe Murphy, 'Nearly Half of Black and Ethnic Minority Londoners "Have Faced Racist Abuse", Study Finds,' The Independent, 2017, https://www.standard.co.uk/news/crime/nearly-half-of-black-and-ethnic-minority-londoners-have-faced-racist-abuse-study-

finds-a3252851.html.

469 Greater London Authority, 'Ethnicity Pay Gap Reporting: March 2017 Data' (London, 2017), https://www.london.gov.uk/sites/default/files/gla-ethnicity-pay-gap-report-2017.pdf.

470 'Low Pay and High Stress: Survey Lifts Lid on Life as a Struggling Performer,' BBC News, 2018, https://www.bbc.co.uk/news/entertainment-arts-46356689.

471 A McRobbie, 'Re-Thinking Creative Economy as Radical Social Enterprise,' *Variant* 41 (2011): 32–33.

472 Daniel Ashton, 'Creative Work Careers: Pathways and Portfolios for the Creative Economy,' *Journal of Education and Work* 28, no. 4 (2015). I have personal experience of this, not only in tailoring my CV for retail work when I couldn't even get an interview for university positions, but also when I taught a session called 'Art Works' on CV building for Arts students. It made me sad.

473 Brook, O'Brien, and Taylor, 'Panic! Social Class, Taste and Inequalities in the Creative Industries.'

474 This is not at all to suggest that Mandla is involved in anything of questionable legality.

475 Alistair Smith, 'London Theatre Report' (London, 2014), https://www.londontheatre1.com/londontheatrereportv7.pdf.

476 Nick Clark, 'Just One Actor in 50 Makes More than £20,000 per Year, Survey Shows,' The Independent, 2014, https://www.independent.co.uk/incoming/just-one-actor-in-50-makes-more-than-20000-per-year-survey-shows-9448922.html.

477 Levitt and Venkatesh, 'An Economic Analysis of a Drug-Selling Gang's Finances.'

478 Emma Youle, 'Camden Fringe Theatre Thrives but Actors Pay Remains Too Low: Only One in Five on Minimum Wage,' Ham & High, 2014, https://www.hamhigh.co.uk/news/camden-fringe-theatre-thrives-but-actors-pay-remains-too-low-only-one-in-five-on-minimum-wage-1-3785159.

479 'Plays in London,' Official London Theatre, 2018, https://officiallondontheatre.com/plays-in-london/.

480 Smith, 'London Theatre Report.'

481 Smith.

482 Emma Holland, 'Where to Find Australian Flat Whites and Coffees in London,' The Upsider, 2018, https://theupsider.com.au/london-coffee/8768.

483 Peter Thomson, 'Origins of the Flat White,' Peter J Thomson, 2014, https://www.peterjthomson.com/coffee/flat-white-coffee-origins/.

484 Jonathan Pearlman, 'Who Invented the Flat White? Row Breaks out between Australian and New Zealand Cafe Owners,' Telegraph, 2015, https://www.telegraph.co.uk/news/worldnews/australiaandthepacific/australia/11895654/Who-invented-the-flat-white-Row-breaks-out-between-Australian-and-New-Zealand-cafe-owners.html.

485 'London's Original Flat White,' Flat White, 2015, http://www.flatwhitesoho.co.uk/.

486 'London's Original Flat White.'

487 Harriet Marsden, 'How the Flat White Conquered the Coffee Scene,' The Independent, 2018, https://www.independent.co.uk/life-style/flat-white-coffee-culture-antipodean-mcdonalds-advert-starbucks-latte-a8246111.html.

488 I feel a little guilty. But not really.

489 'The Changing Face of British Coffee Culture: 5 Key Themes,' Allegra World Coffee Portal, 2018, https://www.worldcoffeeportal.com/Latest/InsightAnalysis/2018/5-key-themes-The-changing-face-of-British-coffee.

490 'The Decline of the Australian in the UK,' BBC News, 2014, https://www.bbc.co.uk/news/magazine-25401024.

491 GLA Intelligence, 'Country of Birth Ward Tools (2011 Census),' Census Information Scheme, 2011, https://data.london.gov.uk/dataset/country-of-birth-ward-tools--2011-census-.

492 Ash London, 'Ten Reasons You Need to Spend a Year Living in London in Your 20s,' news.com.au, 2016, https://www.news.com.au/travel/travel-ideas/adventure/ten-reasons-you-need-to-spend-a-year-living-in-london-in-your-20s/news-story/0278b09c1ac8bdf

de28332fb02e2c3e0.

493 Alex Stanhope, 'An Australian Explains Why London Is the Worst City on Earth,' Vice UK, 2017, https://www.vice.com/en_uk/article/ezz4ke/an-australian-explains-why-london-is-the-worst-city-on-earth.

494 Esther Smith, 'Trial Shifts: To Pay or Not to Pay?,' Big Hospitality, 2017, https://www.bighospitality.co.uk/Article/2017/08/09/Trial-shifts-to-pay-or-not-to-pay.

495 'Jobs Paid Less than the London Living Wage in London in 2015, 2016, 2017, by Industry,' Office for National Statistics, 2018, https://www.ons.gov.uk/employmentandlabourmarket/peopleinwork/earningsandworkinghours/adhocs/008557jobspaidlessthanthelondonlivingwageinlondonin201520162017byindustry.

496 'London Analysis: Estimates of Employee Jobs Paid Less than the Living Wage in London and Other Parts of the UK,' Office for National Statistics, 2015, https://www.ons.gov.uk/employmentandlabourmarket/peopleinwork/earningsandworkinghours/articles/londonanalysis/2015-10-12.

497 Florida, *The New Urban Crisis*.

498 Wainwright, ''Everything Is Gentrification Now': But Richard Florida Isn't Sorry.'

499 Wainwright.

500 Mark Spilsbury, 'Journalists at Work' (London, 2018).

501 Nick Davies, *Flat Earth News* (London: Vintage, 2008).

502 'Journalism and Social Class Briefing,' National Union of Journalists, 2012, https://www.nuj.org.uk/documents/journalism-and-social-class-briefing/milburn.pdf.

503 Neil Thurman, Alessio Cornia and Jessica Kunert, 'Journalists in the UK' (London, 2016), http://openaccess.city.ac.uk/14664/1/Journalists in the UK.pdf.

504 'Journalism and Social Class Briefing.'

505 Spilsbury, 'Journalists at Work.'

506 'One in Five Journalists Earn Less than £20,000,' National Union of Journalists, 2015, https://www.nuj.org.uk/news/one-in-five-

journalists-earn-less-than-20000/.

507 Spilsbury, 'Journalists at Work.'

508 Thurman, Cornia, and Kunert, 'Journalists in the UK.'

509 Montacute, 'Internships - Unpaid, Unadvertised, Unfair.'

510 Spilsbury, 'Journalists at Work.'

511 Dahlgreen, 'Bookish Britain: Literary Jobs Are the Most Desirable'; Laura Hampson, 'This Is the Age Most Adults Land Their Dream Job,' The Evening Standard, 2018, https://www.standard.co.uk/ lifestyle/london-life/how-to-find-dream-job-a4007906.html.

512 '2018 Authors' Earnings' (London, 2018), https://literaturea lliancescotland.co.uk/wp-content/uploads/2018/06/ALCS_ Authors_Earnings_Report_2018.pdf.

513 '2018 Authors' Earnings.'

514 Thurman, Cornia, and Kunert, 'Journalists in the UK.'

515 White, *London in the 19th Century*, 225.

516 White, 227.

517 White, 229.

518 White, 235.

519 White, 236.

520 White, 235.

521 I was offered £50 for my latest submission. I took it.

522 Allen Wood, *Karl Marx* (London: Routledge, 2004), 246.

523 Terry Eagleton, *After Theory* (London: Penguin, 2003), 42.

524 Wood, *Karl Marx*, 135–36.

525 London, *The People of the Abyss*, 65.

526 London, 66.

527 London, 67.

528 Charles Duhigg and David Barboza, 'Apple IPad and the Human Costs for Workers in China,' The New York Times, 2012, http://www. nytimes.com/2012/01/26/business/ieconomy-apples-ipad-and-the-human-costs-for-workers-in-china.html?_r=4&pagewanted=all.

529 James Pomfret, 'Migrants Elbow for Foxconn Jobs despite Labor Probe,' Reuters, 2012, http://www.reuters.com/article/us-apple-labour-china-idUSTRE81M0EA20120223; Rob Waugh, 'Apple's

Chinese Supplier Foxconn Is Recruiting 18,000 People to Build New IPhone - and Device Is "Due in June",' Mail Online, 2012, http://www.dailymail.co.uk/sciencetech/article-2125009/iPhone-5-release-date-Apples-Chinese-supplier-Foxconn-recruiting-18k-people-build-new-device-June.html.

530 Karl Marx, *Capital* (Oxford: Oxford University Press, 1995), 352.

531 Marx, 352.

532 Marx, 357.

533 GLA Economics, 'London's Economic Outlook : Spring 2017 The GLA's Medium-Term Planning Projections' (London: Greater London Authority, 2017).

534 GLA Economics.

535 Jonathan Prynn, 'Record Year as 19 Million Tourists Visit London,' Evening Standard, 2017, https://www.standard.co.uk/news/london/record-year-as-19m-tourists-visit-london-a3542271.html.

536 'Annual Survey of Visits to Visitor Attractions: Latest Results,' Visit Britain, 2016, https://www.visitbritain.org/annual-survey-visits-visitor-attractions-latest-results.

537 Such was the success of the event that a surplus of £186,000 was achieved, the equivalent of £23 million today.

538 'Whitehall, May 18 1899,' *The London Gazette*, May 19, 1899, https://www.thegazette.co.uk/London/issue/27081/page/3186.

539 As is the case across London, our landlord has sub-divided this address into four separate dwellings. Without irony, he complains that his daughters still live with him as they cannot afford property in London.

540 I'm not succeeding.

541 Kathryn Hughes, 'The Middle Classes: Etiquette and Upward Mobility,' The British Library, 2014, https://www.bl.uk/romantics-and-victorians/articles/the-middle-classes-etiquette-and-upward-mobility.

542 'Domestic Workers,' Women in Informal Employment: Globalizing and Organizing, 2018, http://www.wiego.org/informal-economy/occupational-groups/domestic-workers.

543 William Cavert, *The Smoke of London: Energy and Environment in the Early Modern City* (Cambridge: Cambridge University Press, 2016), 14.

544 White, *London in the 20th Century*, 193–194.

545 German and Rees, *A People's History of London*, 233.

546 'Employment by Occupation Type and Gender, Borough,' London Datastore, 2017, https://data.london.gov.uk/dataset/employment-occupation-type-and-gender-borough.

547 Harry Mount, 'Are You Being Served?,' The Telegraph, 2013, http://www.telegraph.co.uk/lifestyle/10024092/Are-you-being-served.html.

548 Kalayaan, 'Britain's Forgotten Slaves; Migrant Domestic Workers in the UK Three Years after the Introduction of the Tied Overseas Domestic Worker Visa,' Kalayaan Three Year Briefing, 2015, http://www.kalayaan.org.uk/wp-content/uploads/2014/09/Kalayaan-3-year-briefing.pdf.

549 Mount, 'Are You Being Served?'

550 Clive Coleman, '"Outsourced" Workers Seek Better Deal in Landmark Case,' BBC News, 2017, http://www.bbc.co.uk/news/uk-42056769.

551 Equality and Human Rights Commission, 'The Invisible Workforce: Employment Practices in the Cleaning Sector - Findings Report,' no. August (2014): 1–92, https://www.equalityhumanrights.com/sites/default/files/the_invisible_workforce_full_report_08-08-14.pdf; Trust for London, 'Low Pay,' London's Poverty Profile, 2016, http://www.londonpovertyprofile.org.uk/indicators/topics/low-pay/.

552 Katie Morley, 'Half of Millennials Hiring Cleaners as They Are "too Busy" to Clean One-Bed Flats,' The Telegraph, 2017, http://www.telegraph.co.uk/news/2017/06/18/half-millenials-hiring-cleaners-busy-clean-one-bed-flats/.

553 Tristram Hunt, 'Urban Britain Is Heading for Victorian Levels of Inequality,' The Guardian, 2007, https://www.theguardian.com/commentisfree/2007/jul/18/comment.money; David Olusoga,

'The Victorian Slums Are Back – and Housing Developers Are to Blame Again,' The Guardian, 2018, https://www.theguardian.com/commentisfree/2018/jan/16/victorian-slums-housing-developers-housebuilding-inequality; Haddad, 'The Perfect Storm: Economic Stagnation, the Rising Cost of Living, Public Spending Cuts, and the Impact on UK Poverty'; Graham Snowdon, 'Pay Gap Widening to Victorian Levels,' The Guardian, 2012, https://www.theguardian.com/business/2011/may/16/high-pay-commission-wage-disparity.

554 'Spain Youth Unemployment Rate,' Trading Economics, 2018, https://tradingeconomics.com/spain/youth-unemployment-rate.

555 'Population by Nationality.'

556 D. McIlwaine, C. and Bunge, 'Towards Visibility: The Latin American Community in London' (London, 2016).

557 Equality and Human Rights Commission, 'The Invisible Workforce: Employment Practices in the Cleaning Sector - Findings Report,' 23.

558 Keijonen, 'London's Sectors: More Detailed Jobs Data.'

559 ONS, 'London Analysis: Estimates of Employee Jobs Paid Less than the Living Wage in London and Other Parts of the UK,' London Analysis: Estimates of employee jobs paid less than the Living Wage in London and Other Parts of the UK, 2015, https://www.ons.gov.uk/employmentandlabourmarket/peopleinwork/earningsandworkinghours/articles/londonanalysis/2015-10-12.

560 Mayhew, London Labour and the London Poor, 10.

561 ONS, 'People in Employment on a Zero-Hours Contract: March 2017,' People in employment on a zero-hours contract: Mar 2017, 2017, https://www.ons.gov.uk/employmentandlabourmarket/peopleinwork/earningsandworkinghours/articles/contractsthatdonotguaranteeaminimumnumberofhours/mar2017.

562 ADS, 'UK Security Sector Outlook 2016,' UK security sector outlook 2016, 2016, https://www.adsgroup.org.uk/wp-content/uploads/sites/21/2016/12/SecurityOutlook2016-E-Res.pdf.

563 London Stock Exchange, 'GFS G4S PLC ORD 25P,' London Stock Exchange, 2017.

564 Shane Croucher, 'G4S Scandals: From London 2012 Security Fiasco to Jimmy Mubenga Death,' International Business Times, 2014.

565 BBC, 'FTSE 100 Closes at Another Record High,' BBC News, 2017, http://www.bbc.co.uk/news/business-39301556.

566 Trust for London, 'Low Pay.'

567 Frank Field and Andrew Forsey, 'Sweated Labour: Uber and the "Gig Economy"' (London, 2016), http://www.frankfield.co.uk/upload/docs/Sweated Labour - Uber and the 'gig economy'.pdf.

568 Select Committee on the Sweating System, 'Report from the Select Committee of the House of Lords on the Sweating System, with Proceedings of the Committee,' 1890.

569 Even Marx did not write of unemployment, relying instead upon notions of surplus labour and the reserve army, terms taken from the British Labour movement of the time.

570 White, London in the 19th Century, 184.

571 'Drive with Uber Make Money on Your Schedule,' Uber, 2019, https://www.uber.com/a/join-new/gb.

572 Field and Forsey, 'Sweated Labour: Uber and the "Gig Economy."'

573 'PHVs and the Congestion Charge,' Transport for London, 2019, https://tfl.gov.uk/info-for/taxis-and-private-hire/phvs-and-the-congestion-charge.

574 'Taxi and Private Hire Driver Demographic Statistics,' Transport for London, 2018, http://content.tfl.gov.uk/taxi-and-phv-demographic-stats.pdf.

575 White, London in the 19th Century, 186.

576 White, 187.

577 Booth, Life and Labour of the People in London, 322.

578 Sean Morrison, Hatty Collier and Johnathan Mitchell, 'Uber London Ban Reaction as It Happened: TfL Strips App of Its Licence,' The Evening Standard, 2017, https://www.standard.co.uk/news/transport/uber-stripped-of-london-licence-live-updates-and-reaction-a3641111.html.

579 'IWGB Reaction to TfL Decision to Revoke UBER's License,' IWGB, 2017, https://www.forbes.com/sites/oliversmith/2018/03/16/the-

londoner-who-brought-uber-to-its-knees/#6ec6d6dd6933.

580 Samuel Fishwick, 'Uber Drivers React to News of TfL's London Ban: 'I Finished the Job, Then Pulled over and Cried,'' The Evening Standard, 2017, https://www.standard.co.uk/lifestyle/london-life/ uber-drivers-react-over-news-of-tfl-ban-a3643966.html.

581 'Uber Granted Short-Term Licence to Operate in London,' BBC News, 2018, https://www.bbc.co.uk/news/business-44612837.

582 Sarah Butler, 'Uber Loses Appeal over Driver Employment Rights,' The Guardian, 2018, https://www.theguardian. com/technology/2018/dec/19/uber-loses-appeal-over-driver-employment-rights.

583 Field and Forsey, 'Wild West Workplace: Self-Employment in Britain's "Gig Economy."'

584 Chris Yuill, 'Identity and Solidarity in the Gig Economy,' in BSA 2018 Annual Conference (Northumbria: British Sociological Association, 2018).

585 'Keep Deliveroo'in,' Reddit, 2019, https://www.reddit.com/r/ deliveroos/.

586 'Tech Round-Up: Why Am I Offered Specific Orders?,' Roo Community, 2019, https://roocommunity.com/tech-round-up-how-and-why-am-i-offered-specific-orders/.

587 'Introduction to Deliveroo,' European Commission, 2016, http://ec.europa.eu/information_society/newsroom/image/ document/2016-6/deliveroo_13855.pdf.

588 'Deliveroo Claims Victory in Self-Employment Case,' BBC News, 2017, https://www.bbc.co.uk/news/business-41983343.

589 Anoosh Chakelian, ''I Don't Even Go to the Toilet': Deliveroo Riders Will Fight to Be Recognised as Workers,' The New Statesman, 2018, https://www.newstatesman.com/politics/economy/2018/06/i-don-t-even-go-toilet-deliveroo-riders-will-fight-be-recognised-workers.

590 Patrick Collinson, 'How Do Deliveroo and Uber Workers Cope with Precarious Pay?,' The Guardian, 2018, https://www.theguardian. com/business/2018/oct/20/deliveroo-uber-workers-pay-gig-

economy.

591 White, *London in the 19th Century*, 198.

592 Field and Forsey, 'Sweated Labour: Uber and the "Gig Economy."'

593 London, *The People of the Abyss*, 18.

594 Bauman, *Wasted Lives: Modernity and Its Outcasts* (London: Polity, 2004).

595 Michael Denning, 'Wageless Life,' *New Left Review*, 2010, 79–97.

596 Guy Vincent, 'Sustainable Microentrepreneurship: The Roles of Microfinance, Entrepreneurship and Sustainability in Reducing Poverty in Developing Countries,' The Global Development Research Centre, 2005.

597 Henrik Huitfeldt and Johannes Jütting, 'Informality and Informal Employment,' 2009; Thanos Maroukis, Krystyna Iglicka and Katarzyna Gmaj, 'Irregular Migration and Informal Economy in Southern and Central-Eastern Europe: Breaking the Vicious Cycle?' *International Migration* 49, no. 5 (October 16, 2011): 129–56, https://doi.org/10.1111/j.1468-2435.2011.00709.x.

598 White, *London in the 19th Century*, 198.

599 Marx, *Das Kapital*, 362.

600 Marx, *Das Kapital*.

601 Yvonne Roberts, 'The Tiny Union Beating the Gig Economy Giants,' The Guardian, 2018, https://www.theguardian.com/politics/2018/jul/01/union-beating-gig-economy-giants-iwgb-zero-hours-workers.

602 'About Us,' The University of London, 2019, https://london.ac.uk/about-us.

603 'Boycott Senate House,' IWGB, 2019, https://iwgb.org.uk/boycottsenatehouse.

604 'Why Support the Boycott?,' IWGB, 2019, https://iwgb.org.uk/page/hidden/why-support-the-boycott.

605 Richard J Evans, 'Eric Hobsbawm Would Not Have Backed University of London Boycott,' The Guardian, 2019, https://www.theguardian.com/education/2019/feb/11/eric-hobsbawm-would-not-have-backed-university-of-london-boycott.

606 Sarah Marsh, 'London University Criticised for Spending £415,000 on Protest Security,' The Guardian, 2018, https://www.theguardian. com/education/2018/jun/04/university-of-london-criticised-for-spending-415000-on-student-protest-security.

607 Simon Childs, 'The University of London's "Theatre of Security" Is Clamping Down on Student Dissent,' Vice, 2018, https://www. vice.com/en_uk/article/wjbn5n/the-university-of-londons-theatre-of-security-is-clamping-down-on-student-dissent.

608 '10 December 2018 - University of London Statement on Boycott of Senate House,' University of London, 2018, https://london. ac.uk/10-december-2018-university-london-statement-boycott-senate-house.

609 '10 December 2018 - University of London Statement on Boycott of Senate House.'

610 Butler, 'Uber Loses Appeal over Driver Employment Rights.'

611 Sarah Butler, 'Deliveroo Riders Lose High Court Battle to Gain Union Recognition,' The Guardian, 2018, https://www.theguardian. com/business/2018/dec/05/deliveroo-riders-lose-high-court-battle-gain-union-recognition.

612 @boycottUoL, 'Around 50 @UoLondon Cleaners Have Written a Letter Thanking Academics for Boycotting @londonu and Telling Them Why Their Resolve to Campaign to End Outsourcing Is Stronger than Ever. 😊😊😊 #BoycottSenateHouse Http:// Boycottsenatehouse.Com,' BOYCOTT SENATE HOUSE, 2019.

613 Tito Boeri and Juan F. Jimeno, 'The Unbearable Divergence of Unemployment in Europe' (Madrid, 2015), https://www.bde. es/f/webbde/SES/Secciones/Publicaciones/PublicacionesSeriadas/ DocumentosTrabajo/15/Fich/dt1534e.pdf.

614 Rupert Neate, 'Two-Thirds of UK's Highest Paid Live in London or South-East, HMRC Data Shows,' The Guardian, 2019, https:// www.theguardian.com/inequality/2019/mar/18/two-thirds-of-uks-highest-paid-live-in-london-or-south-east-hmrc-data-shows.

615 Oxford Economics, 'London 2030: How Will the Capital's Economy Change?' (Oxford, 2018).

616 Julia Kollewe, 'High Times: 76 Tall Buildings to Join London's Skyline in 2019,' The Guardian, 2019, https://www.theguardian.com/business/2019/mar/05/tall-buildings-london-skyline-2019.

617 GLA Intelligence, 'Interim 2015-Based Trend Projection Results' (London, 2017).

618 Ashley Kirk, 'Seven Things You Did Not Know about Migration in the UK,' The Telegraph, 2015, https://www.telegraph.co.uk/news/uknews/immigration/11942613/Seven-things-you-did-not-know-about-migration-in-the-UK.html.

619 'More than Half of Children Now Live in Poverty in Some Parts of the UK.'

620 Sarah Marsh, 'Record Number of People Sleeping Rough in London,' The Guardian, 2018, https://www.theguardian.com/society/2018/oct/31/record-number-of-people-are-sleeping-rough-in-london.

621 'Northern European Cities Offer Best Living Conditions,' ECA International, 2018, https://www.eca-international.com/news/march-2018/northern-european-cities-offer-best-living-conditi.

622 '2019 World's Best Cities,' Resonance Consultancy, 2018, http://resonanceco.com/reports/2019-worlds-best-cities/.

623 Prynn, 'Record Year as 19 Million Tourists Visit London.'

624 Ackroyd, London: The Concise Biography, 492.

References

@boycottUoL. 'Around 50 @UoLondon Cleaners Have Written a Letter Thanking Academics for Boycotting @londonu and Telling Them Why Their Resolve to Campaign to End Outsourcing Is Stronger than Ever. 😬😬😬 #BoycottSenateHouse Http://Boycottsenatehouse.Com.' BOYCOTT SENATE HOUSE, 2019.

@mattb. ''Silicon Roundabout': The Ever-Growing Community of Fun Startups in London's Old Street Area [Tweet],' 2018. https://twitter.com/mattb/status/866136681.

'#GOODBYESHOREDITCH.' Last Days of Shoreditch, 2018. http://lastdaysofshoreditch.co.uk/.

'10 December 2018- University of London Statement on Boycott of Senate House.' University of London, 2018. https://london.ac.uk/10-december-2018-university-london-statement-boycott-senate-house.

'20 Facts About London's Culture.' Mayor of London, 2018. https://www.london.gov.uk/what-we-do/arts-and-culture/vision-and-strategy/20-facts-about-london's-culture#.

'2011 Census: Key Statistics and Quick Statistics for Local Authorities in the United Kingdom.' Office for National Statistics, 2011. https://www.ons.gov.uk/peoplepopulationandcommunity/populationandmigration/populationestimates/bulletins/key-statisticsandquickstatisticsforlocalauthoritiesintheunitedkingdom/2013-10-11.

'2018 Authors' Earnings.' London, 2018. https://literatureall iancescotland.co.uk/wp-content/uploads/2018/06/ALCS_Authors_Earnings_Report_2018.pdf.

'2019 World's Best Cities.' Resonance Consultancy, 2018. http://resonanceco.com/reports/2019-worlds-best-cities/.

'A Guide to the Hostile Environment.' Liberty, 2018. https://www.libertyhumanrights.org.uk/sites/default/files/HE web.pdf.

'About Us.' Goldsmiths University of London, 2018. https://www.

gold.ac.uk/about/.

'About Us.' The University of London, 2019. https://london.ac.uk/about-us.

Ackroyd, Peter. *London: The Concise Biography*. London: Vintage, 2001.

Adams, Geraldine Kendall. 'Campaign Launched against Privatisation in Museums.' Museums Association, 2018. https://www.museumsassociation.org/museums-journal/news/21032018-campaign-launched-against-privatisation.

Addison, Joseph. 'Thursday, June 12, 1712.' The Spectator, 1712. https://www.gutenberg.org/files/12030/12030-h/SV2/Spectator2.html#section403.

Aditya Chakrabortty, and Sally Weale. 'Universities Accused of 'importing Sports Direct Model' for Lecturers' Pay.' The Guardian, 2016. https://www.theguardian.com/uk-news/2016/nov/16/universities-accused-of-importing-sports-direct-model-for-lecturers-pay.

ADS. 'UK Security Sector Outlook 2016.' UK security sector outlook 2016, 2016. https://www.adsgroup.org.uk/wp-content/uploads/sites/21/2016/12/SecurityOutlook2016-E-Res.pdf.

Afonso, Alexandre. 'How Academia Resembles a Drug Gang.' LSE Impact Blog, 2013. http://blogs.lse.ac.uk/impactofsocialsciences/2013/12/11/how-academia-resembles-a-drug-gang/.

Ahmed, Murad. 'Strong 2017 Movie Slate Lifts Cineworld Sales, Profits.' Financial Times, 2018. https://www.ft.com/content/efdc62fc-2821-11e8-b27e-cc62a39d57a0.

Allen, Katie. 'Economic Output per Person in London More than Double Rest of UK.' The Guardian, 2016. https://www.theguardian.com/business/2016/dec/15/economic-output-of-london-more-than-double-rest-of-uk.

'Analysis of Real Earnings and Contributions to Nominal Earnings Growth, Great Britain: May 2018.' Office for National Statistics, 2018. https://www.ons.gov.uk/employmentandlabourmarket/

peopleinwork/earningsandworkinghours/articles/
supplementaryanalysisofaverageweeklyearnings/may2018.

'Annual Commuting Time Is up 18 Hours Compared to a Decade Ago, Finds TUC.' TUC, 2018. https://www.tuc.org.uk/news/annual-commuting-time-18-hours-compared-decade-ago-finds-tuc.

'Annual Survey of Visits to Visitor Attractions: Latest Results.' Visit Britain, 2016. https://www.visitbritain.org/annual-survey-visits-visitor-attractions-latest-results.

Anonymous academic. 'I Just Got a Permanent Academic Job – but I'm Not Celebrating.' The Guardian, 2018. https://www.theguardian.com/higher-education-network/2018/jun/22/permanent-academic-job-university-system-unfair-exploitative.

Anonymous Academic. 'Academia Is Built on Exploitation. We Must Break This Vicious Circle.' The Guardian, 2018. https://www.theguardian.com/higher-education-network/2018/may/18/academia-exploitation-university-mental-health-professors-plagiarism.

Archer, Graeme. 'Let's Talk about the Exodus of 600,000 Whites from London.' Daily Telegraph, 2013. https://www.telegraph.co.uk/news/uknews/immigration/9888310/Lets-talk-about-the-exodus-of-600000-whites-from-London.html.

'Aristocrats Own Third of Land in England and Wales.' The Independent, 2010. https://www.independent.co.uk/news/uk/home-news/aristocrats-own-third-of-land-in-england-and-wales-2130392.html.

Ashton, Daniel. 'Creative Work Careers: Pathways and Portfolios for the Creative Economy.' *Journal of Education and Work* 28, no. 4 (2015).

'Battersea Power Station.' South Chelsea. Accessed March 7, 2018. https://web.archive.org/web/20120310153152/http://www.southchelsea.freeserve.co.uk/page11.html.

Batty, David. *My Generation*. United Kingdom: Lionsgate, 2017.

Bauman, Zygmunt. *Wasted Lives: Modernity and Its Outcasts*. London:

Polity, 2004.

Bauman, Zygmunt. *Work, Consumerism and the New Poor*. Berkshire: Open University Press, 2005.

BBC. 'FTSE 100 Closes at Another Record High.' BBC News, 2017. http://www.bbc.co.uk/news/business-39301556.

——. 'Tate Modern Drew in Record Visitors in 2016.' BBC News, 2017. http://www.bbc.co.uk/news/entertainment-arts-39404206.

BECTU. 'Living Staff Living Wage.' Campaigns, 2018. https://www.bectu.org.uk/get-involved/campaigns/picturehouse.

——. 'Production Branch Ratecard 2018.' Production branch ratecard 2018, 2017. https://www.bectu.org.uk/advice-resources/library/2449.

Bell, Daniel. *The Coming of Post-Industrial Society*. New York: Basic Books, 1976.

'Berkeley Square vs Canary Wharf – Which Is London's Premium Business Address?' Morgan Pryce, 2011. https://www.morganpryce.co.uk/knowledge-centre/exclusive-news-articles/berkeley-square-vs-canary-wharf-which-is-london-s-premium-business-address.

BFI. 'UK Films and British Talent Worldwide.' London, 2018.

Biddulph, Matt. 'How London's Silicon Roundabout Really Got Started.' Gigaom, 2012. https://gigaom.com/2012/12/11/how-londons-silicon-roundabout-really-got-started/.

Blair, Tony. 'Full Text of Tony Blair's Speech on Education.' The Guardian, 2001. https://www.theguardian.com/politics/2001/may/23/labour.tonyblair.

Bloomfield, Ruth. 'Hotspot in Waiting: Bethnal Green Set to Rival Shoreditch with Trendy Bars and New Homes in the Victorian Chest Hospital.' The Evening Standard, 2018. https://www.homesandproperty.co.uk/property-news/buying/new-homes/bethnal-green-set-to-rival-shoreditch-with-trendy-bars-and-new-homes-in-the-victorian-chest-hospital-a119346.html.

——. 'It's Battersea Poor Station: First-Time Buyers Banished to Former Industrial Estate Half a Mile from Luxury Homes.'

Evening Standard, 2015. https://www.homesandproperty.co.uk/ property-news/its-battersea-poor-station-firsttime-buyers-banished-to-former-industrial-estate-half-a-mile-from-47706. html.

Booth, Charles. *Life and Labour of the People in London*. London and New York: Macmillan, 1890.

Booth, Robert, and Caelainn Barr. 'Number of Londoners Abandoning Capital Hits 10-Year High.' The Guardian, 2017. https://www.theguardian.com/uk-news/2017/dec/29/londoners-leaving-capital-for-brighton-birmingham-and-bristol.

Booth, William. *In Darkest England and the Way Out*. Cambridge: Cambridge University Press, 1890.

BOP Consulting. 'Soho: The World's Creative Hub.' London, 2013. http://www.thecreativeindustries.co.uk/media/232461/soho-bop-report.pdf.

BOP Consulting & Graham Devlin Associates. 'Arts Council England Analysis of Theatre in England.' London, 2016. https://www. artscouncil.org.uk/sites/default/files/download-file/Analysis of Theatre in England - Final Report.pdf.

Boswell, James. *The Life of Samuel Johnson*. London: Hutchinson and Co, 1791.

Bourdieu, Pierre. *Distinction*. London: Routledge, 1984.

'Box Park Shoreditch: About.' Box Park Shoreditch, 2018. https:// www.boxpark.co.uk/shoreditch/about/.

'Boycott Senate House.' IWGB, 2019. https://iwgb.org.uk/ boycottsenatehouse.

Bradley, Lloyd. 'Calypso and the Birth of British Black Music.' British Library, 2018. https://www.bl.uk/windrush/articles/ calypso-and-the-birth-of-british-black-music.

Bradshaw, Tim. 'Silicon Roundabout: Is This the Heart of the UK's New Dotcom Boom?' Financial Times, 2008. https://www.ft.com/ content/f815bdd4-4bfa-3e47-bfda-5948428001b7.

'Britain and the Slave Trade.' The National Archives. Accessed October 30, 2017. http://www.nationalarchives.gov.uk/slavery/

pdf/britain-and-the-trade.pdf.

Brook, Orian, David O'Brien and Mark Taylor. 'Panic! Social Class, Taste and Inequalities in the Creative Industries.' London, 2018.

Brown, Richard, and Brell Wilson. 'Running on Fumes: London's Council Services in Austerity.' Centre for London, 2015. https:// www.centreforlondon.org/wp-content/uploads/2016/08/ CFL3888_Running-on-fumes_short_paper_12.11.15_WEB.pdf.

Butcher, Mike. 'Now We Have Silicon Roundabout Where Are London's Existing, Organic, Tech Hubs?' Tech Crunch, 2008.

Butler, Sarah. 'Deliveroo Riders Lose High Court Battle to Gain Union Recognition.' The Guardian, 2018. https://www. theguardian.com/business/2018/dec/05/deliveroo-riders-lose-high-court-battle-gain-union-recognition.

— — —. 'Uber Loses Appeal over Driver Employment Rights.' The Guardian, 2018. https://www.theguardian.com/technology/2018/ dec/19/uber-loses-appeal-over-driver-employment-rights.

Cadwalladr, Carole. 'Whatever the Party, Our Political Elite Is an Oxbridge Club.' The Guardian, 2015. https://www.theguardian. com/commentisfree/2015/aug/24/our-political-elite-oxbridge-club.

Carey, Heather, Lizzie Crowley, Cicely Dudley, Helen Sheldon and Lesley Giles. 'A Skills Audit of the UK Film and Screen Industries.' London, 2017.

Cavert, William. The Smoke of London: Energy and Environment in the Early Modern City. Cambridge: Cambridge University Press, 2016.

Chakelian, Anoosh. '"I Don't Even Go to the Toilet": Deliveroo Riders Will Fight to Be Recognised as Workers.' The New Statesman, 2018. https://www.newstatesman.com/politics/ economy/2018/06/i-don-t-even-go-toilet-deliveroo-riders-will-fight-be-recognised-workers.

'Changing Shadows.' The Economist, 2003. https://www.economist. com/christmas-specials/2003/12/18/changing-shadows.

'Chasing Cool.' The Economist, 2014. https://www.economist.com/

blighty/2014/04/08/chasing-cool.

Childs, Simon. 'The University of London's 'Theatre of Security' Is Clamping Down on Student Dissent.' Vice, 2018. https://www. vice.com/en_uk/article/wjbn5n/the-university-of-londons-theatre-of-security-is-clamping-down-on-student-dissent.

Clark, Nick. 'Just One Actor in 50 Makes More than £20,000 per Year, Survey Shows.' The Independent, 2014. https://www. independent.co.uk/incoming/just-one-actor-in-50-makes-more-than-20000-per-year-survey-shows-9448922.html.

Clive Emsley; Tim Hitchcock; Robert Shoemaker. 'A Population History of London.' Old Bailey Proceedings Online, 2017. https:// www.oldbaileyonline.org/static/Population-history-of-london. jsp.

'Coal-Fired Power Stations.' Hansard, 1984. http://hansard. millbanksystems.com/written_answers/1984/jan/16/coal-fired-power-stations#S6CV0052P0_19840116_CWA_281.

Cobb, Jason. 'Exclusive: Grow Brixton to Pop Brixton – How a Green Oasis for the Community Turned into a 21st Century Business Park.' Brixton Buzz, 2016. http://www.brixtonbuzz.com/2016/06/exclusive-grow-brixton-to-pop-brixton-how-a-green-oasis-for-the-community-turned-into-a-21st-century-business-park/.

— — —. 'Lambeth Council Extends Pop Brixton Lease for Two Years as Business Park Fails to Deliver Any Profit.' Brixton Buzz, 2018. http://www.brixtonbuzz.com/2018/01/lambeth-council-extends-pop-brixton-lease-for-two-years-as-business-park-fails-to-deliver-any-profit/.

— — —. 'Planning Permission Recommended for Grow:Brixton to Transform Site of Old Pope's Road Car Park.' Brixton Buzz, 2014. http://www.brixtonbuzz.com/2014/09/planning-permission-recommended-for-growbrixton-to-transform-site-of-old-popes-road-car-park/.

Cockburn, Cynthia. Looking to London. London: Pluto Press, 2017.

'Coldharbour.' City Population, 2011. https://www.citypopulation. de/php/uk-wards-london.php?adm2id=E05000420.

Coleman, Clive. '''"Outsourced" Workers Seek Better Deal in Landmark Case.' BBC News, 2017. http://www.bbc.co.uk/news/uk-42056769.

Collinson, Patrick. 'How Do Deliveroo and Uber Workers Cope with Precarious Pay?' The Guardian, 2018. https://www.theguardian.com/business/2018/oct/20/deliveroo-uber-workers-pay-gig-economy.

Conner, Kimberly. '20 Reasons London Is the Most Exciting City in the World.' Huffington Post, 2016. https://www.huffingtonpost.com/kimberly-conner/20-reasons-london-is-the-_b_9633332.html.

Corporate Research Unit. 'Bethnal Green Ward Profile.' London Borough of Tower Hamlets, 2014. https://www.towerhamlets.gov.uk/Documents/Borough_statistics/Ward_profiles/Bethnal_Green.pdf.

———. 'Spitalfields and Banglatown Ward Profile.' London Borough of Tower Hamlets. London, 2014. https://www.towerhamlets.gov.uk/Documents/Borough_statistics/Ward_profiles/Spitalfields-and-Banglatown-FINAL-10062014.pdf.

'Craft Content. Make Bank.' TRIBE, 2019. https://www.tribegroup.co/influencers.

Cremin, Colin. Capitalism's New Clothes. London: Pluto Press, 2011.

Croucher, Shane. 'G4S Scandals: From London 2012 Security Fiasco to Jimmy Mubenga Death.' International Business Times, 2014.

Cunningham, S. 'Developments in Measuring the 'Creative Workforce.'' Cultural Trends 20, no. 1 (2011): 25–40.

Dahlgreen, Will. 'Bookish Britain: Literary Jobs Are the Most Desirable.' YouGov, 2015. https://yougov.co.uk/topics/politics/articles-reports/2015/02/15/bookish-britain-academic-jobs-are-most-desired.

Dalrymple, William. 'The East India Company: The Original Corporate Raiders.' The Guardian, 2015. https://www.theguardian.com/world/2015/mar/04/east-india-company-original-corporate-raiders.

Daly, Glyn. 'Politics of the Political: Psychoanalytic Theory and the Left(S).' *Journal of Political Ideologies* 14 (2009): 279–300.

'DataShine: Census.' DataShine, 2019. http://datashine.org.uk/#tab le=QS112EW&col=QS112EW0031&ramp=YlOrRd&layers=BTTT &zoom=14&lon=-0.0636&lat=51.5280.

Davidsson, Johan, and Marek Naczyk. 'The Ins and Outs of Dualisation: A Literature Review.' *Working Papers on the Reconciliation of Work and Welfare in Europe* 2 (2009).

Davies, Nick. *Flat Earth News*. London: Vintage, 2008.

Defoe, Daniel. *A Tour Thro' the Whole Island of Great Britain, Divided into Circuits or Journies*. London: JM Dent and Co, 1927.

Degen, Monica, Clare Melhuish, and Gillian Rose. 'Producing Place Atmospheres Digitally: Architecture, Digital Visualisation Practices and the Experience Economy.' *Journal of Consumer Culture* 27 (2015): 1–22.

'Deliveroo Claims Victory in Self-Employment Case.' BBC News, 2017. https://www.bbc.co.uk/news/business-41983343.

Denning, Michael. 'Wageless Life.' *New Left Review*, 2010, 79–97.

Dickens, Charles. *Oliver Twist*. London: Penguin, 2003.

'Domestic Workers.' Women in Informal Employment: Globalizing and Organizing, 2018. http://www.wiego.org/informal-economy/occupational-groups/domestic-workers.

Dorling, Danny. 'The New Urban Crisis by Richard Florida Review – 'Flawed and Elitist Ideas.'' The Observer, 2017. https://www.theguardian.com/books/2017/sep/26/richard-florida-new-urban-crisis-review-flawed-elitist-ideas.

Douglas-Fairhurst, Robert. 'London Labour and the London Poor by Henry Mayhew.' The Guardian, 2010. https://www.theguardian.com/books/2010/oct/16/rereading-henry-mayhew-london-poor.

'Drive with Uber Make Money on Your Schedule.' Uber, 2019. https://www.uber.com/a/join-new/gb.

Duhigg, Charles, and David Barboza. 'Apple IPad and the Human Costs for Workers in China.' The New York Times, 2012. http://www.nytimes.com/2012/01/26/business/ieconomy-apples-

ipad-and-the-human-costs-for-workers-in-china.html?_
r=4&pagewanted=all.

Eagleton, Terry. *After Theory*. London: Penguin, 2003.

Ehrenhalt, Alan. *The Great Inversion and the Future of the American City*. New York: Vintage, 2013.

Elliott, Coran. 'Landlords Spending Thousands on Flowers to Create 'Instagram Friendly' Pubs to Boost Trade.' The Telegraph, 2018. https://www.telegraph.co.uk/news/2018/08/04/landlords-spending-thousands-flowers-create-instagram-friendly/.

Ellis-Petersen, Hannah. 'Anger as Tate Asks Staff to Contribute towards Boat for Nicholas Serota.' The Guardian, 2017. https://www.theguardian.com/artanddesign/2017/apr/27/tate-asks-staff-to-pitch-in-to-buy-boat-for-departing-chief-nicholas-serota.

Emmenegger, Partick; Häusermann, Silja; Palier, Bruno; Seeleib-Kaiser, Martin, ed. *The Age of Dualization: The Changing Face of Inequality in Deindustrializing Societies*. Oxford: Oxford University Press, 2012.

'Employment and Place of Employment in the Film Industry, 2017.' Office for National Statistics, 2017. https://www.ons.gov.uk/employmentandlabourmarket/peopleinwork/employmentandemployeetypes/adhocs/008458employmentandplaceofemploymentinthefilmindustry2017?:uri=employmentandlabourmarket/peopleinwork/employmentandemployeetypes/adhocs/008458employmentandplac.

'Employment by Occupation Type and Gender, Borough.' London Datastore, 2017. https://data.london.gov.uk/dataset/employment-occupation-type-and-gender-borough.

'Employment in the Film Industry.' London, 2017.

Engels, Fredrich. *The Condition of the Working Class in England*. London: Penguin, 1845.

'Enoch Powell's 'Rivers of Blood' Speech.' The Telegraph, 2007. https://www.telegraph.co.uk/comment/3643823/Enoch-Powells-Rivers-of-Blood-speech.html.

Equality and Human Rights Commission. 'The Invisible Workforce:

Employment Practices in the Cleaning Sector - Findings Report,'
no. August (2014): 1–92. https://www.equalityhumanrights.com/
sites/default/files/the_invisible_workforce_full_report_08-08-14.
pdf.

'EU Referendum: The Results in Maps and Charts.' BBC News, 2016.
http://www.bbc.co.uk/news/uk-politics-36616028.

Evans, Richard J. 'Eric Hobsbawm Would Not Have Backed
University of London Boycott.' The Guardian, 2019. https://
www.theguardian.com/education/2019/feb/11/eric-hobsbawm-
would-not-have-backed-university-of-london-boycott.

'Facing Facts: The Impact of Migrants on London, Its Workforce
and Economy.' PWC, 2017. https://www.pwc.co.uk/services/
legal-services/services/immigration/facing-facts--the-impact-of-
migrants-on-london--its-workforce-an.html.

Field, Frank, and Andrew Forsey. 'Sweated Labour: Uber and the
'Gig Economy.'' London, 2016. http://www.frankfield.co.uk/
upload/docs/Sweated Labour - Uber and the 'gig economy'.pdf.

— — —. 'Wild West Workplace: Self-Employment in Britain's 'Gig
Economy.'' London, 2016. http://www.frankfield.co.uk/upload/
docs/Wild West Workplace.pdf.

Fielding, Henry. 'An Enquiry Into the Causes of the Late Increase
of Robbers.' Internet Archive, 1751. https://archive.org/details/
anenquiryintoca00fielgoog.

Fishwick, Samuel. 'Uber Drivers React to News of TfL's London Ban:
'I Finished the Job, Then Pulled over and Cried.'' The Evening
Standard, 2017. https://www.standard.co.uk/lifestyle/london-
life/uber-drivers-react-over-news-of-tfl-ban-a3643966.html.

Florida, Richard. 'Class-Divided Cities: London Edition.' CityLab,
2013. https://www.citylab.com/life/2013/11/londons-class-divid
es/6056/.

— — —. 'Mapping the World's Knowledge Hubs.' CityLab, 2017.
https://www.citylab.com/life/2017/01/mapping-the-worlds-
knowledge-hubs/505748/.

— — —. 'The Economic Power of Cities Compared to Nations.'

CityLab, 2017. https://www.citylab.com/life/2017/03/the-econo mic-power-of-global-cities-compared-to-nations/519294/.

— — —. *The New Urban Crisis*. London: OneWorld, 2017.

— — —. *The Rise of the Creative Class, Revisited*. New York: Basic Books, 2014.

— — —. *The Rise of the Creative Class: And How It's Transforming Work, Leisure, Community and Everyday Life*. New York: Basic Books, 2002.

Fox, Kate. *Watching the English*. London: Hodder and Stoughton, 2004.

Fox, Susan. *The New Cockney: New Ethnicities and Adolescent Speech in the Traditional East End of London*. Basingstoke: Palgrave Macmillan, 2015.

Francis, Sam. 'Londoners Work 'Three Weeks a Year More than Rest of UK.'' BBC News, 2017. https://www.bbc.co.uk/news/uk-england-london-39516134.

Frank, Thomas. *The Conquest of Cool*. Chicago: The University of Chicago Press, 1997.

Friedman, Thomas. *The World Is Flat: The Globalized World in the Twenty-First Century*. London: Penguin Books, 2005.

Future Brixton. 'Have Your Say What Happens 'Meanwhile at Pope's Road'.' Love Lambeth, 2014. https://love.lambeth.gov.uk/have-your-say-what-happens-meanwhile-at-popes-road/.

Gallas, Alexander. 'The Proliferation Of Precarious Labour in Academia.' Progress in Political Economy, 2018. http://ppesydney.net/proliferation-precarious-labour-academia/.

'Gallery Staff's Pay Should Reflect Success of Tate Modern 2.' Public and Commercial Services Union, 2016. https://www.pcs.org.uk/news/gallery-staffs-pay-should-reflect-success-of-tate-modern-2.

German, Lindsey, and John Rees. *A People's History of London*. London and New York: Verso, 2012.

'Get to Know Us.' Impact Hub Global Community, 2019. https://impacthub.net/get-to-know-us/#frequent.

Gill, R. 'Academics, Cultural Workers and Critical Labour Studies.' *Journal of Cultural Economy* 7, no. 1 (2014): 12–30.

GLA Economics. 'London's Economic Outlook : Spring 2017 The GLA's Medium-Term Planning Projections.' London: Greater London Authority, 2017.

GLA Intelligence. 'Country of Birth Ward Tools (2011 Census).' Census Information Scheme, 2011. https://data.london.gov.uk/dataset/country-of-birth-ward-tools--2011-census-.

———. 'Interim 2015-Based Trend Projection Results.' London, 2017.

Goldberg, David. *This Is Not the Way: Jews, Judaism and the State of Israel*. London: Faber and Faber, 2012.

Golden, Catherine J. *Posting It: The Victorian Revolution in Letter Writing*. Gainesville, Florida: University Press of Florida, 2009.

Goldsmith, Zac. 'On Thursday, Are We Really Going to Hand the World's Greatest City to a Labour Party That Thinks Terrorists Is Its Friends? A Passionate Plea from ZAC GOLDSMITH Four Days before Mayoral Election.' Mail Online, 2016. http://www.dailymail.co.uk/debate/article-3567537/On-Thursday-really-going-hand-world-s-greatest-city-Labour-party-thinks-terrorists-friends-passionate-plea-ZAC-GOLDSMITH-four-days-Mayoral-election.html.

Goodley, Simon, and Jonathan Ashby. 'Revealed: How Sports Direct Effectively Pays below Minimum Wage.' The Guardian, 2015. https://www.theguardian.com/business/2015/dec/09/how-sports-direct-effectively-pays-below-minimum-wage-pay.

Gorczynski, Paul F., Denise Hill, and Shanaya Rathod. 'Examining the Construct Validity of the Transtheoretical Model to Structure Workplace Physical Activity Interven- Tions to Improve Mental Health in Academic Staff.' *EMS Community Medicine Journal* 1, no. 1 (2017).

Greater London Authority. 'Ethnicity Pay Gap Reporting: March 2017 Data.' London, 2017. https://www.london.gov.uk/sites/default/files/gla-ethnicity-pay-gap-report-2017.pdf.

Greenfield, Patrick. 'Middle-Class Cocaine Use Fuels London's Rising Violence, Says Sadiq Khan.' The Guardian, 2018. https://www.theguardian.com/society/2018/jul/27/middle-class-cocaine-use-fuels-londons-rising-violence-says-sadiq-khan-knife-crime.

Gutteridge, Nick. 'REVEALED: EU Migrants Pocket MORE Tax Credits Cash and Child Benefits than BRITISH Workers.' Express, 2016. https://www.express.co.uk/news/uk/655145/Brexit-EU-referendum-European-migrants-benefits-tax-credits-British-workers.

Haddad, Moussa. 'The Perfect Storm: Economic Stagnation, the Rising Cost of Living, Public Spending Cuts, and the Impact on UK Poverty.' Oxfam, 2012. https://policy-practice.oxfam.org.uk/publications/the-perfect-storm-economic-stagnation-the-rising-cost-of-living-public-spending-228591.

''Half of Women' Sexually Harassed at Work, Says BBC Survey.' BBC News, 2017. https://www.bbc.co.uk/news/uk-41741615.

Hall, Catherine, Nicholas Draper, Keith McClelland, Katie Donington, and Rachel Lang. 'Introduction.' In Legacies of British Slave Ownership. Cambridge: Cambridge University Press, 2014.

Hampson, Laura. 'This Is the Age Most Adults Land Their Dream Job.' The Evening Standard, 2018. https://www.standard.co.uk/lifestyle/london-life/how-to-find-dream-job-a4007906.html.

Harman, Chris. A People's History of the World. 2nd ed. London: Verso, 2008.

Harris, John. 'Cool Britannia: Where Did It All Go Wrong?' New Statesman, 2017. https://www.newstatesman.com/1997/2017/05/cool-britannia-where-did-it-all-go-wrong.

'Hidden Homelessness in London.' London Assembly, 2017. https://www.london.gov.uk/sites/default/files/london_assembly_-_hidden_homelessness_report.pdf.

Higgins, Charlotte. 'How Nicholas Serota's Tate Changed Britain.' The Guardian, 2017. https://www.theguardian.com/artanddesign/2017/jun/22/how-nicholas-serota-tate-changed-britain.

Hills, John, Brewer, Mike, Jenkins, Stephen P, Lister, Ruth, Lupton, Ruth, Machin, Stephen, Mills, Colin, Modood, Tariq, Rees, Teresa and Riddell, Sheila. 'An Anatomy of Economic Inequality in the UK: Report of the National Equality Panel.' London, 2010.

Hinds, Donald. *Journey to an Illusion: The West Indian in Britain.* London: Heinemann, 1966.

'History of University of London.' University of London, 2018. https://london.ac.uk/about-us/history-university-london.

Holland, Emma. 'Where to Find Australian Flat Whites and Coffees in London.' The Upsider, 2018. https://theupsider.com.au/london-coffee/8768.

Holmes, David. *Communication Theory: Media, Technology and Society.* London: SAGE, 2005.

Hopkins, Jack. 'Bridging the Gap between Bedroom and High Street: A Space for Start-Ups to POP up in Brixton.' jackhopkins, 2015. https://jackhopkins.wordpress.com/2015/04/14/bridging-the-gap-between-bedroom-and-high-street-a-space-for-start-ups-to-pop-up-in-brixton/.

'House Price Calculator: Where Can I Afford to Rent or Buy?' BBC News, 2018. https://www.bbc.co.uk/news/business-23234033.

Hudson, Pat. 'The Workshop of the World.' BBC History, 2011. http://www.bbc.co.uk/history/british/victorians/workshop_of_the_world_01.shtml.

'Huge Survey Reveals Seven Social Classes in UK.' BBC News, 2013. https://www.bbc.co.uk/news/uk-22007058.

Hughes, Kathryn. 'The Middle Classes: Etiquette and Upward Mobility.' The British Library, 2014. https://www.bl.uk/romantics-and-victorians/articles/the-middle-classes-etiquette-and-upward-mobility.

Huitfeldt, Henrik, and Johannes Jütting. 'Informality and Informal Employment,' 2009.

Hunt, Tristram. 'Urban Britain Is Heading for Victorian Levels of Inequality.' The Guardian, 2007. https://www.theguardian.com/

commentisfree/2007/jul/18/comment.money.

'Immigration and Emigration: East End Jews.' BBC, 2003. http://www.bbc.co.uk/legacies/immig_emig/england/london/article_2.shtml.

'Immigration and Emigration: The Huguenots.' BBC, 2003. http://www.bbc.co.uk/legacies/immig_emig/england/london/article_1.shtml.

'Impact Hub.' Pop Brixton, 2019. https://www.popbrixton.org/members/impact-hub/.

'Insight: Focus on the Southwest Ontario Region.' Martin Prosperity Insights, 2009. http://martinprosperity.org/tag/service-class/.

'Introduction to Deliveroo.' European Commission, 2016. http://ec.europa.eu/information_society/newsroom/image/document/2016-6/deliveroo_13855.pdf.

'IWGB Reaction to TfL Decision to Revoke UBER's License.' IWGB, 2017. https://www.forbes.com/sites/oliversmith/2018/03/16/the-londoner-who-brought-uber-to-its-knees/#6ec6d6dd6933.

James, Henry. *The Notebooks of Henry James*. Chicago: The University of Chicago Press, 1947.

Jameson, Fredric. *Postmodernism, or, the Cultural Logic of Late Capitalism*. Durham, NC: Duke University Press, 1991.

Jerrold, Blanchard. *London, a Pilgrimage*. London: Anthem Press, 2005.

Jimeno, Tito Boeri and Juan F. 'The Unbearable Divergence of Unemployment in Europe.' Madrid, 2015. https://www.bde.es/f/webbde/SES/Secciones/Publicaciones/PublicacionesSeriadas/DocumentosTrabajo/15/Fich/dt1534e.pdf.

'Jobs Paid Less than the London Living Wage in London in 2015, 2016, 2017, by Industry.' Office for National Statistics, 2018. https://www.ons.gov.uk/employmentandlabourmarket/peoplein-work/earningsandworkinghours/adhocs/008557jobspaidlessthanthelondonlivingwageinlondonin201520162017byindustry.

'Johnson: How British Values Help to Make the World Richer and Safer.' CCHQ Press, 2016. http://press.conservatives.com/

post/151242631480/johnson-how-british-values-help-to-make-the-world.

Johnson, Jamie. 'London Is Europe's Cocaine Capital – but Only during the Week.' The Telegraph, 2016. https://www.telegraph.co.uk/news/2016/12/13/london-overtaken-antwerp-europes-weekend-cocaine-capital/.

Jones, Owen. *The Establishment*. London: Penguin, 2014.

'Journalism and Social Class Briefing.' National Union of Journalists, 2012. https://www.nuj.org.uk/documents/journalism-and-social-class-briefing/milburn.pdf.

Judah, Ben. *This Is London*. London: Picador, 2016.

Kalayaan. 'Britain's Forgotten Slaves; Migrant Domestic Workers in the UK Three Years after the Introduction of the Tied Overseas Domestic Worker Visa.' Kalayaan Three Year Briefing, 2015. http://www.kalayaan.org.uk/wp-content/uploads/2014/09/Kalayaan-3-year-briefing.pdf.

Kamp, David. 'London Swings! Again!' Vanity Fair, 1997. https://www.vanityfair.com/magazine/1997/03/london199703.

Kapp, Yvonne. *Eleanor Marx: Vol 1 Family Life*. London: Virago Press, 1972.

'Keep Deliveroo'in.' Reddit, 2019. https://www.reddit.com/r/deliveroos/.

Keijonen, Milja. 'London's Sectors: More Detailed Jobs Data.' GLA Economics, 2015. https://www.london.gov.uk/sites/default/files/gla_migrate_files_destination/London%27s sectors - more detailed jobs data.pdf.

Kettell, Steven. 'Circuits of Capital and Overproduction: A Marxist Analysis of the Present World Economic Crisis.' *Review of Radical Political Economics2* 38, no. 1 (2006): 24–44.

Kettle, Martin and Lucy Hodges. *Uprising!: Police, the People and the Riots in Britain's Cities*. London: Macmillan, 1982.

Khamis, Susie, Lawrence Ang, and Raymond Welling. 'Self-Branding, 'Micro-Celebrity' and the Rise of Social Media Influencers.' *Celebrity Studies*, 2016. https://doi.org/10.1080/1939

2397.2016.1218292.

Kirby, Philip. 'Leading People 2016: The Educational Backgrounds of the UK Professional Elite,' 2016. https://www.suttontrust.com/wp-content/uploads/2016/02/Leading-People_Feb16.pdf.

Kirk, Ashley. 'Seven Things You Did Not Know about Migration in the UK.' The Telegraph, 2015. https://www.telegraph.co.uk/news/uknews/immigration/11942613/Seven-things-you-did-not-know-about-migration-in-the-UK.html.

Klein, Naomi. No Logo. Picador: Knopf Canada, 1999.

Knights, David, and Caroline Clarke. 'It's a Bittersweet Symphony, This Life: Fragile Academic Selves and Insecure Identities at Work.' Organization Studies 35, no. 3 (2014): 335–57.

Kollewe, Julia. 'Battersea Power Station Developer Slashes Number of Affordable Homes.' The Guardian, 2017. http://www.thisismoney.co.uk/money/mortgageshome/article-2328459/Almost-866-flats-Battersea-Power-Station-development-sold-foreign-investors.htm.

———. 'High Times: 76 Tall Buildings to Join London's Skyline in 2019.' The Guardian, 2019. https://www.theguardian.com/business/2019/mar/05/tall-buildings-london-skyline-2019.

Lambeth Council. 'Future Brixton Masterplan.' London, 2009. https://moderngov.lambeth.gov.uk/documents/s57901/01 Future Brixton Masterplan 1.pdf.

———. 'Officer Delegated Decision.' Brixton High Street Fund, Pop Brixton co-working space, 2014.

———. 'Pop Brixton - Lease Extension until November 2020,' 2017. https://moderngov.lambeth.gov.uk/documents/s92926/Pop Brixton ODDR - SLA and Lease extension 003.docx.pdf.

———. 'State of the Borough 2016.' London, 2016. https://www.lambeth.gov.uk/sites/default/files/State of Borough 2016 - v3.pdf.

Levecque, Katia, Frederik Anseel, Alain De Beuckelaer, Johan Van der Heyden, and Lydia Gisle. 'Work Organization and Mental Health Problems in PhD Students.' Research Policy 46, no. 4 (2017).

Levitt, Steven, and Sudhir Venkatesh. 'An Economic Analysis of a

Drug-Selling Gang's Finances.' *Quarterly Journal of Economics* 115, no. 3 (2000): 755–89.

Lichtenstein, Rachel. *On Brick Lane*. London: Hamish Hamilton, 2007.

'London's Original Flat White.' Flat White, 2015. http://www. flatwhitesoho.co.uk/.

'London's Population by Age.' Trust for London, 2018. https://www. trustforlondon.org.uk/data/londons-population-age/.

'London Analysis: Estimates of Employee Jobs Paid Less than the Living Wage in London and Other Parts of the UK.' Office for National Statistics, 2015. https://www.ons. gov.uk/employmentandlabourmarket/peopleinwork/ earningsandworkinghours/articles/londonanalysis/2015-10-12.

London, Ash. 'Ten Reasons You Need to Spend a Year Living in London in Your 20s.' news.com.au, 2016. https://www.news. com.au/travel/travel-ideas/adventure/ten-reasons-you-need-to-spend-a-year-living-in-london-in-your-20s/news-story/0278b09c 1ac8bdfde28332fb02e2c3e0.

London, Jack. *The People of the Abyss*. London: Macmillan, 1903.

'London Loses One Pub a Week, According to New Figures.' BBC News, 2018. https://www.bbc.co.uk/news/uk-england-london-44659180.

London Stock Exchange. 'GFS G4S PLC ORD 25P.' London Stock Exchange, 2017.

Lopes, Ana, and Indra Angeli Dewan. 'Precarious Pedagogies? The Impact of Casual and Zero-Hour Contracts in Higher Education.' *Journal of Feminist Scholarship* 7, no. 8 (2014): 28–42.

Lorenz, Taylor. 'Rising Instagram Stars Are Posting Fake Sponsored Content.' The Atlantic, 2018. https://www.theatlantic.com/ technology/archive/2018/12/influencers-are-faking-brand-deals/578401/.

'Low Pay and High Stress: Survey Lifts Lid on Life as a Struggling Performer.' BBC News, 2018. https://www.bbc.co.uk/news/ entertainment-arts-46356689.

LSE. 'Prosperity, Poverty and Inequality in London 2000/01 to 2010/11.' Social Policy in a Cold Climate, 2013. http://sticerd.lse. ac.uk/dps/case/spcc/srr03.pdf.

MacGillis, Alec. 'The Ruse of the Creative Class.' The American Prospect, 2009. http://prospect.org/article/ruse-creative-class-0.

Malik, Nesrine. 'Theresa May Has a Dream. A Mawkish, Shabby "British Dream".' The Guardian, 2018. https://www.theguardian. com/commentisfree/2018/feb/01/theresa-may-british-dream.

Maroukis, Thanos, Krystyna Iglicka, and Katarzyna Gmaj. 'Irregular Migration and Informal Economy in Southern and Central-Eastern Europe: Breaking the Vicious Cycle?' *International Migration* 49, no. 5 (October 16, 2011): 129–56. https://doi. org/10.1111/j.1468-2435.2011.00709.x.

Marsden, Harriet. 'How the Flat White Conquered the Coffee Scene.' The Independent, 2018. https://www.independent.co.uk/life-style/flat-white-coffee-culture-antipodean-mcdonalds-advert-starbucks-latte-a8246111.html.

Marsh, Sarah. 'How Has Brixton Really Changed? The Data behind the Story.' The Guardian, 2016. https://www.theguardian.com/ cities/datablog/2016/jan/14/how-has-brixton-really-changed-the-data-behind-the-story.

— — —. 'London University Criticised for Spending £415,000 on Protest Security.' The Guardian, 2018. https://www.theguardian. com/education/2018/jun/04/university-of-london-criticised-for-spending-415000-on-student-protest-security.

— — —. 'Record Number of People Sleeping Rough in London.' The Guardian, 2018. https://www.theguardian.com/society/2018/ oct/31/record-number-of-people-are-sleeping-rough-in-london.

Martell, Nevin. 'Brett Anderson and Mat Osman on Suede's Discography.' Filter, 2011. http://filtermagazine.com/index.php/ exclusives/entry/brett_anderson_and_mat_osman_on_suedes_ discography.

Martin Prosperity Insights. 'London, Brilliant!,' 2013. http:// martinprosperity.org/wp-content/uploads/2013/06/London-

Insight_v01.pdf.

Marx, Karl. *Capital*. Oxford: Oxford University Press, 1995.

— — —. *Das Kapital*. Oxford: Oxford University Press, 1995.

Marx, Karl, and Fredrich Engels. *Marx and Engels: 1844-51: Vol. 38*. London: Lawrence and Wishart, 1982.

Maximus, Taffus. 'Pop Brixton (Formerly Grow Brixton) Pope's Road Developmen.' Urban75.net, 2015. https://www.urban75. net/forums/threads/pop-brixton-formerly-grow-brixton-popes-road-development.322188/page-96.

— — —. 'Pop Brixton (Formerly Grow Brixton) Pope's Road Development.' Urban75.net, 2014. https://www.urban75.net/ forums/threads/pop-brixton-formerly-grow-brixton-popes-road-development.322188/.

'Mayfair.' Instant Offices, 2018. https://www.instantoffices.com/en/ gb/a-guide-to-office-space-in-mayfair.

Mayhew, Henry. *London Labour and the London Poor*. Ware: Wordsworth Editions, 2008.

— — —. 'Victorian London - Publications - Social Investigation/ Journalism - The Criminal Prisons of London and Scenes of London Life.' The Great World of London, 1862. http://www. victorianlondon.org/publications5/prisons-01.htm.

Mayhew, Ken, Cecile Deer, and Mehak Dua. 'The Move to Mass Higher Education in the UK: Many Questions and Some Answers.' *Oxford Review of Education* 30, no. 1 (2004).

Mayor of London. 'Culture for All Londoners.' London, 2018. https:// www.london.gov.uk/sites/default/files/2017_draft_strategies_ culture_2.0.pdf.

— — —. 'London Datastore.' Historical Census Population, 2011. https://data.london.gov.uk/dataset/historic-census-population/ resource/2c7867e5-3682-4fdd-8b9d-c63e289b92a6#.

— — —. 'Sadiq Khan Places Culture at the Heart of the London Plan,' 2017. https://www.london.gov.uk/press-releases/mayoral/ mayor-places-culture-at-heart-of-london-plan.

McGuigan, Jim. *Cool Capitalism*. London: Pluto Press, 2009.

———. 'The Coolness of Capitalism Today.' *TripleC* 10, no. 2 (2012): 425–38.

———. 'The Politics of Cultural Studies.' *Cultural Politics* 2, no. 2 (2006): 137–58.

McGuire, Stryker, and Michael Elliott. 'Hot Fashion, a Pulsating Club Scene and Lots of New Money Have Made This the Coolest City on the Planet.' *Newsweek*, November 1996.

McIlwaine, C. and Bunge, D. 'Towards Visibility: The Latin American Community in London.' London, 2016.

McMillan, Chris. '#MakeAmericaGreatAgain: Ideological Fantasy, American Exceptionalism and Donald Trump.' *Subjectivity* 10, no. 2 (2017): 1–19.

McRobbie, A. 'Re-Thinking Creative Economy as Radical Social Enterprise.' *Variant* 41 (2011): 32–33.

McWilliams, Douglas. *The Flat White Economy*. London: Douglas Overlook, 2015.

Mintz, Sidney W. *Sweetness and Power: The Place of Sugar in Modern History*. New York: Penguin Books, 1985.

Montacute, Rebecca. 'Internships - Unpaid, Unadvertised, Unfair.' Sutton Trust, 2018. https://www.suttontrust.com/wp-content/uploads/2018/01/Internships-2018-briefing.pdf.

Mooney, Graham. 'Shifting Sex Differentials in Mortality During Urban Epidemiological Transition: The Case of Victorian London.' *International Journal of Population Geography* 8 (2002): 17–47.

Moore, Rowan. *Slow Burn City*. London: Picador, 2016.

'More than Half of Children Now Live in Poverty in Some Parts of the UK.' End Child Poverty, 2018. https://www.endchildpoverty.org.uk/more-than-half-of-children-now-living-in-poverty-in-some-parts-of-the-uk/.

Morley, Katie. 'Half of Millennials Hiring Cleaners as They Are 'too Busy' to Clean One-Bed Flats.' The Telegraph, 2017. http://www.telegraph.co.uk/news/2017/06/18/half-millenials-hiring-cleaners-busy-clean-one-bed-flats/.

Morrison, Sean, Hatty Collier, and Johnathan Mitchell. 'Uber London Ban Reaction as It Happened: TfL Strips App of Its Licence.' The Evening Standard, 2017. https://www.standard.co.uk/news/transport/uber-stripped-of-london-licence-live-updates-and-reaction-a3641111.html.

Mount, Harry. 'Are You Being Served?' The Telegraph, 2013. http://www.telegraph.co.uk/lifestyle/10024092/Are-you-being-served.html.

Muggs, Joe. 'Is New Cross the New Camden?' Evening Standard. Accessed August 5, 2018. https://www.standard.co.uk/go/london/clubbing/is-new-cross-the-new-camden-6695175.html.

Murphy, Joe. 'Nearly Half of Black and Ethnic Minority Londoners 'Have Faced Racist Abuse', Study Finds.' The Independent, 2017. https://www.standard.co.uk/news/crime/nearly-half-of-black-and-ethnic-minority-londoners-have-faced-racist-abuse-study-finds-a3252851.html.

National Committee of Inquiry into Higher Education. 'Higher Education in the Learning Society (The Dearing Report),' 1997. http://www.leeds.ac.uk/educol/ncihe/.

'National Statistics: Asylum.' Home Office, 2017. https://www.gov.uk/government/publications/immigration-statistics-october-to-december-2016/asylum.

Neate, Rupert. 'Two-Thirds of UK's Highest Paid Live in London or South-East, HMRC Data Shows.' The Guardian, 2019. https://www.theguardian.com/inequality/2019/mar/18/two-thirds-of-uks-highest-paid-live-in-london-or-south-east-hmrc-data-shows.

'New Cross.' UK Census Data, 2011. http://www.ukcensusdata.com/new-cross-e05000449#sthash.eAlmTa7g.dpbs.

'Northern European Cities Offer Best Living Conditions.' ECA International, 2018. https://www.eca-international.com/news/march-2018/northern-european-cities-offer-best-living-conditi.

O'Brien, Ollie. 'Cool London?' Mapping London, 2014. http://mappinglondon.co.uk/2014/cool-london/.

O'Suvillan, Olivia. 'Cine-Files: Ritzy, Brixton, London.' The Guardian, 2011. https://www.theguardian.com/film/2011/oct/05/cine-files-ritzy-cinema-brixton.

Office for National Statistics. 'Births by Parents' Country of Birth, England and Wales: 2017,' 2018. https://www.ons.gov.uk/peoplepopulationandcommunity/birthsdeathsandmarriages/livebirths/bulletins/parentscountryofbirthenglandandwales/2017.

— — —. 'Population Estimates for the UK, England and Wales, Scotland and Northern Ireland: Mid-2017.' Population Estimates, 2018. https://www.ons.gov.uk/peoplepopulationandcommunity/populationandmigration/populationestimates/bulletins/annualmidyearpopulationestimates/mid2017#growth-varies-less-across-the-uk-london-no-longer-growing-fastest.

Olusoga, David. 'The Victorian Slums Are Back – and Housing Developers Are to Blame Again.' The Guardian, 2018. https://www.theguardian.com/commentisfree/2018/jan/16/victorian-slums-housing-developers-housebuilding-inequality.

'One in Five Journalists Earn Less than £20,000.' National Union of Journalists, 2015. https://www.nuj.org.uk/news/one-in-five-journalists-earn-less-than-20000/.

ONS. 'London Analysis: Estimates of Employee Jobs Paid Less than the Living Wage in London and Other Parts of the UK.' London Analysis: Estimates of employee jobs paid less than the Living Wage in London and Other Parts of the UK, 2015. https://www.ons.gov.uk/employmentandlabourmarket/peopleinwork/earningsandworkinghours/articles/londonanalysis/2015-10-12.

— — —. 'People in Employment on a Zero-Hours Contract: Mar 2017.' People in employment on a zero-hours contract: Mar 2017, 2017. https://www.ons.gov.uk/employmentandlabourmarket/peopleinwork/earningsandworkinghours/articles/contractsthatdonotguaranteeaminimumnumberofhours/mar2017.

— — —. 'Population Dynamics of UK City Regions since Mid-2011.'

Population dynamics of UK city regions since mid-2011, 2016. https://www.ons.gov.uk/peoplepopulationandcommunity/ populationandmigration/populationestimates/articles/ populationdynamicsofukcityregionssincemid2011/2016-10-11.

— — —. 'UK Labour Market: May 2017.' UK labour market: May 2017, 2017. https://www.ons.gov.uk/employmentandlabourmarket/ peopleinwork/employmentandemployeetypes/bulletins/ uklabourmarket/may2017.

Osborne, Hilary. 'Average Price of London Home Almost Doubles to £600,625 since 2009.' The Guardian, 2016. https://www. theguardian.com/money/2016/may/11/average-london-home-doubles-price-house-property.

'Our #LondonisOpen Campaign.' Mayor of London, 2017. https:// www.london.gov.uk/about-us/mayor-london/londonisopen.

Oxford Economics. 'London 2030: How Will the Capital's Economy Change?' Oxford, 2018.

Parsons, Tony. 'London Is the Greatest City in the World.' GQ, 2016. http://www.gq-magazine.co.uk/article/tony-parsons-london-capital-world.

Patterson, Sheila. *Dark Strangers: A Sociological Study of the Absorption of a Recent West Indian Migrant Group in Brixton, South London.* Bloomington: Indiana University Press, 1963.

Paytner, Ben. 'Female Freelancers Are Paid Way Less Than Men For The Same Creative Jobs.' Fast Company, 2017. https://www. fastcompany.com/40482750/female-freelancers-are-paid-way-less-than-men-for-the-same-creative-jobs.

Pearlman, Jonathan. 'Who Invented the Flat White? Row Breaks out between Australian and New Zealand Cafe Owners.' Telegraph, 2015. https://www.telegraph.co.uk/news/worldnews/ australiaandthepacific/australia/11895654/Who-invented-the-flat-white-Row-breaks-out-between-Australian-and-New-Zealand-cafe-owners.html.

'Peckham Levels.' Peckham Levels, 2019. https://www.peck hamlevels.org/.

'Personal Well-Being Estimates.' Office for National Statistics, 2018. https://www.ons.gov.uk/peoplepopulationandcommunity/ wellbeing/datasets/headlineestimatesofpersonalwellbeing.

'Personal Well-Being in the UK: 2015 to 2016.' Office for National Statistics, 2016. https://www.ons.gov.uk/peoplepop ulationandcommunity/wellbeing/bulletins/measuringnatio nalwellbeing/2015to2016#people-in-london-reported-lower-worthwhile-ratings-than-uk-overall.

'PHVs and the Congestion Charge.' Transport for London, 2019. https://tfl.gov.uk/info-for/taxis-and-private-hire/phvs-and-the-congestion-charge.

Picard, Liza. 'The Great Exhibition.' British Library, 2009. https:// www.bl.uk/victorian-britain/articles/the-great-exhibition.

Pierucci, Sidney. 'Why MICRO-INFLUENCER Marketing Is Still 'The Game' in 2019.' The StartUp, 2018. https://medium.com/ swlh/why-micro-influencer-marketing-is-the-game-in-2018-fdeda0993c36.

Plato. *The Republic*. New York: Cosimos, 2008.

'Plays in London.' Official London Theatre, 2018. https:// officiallondontheatre.com/plays-in-london/.

Pomfret, James. 'Migrants Elbow for Foxconn Jobs despite Labor Probe.' Reuters, 2012. http://www.reuters.com/article/us-apple-labour-china-idUSTRE81M0EA20120223.

'Population by Nationality.' Office for National Statistics, 2017. https://data.london.gov.uk/dataset/nationality.

Pountain, Dick, and David Robins. *Cool Rules: An Anatomy of an Attitude*. London: Reaktion, 2000.

'Precarious Work in Higher Education.' UCU, 2016. https://www. ucu.org.uk/media/7995/Precarious-work-in-higher-education-a-snapshot-of-insecure-contracts-and-institutional-attitudes-Apr-16/pdf/ucu_precariouscontract_hereport_apr16.pdf.

Prime Minster's Office. 'PM Announces East London 'Tech City.'' Gov.uk, 2010. https://www.gov.uk/government/news/pm-anno unces-east-london-tech-city.

Prynn, Jonathan. 'Record Year as 19 Million Tourists Visit London.' Evening Standard, 2017. https://www.standard.co.uk/news/london/record-year-as-19m-tourists-visit-london-a3542271.html.

Queen Mary University. 'The Queen Mary Statement of Graduate Attributes,' 2015. http://www.qmul.ac.uk/gacep/statement/.

Quetteville, Harry de. 'The Silicon Joke?' The Telegraph, 2018. https://www.telegraph.co.uk/technology/the-silicon-joke/.

'Rent a Space - Ebor Street Wall.' Rent a Space, 2018. https://www.appearhere.co.uk/spaces/ebor-street-wall-shoreditch.

Reynolds, Z. Nia. *When I Came to England: An Oral History of Life in 1950s and 1960s Britain*. London: Black Stock, 2001.

Robbins, Lord. 'The Robbins Report.' London, 1963.

Roberts, Yvonne. 'The Tiny Union Beating the Gig Economy Giants.' The Guardian, 2018. https://www.theguardian.com/politics/2018/jul/01/union-beating-gig-economy-giants-iwgb-zero-hours-workers.

Rocks, Christopher. *London's Creative Industries - 2017 Update*, 2017. https://www.london.gov.uk/sites/default/files/working_paper_89-creative-industries-2017.pdf.

Rozario, Daryl. 'London's Creative Industries – 2017 Update.' London Datastore, 2017. https://data.london.gov.uk/apps_and_analysis/londons-creative-industries-2017-update/.

Rustin, Susanna. 'Modern Master: How Nick Serota's Tate Skyrocketed to Success.' The Guardian, 2017. https://www.theguardian.com/artanddesign/2017/may/30/tate-modern-britain-liverpool-st-ives-nicholas-serota.

Sara Selwood, Bill Schwarz, Nick Merriman. *The Peopling of London: Fifteen Thousand Years of Settlement from Overseas : An Evaluation of the Exhibition*. London: Museum of London, 1996.

Savage, Mike. *Social Class in the 21st Century*. London: Pelican Books, 2015.

Savage, Mike, Fiona Devine, Niall Cunningham, Mark Taylor, Yaojun Li, Johs Hjellbrekke, Brigitte Le Roux, Sam Friedman and Andrew Miles. 'A New Model of Social Class? Findings from the

BBC's Great British Class Survey Experiment.' *Sociology* 47, no. 2 (2014).

Sawyerr, Ade. 'Will There Ever Be a British Dream?' Operation Black Vote, 2011. http://www.obv.org.uk/news-blogs/will-there-ever-be-british-dream.

Scorziell, Luke. 'The Experience Economy with Case Lawrence.' The Edge of Ideas, 2018. https://theedgeofideas.com/2018/03/21/ep-33-experience-economy-case-lawrence/.

Select Committee on the Sweating System. 'Report from the Select Committee of the House of Lords on the Sweating System, with Proceedings of the Committee,' 1890.

Selvon, Sam. *The Lonely Londoners*. London: Penguin Books, 2006.

Shannon, H.A. 'Migration and the Growth London, 1841-1891.' *Economic History Review* V, no. 2 (1935): 79–86.

Shorter, Clement. *The Brontes Life and Letters Volume II*. London: Hodder and Stoughton, 1908.

Simpson, Jack. 'Battersea Power Station Deal Delayed Again.' Construction News, 2018. https://www.constructionnews.co.uk/markets/sectors/housing/battersea-power-station-deal-delayed-again/10033827.article.

Sims, Alex. '14 Reasons to Go to New Cross Road, SE14.' Time Out, 2016. https://www.timeout.com/london/blog/14-reasons-to-go-to-new-cross-road-se14-102116.

Smith, Alistair. 'London Theatre Report.' London, 2014. https://www.londontheatre1.com/londontheatrereportv7.pdf.

Smith, Esther. 'Trial Shifts: To Pay or Not to Pay?' Big Hospitality, 2017. https://www.bighospitality.co.uk/Article/2017/08/09/Trial-shifts-to-pay-or-not-to-pay.

Snowdon, Graham. 'Pay Gap Widening to Victorian Levels.' The Guardian, 2012. https://www.theguardian.com/business/2011/may/16/high-pay-commission-wage-disparity.

Social Mobility Commission. 'Social Mobility Index: 2017 Data.' Gov.uk, 2017. https://www.gov.uk/government/publications/social-mobility-index-2017-data.

Solon, Olivia. 'Amazon Patents Wristband That Tracks Warehouse Workers' Movements.' The Guardian, 2018. https://www. theguardian.com/technology/2018/jan/31/amazon-warehouse-wristband-tracking.

'Spain Youth Unemployment Rate.' Trading Economics, 2018. https://tradingeconomics.com/spain/youth-unemployment-rate.

Spilsbury, Mark. 'Journalists at Work.' London, 2018.

'Stamp out Casual Contracts.' UCU, 2018. https://www.ucu.org.uk/ stampout.

Stanhope, Alex. 'An Australian Explains Why London Is the Worst City on Earth.' Vice UK, 2017. https://www.vice.com/en_uk/ article/ezz4ke/an-australian-explains-why-london-is-the-worst-city-on-earth.

'Statistics.' Creative Industries Federation, 2017. https://www. creativeindustriesfederation.com/statistics.

Stevenson, Gabrielle Brace. 'Ben Wilson's Chewing Gum Art On The Millennium Bridge.' Culture Trip, 2016. https://theculturetrip. com/europe/united-kingdom/england/london/articles/ben-wilsons-chewing-gum-art-on-the-millennium-bridge/.

'Strike - QMUL UCU.' Strike, 2018. https://qmucu.wordpress.com/ strike/.

'Student Numbers in London.' London Higher, 2017. https://www. londonhigher.ac.uk/ceo-blog/student-numbers-in-london/.

Swinney, Paul and Maire Williams. 'The Great British Brain Drain.' London, 2016. http://www.centreforcities.org/wp-content/uplo ads/2016/11/16-11-18-The-Great-British-Brain-Drain.pdf.

Tapsfield, Emma and James Glanfield. '"The Most Racist Programme I've Ever Watched": BBC Faces Twitter Backlash over Controversial Documentary The Last Whites of the East End – While Some Viewers Say 'It's Only Telling the Truth.' Mail Online, 2016. http://www.dailymail.co.uk/news/article-3608136/ The-racist-programme-honest-reflection-state-nation-Britain-divided-reaction-Whites-East-End.html.

Tate. 'History of Tate.' Who we are, 2017. http://www.tate.org.uk/

about/who-we-are/history-of-tate#modern.

'Taxi and Private Hire Driver Demographic Statistics.' Transport for London, 2018. http://content.tfl.gov.uk/taxi-and-phv-demographic-stats.pdf.

'Tech Round-Up: Why Am I Offered Specific Orders?' Roo Community, 2019. https://roocommunity.com/tech-round-up-how-and-why-am-i-offered-specific-orders/.

'The Changing Face of British Coffee Culture: 5 Key Themes.' Allegra World Coffee Portal, 2018. https://www.worldcoffeeportal.com/Latest/InsightAnalysis/2018/5-key-themes-The-changing-face-of-British-coffee.

'The Decline of the Australian in the UK.' BBC News, 2014. https://www.bbc.co.uk/news/magazine-25401024.

'The Disposable Academic.' The Economist 397, no. 8713 (2010).

The Economist. 'The Company That Ruled the Waves.' The Economist, 2011. http://www.economist.com/node/21541753.

'The History.' Battersea Power Station, 2018. https://batterseapowerstation.co.uk/about/heritage-history.

The Nudge London. 'Pop Up London.' Pop Up London Entertainment, 2016. http://thenudge.com/london-/pop-up-london.

'The Origin of "Refugee".' Merriam-Weber. Accessed May 10, 2018. https://www.merriam-webster.com/words-at-play/origin-and-meaning-of-refugee.

'The Scale of Economic Inequality in the UK.' The Equality Trust, 2018. https://www.equalitytrust.org.uk/scale-economic-inequality-uk.

'The Values of Queen Mary University of London.' Queen Mary University of London, 2014. https://www.qmul.ac.uk/strategy/the-strategy/values/index.html.

'Things to Do in London This Weekend.' Time Out, 2018. https://www.timeout.com/london/things-to-do-in-london-this-weekend.

Thompson, Robert Farris. African Art in Motion. Berkeley: University of California Press, 1974.

Thomson, Peter. 'Origins of the Flat White.' Peter J Thomson, 2014. https://www.peterjthomson.com/coffee/flat-white-coffee-origins/.

Thurman, Neil, Alessio Cornia and Jessica Kunert. 'Journalists in the UK.' London, 2016. http://openaccess.city.ac.uk/14664/1/ Journalists in the UK.pdf.

Tomkins, Calvin. 'The Modern Man.' The New Yorker, 2012. https://www.newyorker.com/magazine/2012/07/02/the-modern-man.

'Top Ten Facts About Studying in London.' Study London, 2018. https://www.studylondon.ac.uk/why-study-in-london/top-10-facts.

Tristan, Flora. *London Journal 1840*. London: George Prior Publishers, 1980.

Trust for London. 'Children.' London's Poverty Profile, 2016. http://www.londonspovertyprofile.org.uk/indicators/groups/children/.

— — —. 'Low Pay.' London's Poverty Profile, 2016. http://www.londonspovertyprofile.org.uk/indicators/topics/low-pay/.

'Trust for London.' London's population over time, 2018. https://www.trustforlondon.org.uk/data/londons-population-over-time/.

TUC. 'The Gig Is Up: Trade Unions Tackling Insecure Work.' London, 2017. https://www.tuc.org.uk/workplace-issues/employment-rights/gig-trade-unions-tackling-insecure-work.

'Uber Granted Short-Term Licence to Operate in London.' BBC News, 2018. https://www.bbc.co.uk/news/business-44612837.

Urban, Mike. 'Boycott the Ritzy Campaigners Keep up the Pressure into 2018.' Brixton Buzz, 2018. http://www.brixtonbuzz.com/2018/01/boycott-the-ritzy-campaigners-keep-up-the-pressure-into-2018/.

— — —. 'The Death of Brixton's Pope's Road as Sports Direct Take over.' Brixton Buzz, 2018. http://www.brixtonbuzz.com/2018/06/the-death-of-brixtons-popes-road-as-sports-direct-take-over/.

Vincent, Guy. 'Sustainable Microentrepreneurship: The Roles of Microfinance, Entrepreneurship and Sustainability in Reducing Poverty in Developing Countries.' The Global Development Research Centre, 2005.

Wainwright, Oliver. "Everything Is Gentrification Now': But Richard Florida Isn't Sorry.' The Guardian, 2017. https://www. theguardian.com/cities/2017/oct/26/gentrification-richard-florida-interview-creative-class-new-urban-crisis.

Wallace, Tim. 'London Goes from Best to Worst for Gender Pay Gap.' The Telegraph, 2017. https://www.telegraph.co.uk/business/2017/11/27/london-goes-best-worst-gender-pay-gap/.

Walvin, James. *A Short History of Slavery*. London: Penguin, 2007.

Wandsworth Council. 'Battersea Power Station.' History of Battersea Power Station, 2018. http://www.wandsworth.gov.uk/info/200536/nine_elms/2101/battersea_power_station.

'Ward Profiles and Atlas.' Greater London Authority, 2015. https://data.london.gov.uk/dataset/ward-profiles-and-atlas.

Watts, Peter. 'Mosque, Circus, Neverland UK ... the Best Failed Ideas for Battersea Power Station.' The Guardian, 2016. https://www.theguardian.com/cities/2016/may/31/battersea-power-station-london-mosque-circus-neverland.

Watts, Robert. 'The Sunday Times Rich List 2017: Boom Time for Billionaires.' The Times, 2017. https://www.thetimes.co.uk/article/the-sunday-times-rich-list-2017-boom-time-for-billionaires-pzbkrfbv2.

Waugh, Rob. 'Apple's Chinese Supplier Foxconn Is Recruiting 18,000 People to Build New IPhone - and Device Is 'Due in June."' Mail Online, 2012. http://www.dailymail.co.uk/sciencetech/article-2125009/iPhone-5-release-date-Apples-Chinese-supplier-Foxconn-recruiting-18k-people-build-new-device-June.html.

'Welcome to South Bank.' Home Page for South Bank, 2017. https://www.southbanklondon.com/index.

West, Matt. 'Almost All 866 Flats in Battersea Power Station Development Sold to Foreign Investors for £675m - and They

Haven't Even Been Built Yet.' This is Money, 2013. http://www. thisismoney.co.uk/money/mortgageshome/article-2328459/ Almost-866-flats-Battersea-Power-Station-development-sold-foreign-investors.html.

Wheatle, Alex. 'The Gentrification of Brixton: How Did the Area's Character Change so Utterly?' The Independent, 2015. https://www.independent.co.uk/news/uk/home-news/the-gentrification-of-brixton-how-did-the-areas-character-change-so-utterly-a6749276.html.

Wheen, Francis. *Marx's Das Kapital*. London: Atlantic Books, 2006.

White, Alan. 'Literally No One Has A Clue What Theresa May Means By 'The British Dream." Buzzfeed, 2017. https://www.buzzfeed. com/alanwhite/everyone-wants-to-know-what-the-hell-theresa-may-means-by?utm_term=.bmQx0A4RQV#.ahJ21wEmvd.

White, Jerry. *London in the 18th Century*. London: The Bodley Head, 2012.

———. *London in the 19th Century*. London: The Bodley Head, 2007.

———. *London in the 20th Century*. London: The Bodley Head, 2001.

'Whitehall, May 18 1899.' *The London Gazette*, May 19, 1899. https:// www.thegazette.co.uk/London/issue/27081/page/3186.

'Who Owns Central London?' Who Owns England?, 2017. https:// whoownsengland.org/2017/10/28/who-owns-central-london/.

'Why Support the Boycott?' IWGB, 2019. https://iwgb.org.uk/page/ hidden/why-support-the-boycott.

Wills, Clair. 'Passage to England.' Times Literary Supplement, 2017. https://www.the-tls.co.uk/articles/public/punjabi-immigrants-stories/.

Wilson, Andy. "Co-Existence through Calypsos and Cockney Cabaret': The Inter-Racial Movement and Dutiful Citizenship.' London Black Histories, 2017. http://www.blacklondonhistories. org.uk/tag/1960s/.

———. 'Lambeth's Budget Challenge.' Love Lambeth, 2019. https:// love.lambeth.gov.uk/lambeth-budget-challenge/.

Wilson, Rebecca. 'Creative Sector Gender Pay Gap at 28%, Sphere

Salary Survey Reveals.' Recruitment International, 2017. https://www.recruitment-international.co.uk/blog/2017/07/creative-sector-gender-pay-gap-at-28-percent-sphere-salary-survey-reveals.

Wilsona, Jacqueline Z., Genee Marksa, Lynne Noonea and Jennifer Hamilton-Mackenzie. 'Retaining a Foothold on the Slippery Paths of Academia: University Women, Indirect Discrimination and the Academic Marketplace.' Gender and Education 22, no. 5 (2010): 535–545.

Winnett, Robert. 'Get a Job, Iain Duncan Smith Tells Parents on the Dole.' The Telegraph, 2012. https://www.telegraph.co.uk/news/politics/9330574/Get-a-job-Iain-Duncan-Smith-tells-parents-on-the-dole.html.

'With Greater Participation, Even 'Greater Inequality.'' Times Higher Education, 2016. meshighereducation.com/news/expansion-in-global-higher-education-has-increased-inequality.

''Wobbly' Millennium Bridge Fixed.' BBC News, 2002. http://news.bbc.co.uk/1/hi/england/1829053.stm.

'Women.' Trust for London, 2018. https://www.trustforlondon.org.uk/data/populations/women/.

Wood, Allen. Karl Marx. London: Routledge, 2004.

Woods, Adam. 'Who's Who on the Silicon Roundabout?' The Campaign, 2011. https://www.campaignlive.co.uk/article/whos-silicon-roundabout/1053814.

'Working Lives.' Tube Creature, 2011. http://tubecreature.com/#/occupation/current/same/U/940GZZLUBXN/TFTFTF/13/-0.1029/51.4517/.

www.uncsbrp.org. 'London's Finance Industry.' London's Economic Plan, 2017. http://www.uncsbrp.org/finance.htm.

'You Can Walk Across It on Grass.' Time, April 1966.

Youle, Emma. 'Camden Fringe Theatre Thrives but Actors Pay Remains Too Low: Only One in Five on Minimum Wage.' Ham & High, 2014. https://www.hamhigh.co.uk/news/camden-fringe-theatre-thrives-but-actors-pay-remains-too-low-only-one-in-five-on-minimum-wage-1-3785159.

Yuill, Chris. 'Identity and Solidarity in the Gig Economy.' In *BSA 2018 Annual Conference*. Northumbria: British Sociological Association, 2018.

'Zero-Hours Tate Staff Amazed as They're Asked to Stump up for Boss's New Boat.' Freedom News, 2017.

Žižek, Slavoj. *First as Tragedy, Then as Farce*. London: Verso, 2009.

— — —. 'You May!' London Review of Books, 1999. https://www.lrb.co.uk/v21/n06/slavoj-zizek/you-may.

Index

A

Academia, 93, 168, 172, 174, 177-182

Amazon, 92, 111, 232, 240

Australia, 8, 194-202, 205

B

Bangladeshi, 18, 23, 25, 159

Bankside, 58, 74-79

Battersea, 74-76, 147

Bell, Daniel, 80

Berlin, 54, 63, 162, 245

Bermondsey, 154

Bethnal Green, 28, 129, 131-132, 158-161

Biddulph, Matt 88-89

black cabs, 232-233, 238-239

Blair, Tony 29, 31, 57, 59, 174-175

Bloomsbury, 9, 113, 154, 221, 229

Booth, Charles 45, 79, 129,134, 238,

Booth, William 38

Boswell, James 5, 122, 169

box parks, 131, 146

Brexit, 16, 18, 20, 25, 33-34, 67, 96, 119, 162, 173, 257

Brick Lane, 23, 125

Brighton, 161, 245

Bristol, 72, 245

British Museum, 12, 77, 205, 219

Brixton, 132-148, 224

Bourdieu, Pierre 124, 155

C

Camden, 137, 232

Cameron, David 88

capitalism, 1, 12, 14, 46-47, 53, 75, 79-80, 83, 87, 94, 96, 120, 122-123, 126-134, 137, 139, 141, 145, 147, 180, 192, 204, 212, 214, 220, 223, 228, 242, 243

Caribbean, 23-24, 53, 72, 133, 135-136, 141

City of London, 18, 79, 89, 114, 219

cleaning industry, 139, 222, 224-228, 244, 247

Cockney, 27-28, 32-33, 129, 159

coffee, 1, 72, 85, 89, 100, 105, 113-114, 121, 160-161, 170-172, 194-196, 199

creative classes, 15, 55, 61, 91-97, 101, 113-114, 120, 123, 125, 131-132, 141, 145-148, 157, 160-163, 176-177, 181-182, 188, 203, 209, 212, 244

Croydon, 146

journalism, 205-210

K
Khan, Sadiq 34-35, 90-91, 237

L
Lambeth, 135, 137-139, 141, 143
Limehouse, 154
London Living Wage, 148, 156,
196, 201, 215, 222-223, 226,
250

M
Marx, Karl 11-13, 47, 122, 129,
152, 157-158, 161, 164, 166,
179, 204, 212, 214, 222, 242,
246
Marxism, 94
May, Theresa 16
Mayfair 54, 103, 113, 147, 222
Mayhew, Henry 38-39, 45, 73
McWilliams, Douglas 89-90
Millennium Bridge, 59, 77-79,
95
museums, 76-77, 81, 84, 123,
125, 170, 172, 219-220, 223

N
New Cross, 56, 60-61, 66, 80,
85-86
New York, 6, 17, 54, 62, 183, 192
New Zealand, 8-9, 89, 139, 194-
195, 197

O
Obama, Barack 131
Old Street, 88-89, 100, 103-104
Oxbridge, 115, 207

P
Pakistan, 10, 34, 229
Peckham, 146
Pop Brixton, 134, 137-146
Prince Albert, 151
proletariat, 155, 157-158, 161,
212-213

Q
Queen Mary, University of
London 170, 172-173, 175,
177
Queen Elizabeth 77
Queen Victoria, 43, 52, 73, 151,
219-220

R
refugees, 7, 20
reserve army, 13, 15, 166, 178-
179, 212, 214-215, 246
Ritzy Picturehouse, 148
Rotherhithe, 154
Russell Group, 115

S
Senate House, 246-255
Serota, Nicholas 78, 82-84
service classes, 15, 131, 148,
157-158, 165-166, 203, 225

CULTURE, SOCIETY & POLITICS

The modern world is at an impasse. Disasters scroll across our smartphone screens and we're invited to like, follow or upvote, but critical thinking is harder and harder to find. Rather than connecting us in common struggle and debate, the internet has sped up and deepened a long-standing process of alienation and atomization. Zer0 Books wants to work against this trend. With critical theory as our jumping off point, we aim to publish books that make our readers uncomfortable. We want to move beyond received opinions.

Zer0 Books is on the left and wants to reinvent the left. We are sick of the injustice, the suffering, and the stupidity that defines both our political and cultural world, and we aim to find a new foundation for a new struggle.

If this book has helped you to clarify an idea, solve a problem or extend your knowledge, you may want to check out our online content as well. Look for Zer0 Books: Advancing Conversations in the iTunes directory and for our Zer0 Books YouTube channel.

Popular videos include:

Žižek and the Double Blackmain

The Intellectual Dark Web is a Bad Sign

Can there be an Anti-SJW Left?

Answering Jordan Peterson on Marxism

Follow us on Facebook
at https://www.facebook.com/ZeroBooks and Twitter at https://
twitter.com/Zer0Books

Bestsellers from Zer0 Books include:

Give Them An Argument
Logic for the Left
Ben Burgis
Many serious leftists have learned to distrust talk of logic. This is
a serious mistake.
Paperback: 978-1-78904-210-8 ebook: 978-1-78904-211-5

Poor but Sexy
Culture Clashes in Europe East and West
Agata Pyzik
How the East stayed East and the West stayed West.
Paperback: 978-1-78099-394-2 ebook: 978-1-78099-395-9

An Anthropology of Nothing in Particular
Martin Demant Frederiksen
A journey into the social lives of meaninglessness.
Paperback: 978-1-78535-699-5 ebook: 978-1-78535-700-8

In the Dust of This Planet
Horror of Philosophy vol. 1
Eugene Thacker
In the first of a series of three books on the Horror of Philosophy,
In the Dust of This Planet offers the genre of horror as a way of
thinking about the unthinkable.
Paperback: 978-1-84694-676-9 ebook: 978-1-78099-010-1

The End of Oulipo?
An Attempt to Exhaust a Movement
Lauren Elkin, Veronica Esposito
Paperback: 978-1-78099-655-4 ebook: 978-1-78099-656-1

Capitalist Realism
Is There no Alternative?
Mark Fisher
An analysis of the ways in which capitalism has presented itself
as the only realistic political-economic system.
Paperback: 978-1-84694-317-1 ebook: 978-1-78099-734-6

Rebel Rebel
Chris O'Leary
David Bowie: every single song. Everything you want to know,
everything you didn't know.
Paperback: 978-1-78099-244-0 ebook: 978-1-78099-713-1

Kill All Normies
Angela Nagle
Online culture wars from 4chan and Tumblr to Trump.
Paperback: 978-1- 78535-543-1 ebook: 978-1-78535-544-8

Cartographies of the Absolute
Alberto Toscano, Jeff Kinkle
An aesthetics of the economy for the twenty-first century.
Paperback: 978-1-78099-275-4 ebook: 978-1-78279-973-3

Malign Velocities
Accelerationism and Capitalism
Benjamin Noys
Long listed for the Bread and Roses Prize 2015, *Malign Velocities*
argues against the need for speed, tracking acceleration
as the symptom of the ongoing crises of capitalism.
Paperback: 978-1-78279-300-7 ebook: 978-1-78279-299-4

Meat Market
Female Flesh under Capitalism
Laurie Penny
A feminist dissection of women's bodies as the fleshy fulcrum of
capitalist cannibalism, whereby women are both consumers and
consumed.
Paperback: 978-1-84694-521-2 ebook: 978-1-84694-782-7

Babbling Corpse
Vaporwave and the Commodification of Ghosts
Grafton Tanner
Paperback: 978-1-78279-759-3 ebook: 978-1-78279-760-9

New Work New Culture
Work we want and a culture that strengthens us
Frithjoff Bergmann
A serious alternative for mankind and the planet.
Paperback: 978-1-78904-064-7 ebook: 978-1-78904-065-4

Romeo and Juliet in Palestine
Teaching Under Occupation
Tom Sperlinger
Life in the West Bank, the nature of pedagogy and the role of a
university under occupation.
Paperback: 978-1-78279-637-4 ebook: 978-1-78279-636-7

Ghosts of My Life
Writings on Depression, Hauntology and Lost Futures
Mark Fisher
Paperback: 978-1-78099-226-6 ebook: 978-1-78279-624-4

Sweetening the Pill
or How We Got Hooked on Hormonal Birth Control
Holly Grigg-Spall
Has contraception liberated or oppressed women?
Sweetening the Pill breaks the silence on the dark side of hormonal
contraception.
Paperback: 978-1-78099-607-3 ebook: 978-1-78099-608-0

Why Are We The Good Guys?
Reclaiming your Mind from the Delusions of Propaganda
David Cromwell
A provocative challenge to the standard ideology that Western
power is a benevolent force in the world.
Paperback: 978-1-78099-365-2 ebook: 978-1-78099-366-9

The Writing on the Wall
On the Decomposition of Capitalism and its Critics
Anselm Jappe, Alastair Hemmens
A new approach to the meaning of social emancipation.
Paperback: 978-1-78535-581-3 ebook: 978-1-78535-582-0

Enjoying It
Candy Crush and Capitalism
Alfie Bown
A study of enjoyment and of the enjoyment of studying. Bown
asks what enjoyment says about us and what we say about
enjoyment, and why.
Paperback: 978-1-78535-155-6 ebook: 978-1-78535-156-3

Color, Facture, Art and Design
Iona Singh
This materialist definition of fine-art develops guidelines for
architecture, design, cultural-studies and ultimately social
change.
Paperback: 978-1-78099-629-5 ebook: 978-1-78099-630-1

Neglected or Misunderstood
The Radical Feminism of Shulamith Firestone
Victoria Margree
An interrogation of issues surrounding gender, biology,
sexuality, work and technology, and the ways in which our
imaginations continue to be in thrall to ideologies of maternity
and the nuclear family.
Paperback: 978-1-78535-539-4 ebook: 978-1-78535-540-0

How to Dismantle the NHS in 10 Easy Steps (Second Edition)
Youssef El-Gingihy
The story of how your NHS was sold off and why you will have
to buy private health insurance soon. A new expanded second
edition with chapters on junior doctors' strikes and government
blueprints for US-style healthcare.
Paperback: 978-1-78904-178-1 ebook: 978-1-78904-179-8

Digesting Recipes
The Art of Culinary Notation
Susannah Worth
A recipe is an instruction, the imperative tone of the expert, but
this constraint can offer its own kind of potential. A recipe need
not be a domestic trap but might instead offer escape – something
to fantasise about or aspire to.
Paperback: 978-1-78279-860-6 ebook: 978-1-78279-859-0

Most titles are published in paperback and as an ebook.
Paperbacks are available in traditional bookshops. Both print and
ebook formats are available online.
Follow us on Facebook
at https://www.facebook.com/ZeroBooks
and Twitter at https://twitter.com/Zer0Books